Strand

The measurement of household welfare is one of the most compelling yet demanding areas of economics. To place the analysis of inequality and poverty within an economic framework where individuals are making decisions about current and lifetime incomes and expenditures is a difficult task. This is made all the more challenging by the complexity of the decision making process in which households are involved, and the variety of constraints that they face.

Should one use a collective decision making framework to reflect the fact that individuals often belong to households which contain other individuals? Or is it more appropriate to treat the individual as a 'noncooperative' decision maker who nevertheless makes some allowance for interrelationships with other household members?

How should one allow for different households having different demographic compositions at a point in time when making comparisons of living standards across households? Moreover, how does one allow for changes in the composition of households across their life-cycles?

In the face of the conceptual and practical difficulties of making inferences from observed behaviour, would it be useful to have some subjective attitudinal evidence about economic well-being from direct questionnaires?

These issues, and others which are important and topical, are addressed in this volume by contributions from experts from Europe, North America and Australia. A unifying theme is the strong relationship between the theoretical concepts from microeconomics and the appropriate use of micro data in evaluating household welfare.

This book will be of interest to students and researchers in microeconomics, public economics, applied microeconometrics, and social policy.

Contributors: Richard Blundell; Ian Preston; Ian Walker; Charles Blackorby; David Donaldson; François Bourguignon; Pierre-André Chiappori; Bernard van Praag; Daniela Del Boca; Christopher Flinn; Patricia Apps; Mamta Murthi; James Banks; Fiona Coulter; Frank Cowell; Stephen Jenkins; François Laisney; Rolf Schmachtenberg; Martijn Tummers.

The measurement of household welfare

The measurement of household welfare

EDITED BY

RICHARD BLUNDELL,
IAN PRESTON
AND IAN WALKER

CAMBRIDGE
UNIVERSITY PRESS

Published by the Press Syndicate of the University of Cambridge
The Pitt Building, Trumpington Street, Cambridge CB2 1RP
40 West 20th Street, New York, NY 10011-4211, USA
10 Stamford Road, Oakleigh, Melbourne 3166, Australia

First published 1994

Printed in Great Britain at the University Press, Cambridge

A catalogue record for this book is available from the British Library

Library of Congress cataloguing in publication data

The Measurement of household welfare / edited by
Richard Blundell, Ian Preston, and Ian Walker.
    p.   cm.
Includes bibliographical references and index.
ISBN 0 521 45195 7
1. Welfare economics – Mathematical models. 2. Households –
Economic conditions – Mathematical models. 3. Home economics –
Mathematical models.
I. Blundell, Richard. II. Preston, Ian. III. Walker, Ian, 1945– .
HB846.M43   1994
339.2'2–dc20   93-5717   CIP

ISBN 0 521 45195 7 hardback

CE

Contents

Contributors

RICHARD BLUNDELL, University College London and Institute for Fiscal Studies

IAN PRESTON, University College London and Institute for Fiscal Studies

IAN WALKER, University of Keele and Institute for Fiscal Studies

CHARLES BLACKORBY, University of British Columbia

DAVID DONALDSON, University of British Columbia

FRAŊCOIS BOURGUIGNON, DELTA/ENS, Paris

PIERRE-ANDRÉ CHIAPPORI, DELTA/ENS, Paris

BERNARD VAN PRAAG, Erasmus University, Rotterdam

DANIELA DEL BOCA, University of Turin

CHRISTOPHER FLINN, New York University and University of Turin

PATRICIA APPS, Faculty of Law, University of Sydney and Division of Politics and Economics, Research School of Social Sciences, Australian National University

MAMTA MURTHI, University of Sussex

JAMES BANKS, Institute for Fiscal Studies

FIONA COULTER, University of Bath

FRANK COWELL, London School of Economics

STEPHEN JENKINS, University College, Swansea

FRANÇOIS LAISNEY, University of Mannheim and University of Louis Pasteur, Strasbourg

ROLF SCHMACHTENBERG, University of Mannheim and University of Louis Pasteur, Strasbourg

MARTIJN TUMMERS, Social and Cultural Planning Bureau, The Netherlands

1 An introduction to applied welfare analysis

RICHARD BLUNDELL, IAN PRESTON and IAN WALKER

Introduction

The measurement of individual and household welfare stands out in applied economics for its ability to usefully blend economic theory with empirical practice. It is an area where empirical investigation clearly benefits from theoretical insight and where theoretical concepts are brought alive and appropriately focussed by the discipline of empirical relevance and policy design. There are difficult issues to face in identifying who gains and who loses from complex policy reforms. Potential Pareto improvements[1] are scarce and the scope for useful policy recommendations may well be limited unless one is prepared to go further, attempting to evaluate the sizes of the gains and losses to assess whether, in some sense, the gains outweigh the losses.

A wide variety of empirical work has attempted to measure the impact of policy changes on the behaviour and living standards of individuals. This kind of work has flourished in recent years with the increased availability of large micro datasets and significant decreases in the costs of analysing such data using microeconometric methods. The aim of this book is to complement the existing literature by concentrating on the issues that are highlighted in empirical applications.

Earlier empirical work was based on estimated behavioural models obtained using aggregate data. However, this was limited insofar as it, at least implicitly, imposed the conditions required to be able to infer individual behaviour from aggregate data. Important contributions by Muellbauer (1975, 1976), by Jorgenson, Lau and Stoker (1980) and by Jorgenson (1990), building on the pioneering work of Gorman (1953, 1981) established exact conditions under which it is possible to make such inferences from aggregate data. These are restrictive and the increasing availability of accurate micro data allows a much more general analysis of preferences and constraints, opening up a large new set of empirically motivated issues which this volume addresses.

Even in nonbehavioural models the availability of micro data is invaluable since it allows analyses of policy reforms to be conducted in terms of the numbers of gainers and losers, the amounts of gains and losses and the characteristics of gainers and losers, including their initial living standards. One example of such research into the impact of tax reform on net incomes and the distribution of income gains and losses is Musgrave (1987) who looks into the effect of the US Tax Reform Act of 1986. However the main advantage of micro data is that it allows both the behavioural and distributional effects of policy changes to be analysed. For example, King (1983) uses a model of demand for housing services to calculate money metric measures of gains and losses for a large random sample of the population in the face of changes to the tax treatment of housing in the UK.

This volume aims to introduce, to researchers and students, recent developments in literature concerned with the measurement of welfare, and since we are concerned with practical issues we concentrate on individual welfare measurement which in turn motivates our focus on micro data. This introductory chapter sets the scene by detailing the basic ideas associated with the measurement of welfare, showing why the literature has developed in particular directions in recent years. The main themes of these recent developments are also outlined, and this serves to put subsequent chapters in perspective.

Recent themes in applied welfare analysis

A number of important issues have characterised the recent literature on the measurement of welfare: how to incorporate differences in household characteristics into welfare evaluations; how to evaluate the welfare of individuals when they live in households; how to incorporate intertemporal and labour market dimensions; the potential for using subjective survey data for measuring welfare; and how to measure social welfare, inequality and poverty from individual welfare measures.

The problem of incorporating variation in household characteristics into welfare comparisons is addressed by the literature on costs of children and *equivalence scales* which aims to provide a deflator (or a set of deflators) to derive the number of adult equivalents in any given household, so that expenditure or income levels for different household types can be compared. The chapters in this volume by Blackorby and Donaldson, Murthi, and Banks, Blundell and Preston (2, 7, 8) are concerned with this literature, and that by Coulter, Cowell and Jenkins (9) is an example of a study where allowing for demographic composition can be crucial. Typically equivalence scales are computed from estimates of the impact of the number of individuals in the household (allowing for their ages and sexes to have an effect) on expenditure patterns (and labour supply decisions). This literature skates around the problem of interdependencies between household members by implicitly assuming that it is appropriate to treat the welfare of a household as identical to that of the (dictatorial) parents. While the presumption is that households share resources, some items of expenditure may well be subject to indivisibilities which give rise to economies of scale so that equivalence scales capture the idea that two can live more cheaply than one. Most empirical studies concentrate on the impact of the number of children and estimate the number of *adult equivalents* in each household to produce a measure of *adult equivalent income* to compare across households.[2] One difficulty relates to the direct impact of demographic composition on household welfare. Data on expenditure patterns does not reveal how individuals *feel* about their children – that is, children may have a direct effect on their parents' welfare as well as an indirect effect through the consumption demands they impose. Pollak and Wales (1979) point out that demand analysis tells us only about the latter.

In general, the presence of interdependencies between household members undermines the assumption that there is a single *household welfare function*. In recognition of this models of behaviour have developed in which each individual (typically the two that comprise an adult couple) maximises an individual welfare function allowing for interactions between the behaviour of those within the household. Such interdependencies could arise if there are household public goods or if there is altruism (or envy) featured in the individual welfare functions, as well as arising either from strategic noncooperative behaviour between the couple, or from Pareto efficient cooperative behaviour. The work by Chiappori (1988a) represents a pathbreaking contribution to this area. The chapters in this volume by Bourguignon and Chiappori, Apps, and Del Boca and Flinn (3, 6, 5) are further important contributions to this area.

In practice, empirical welfare analysis has concentrated on the modelling of current expenditure patterns and has defined welfare measures over the quantities consumed. There is a large empirical literature on modelling labour supply, although it has had little impact on the empirical analysis of inequality and poverty. There are exceptions, for example, Hurd and Pencavel (1981), who compute the welfare implications of minimum wages using a labour supply model. Similarly, there has been a recent upsurge of interest in modelling intertemporal savings and labour supply decisions, largely because of the macroeconomic implications of intertemporal substitution which, in simple models at least, suggest that changes in consumption may not be highly correlated with changes in income. Although the perfect credit market assumption underlying much of this work may limit its relevance for poorer households, it is somewhat surprising that this work has had little impact on welfare measurement. This despite the pronounced effect of age on one's position in the current income distribution.

Aggregation of individual welfare judgements turns out to be a particularly thorny problem. It has been known since Arrow (1951)[3] that apparently innocuous sounding properties about the nature of social decision rules are mutually incompatible so that it is simply impossible to construct a method of making social choices satisfying these properties. What may be seen as crucial to Arrow's conditions is that they rule out measurement of welfare in anything other than an ordinal and interpersonally noncomparable sense (see Sen, 1970, 1979). Not surprisingly, this is also the most information that market data can reveal. As a result another strand in applied welfare measurement has been an attempt to measure a cardinal dimension to utilities from responses to questionnaire surveys on evolution of incomes. Chapter 4 in this volume is concerned with this issue.

Views, for instance, about the undesirability of inequality and poverty also carry implications for the way in which we can construct judgements about social welfare from data on the welfare of households. Chapter 10, by Blackorby, Laisney and Schmachtenberg, explores the undesirable implications of one popular way of constructing social welfare judgements. Chapter 11 by Tummers considers the usefulness of survey data in identifying who should be considered as poor.

Duality and the measurement of welfare loss

Welfare measurement has typically (but not exclusively) been based on the theory of consumer demand and although the theory neatly extends to allow for labour supply and intertemporal decisions such extensions have not generally been used for purposes of explicit welfare analysis. The Deaton and Muellbauer (1980a) volume is an excellent introduction to the area, and here we simply sketch the background for the sake of completeness and to introduce the concepts and notation.

The dual household problem is that of minimising the expenditure required to attain a specified utility level, u, given a set of prices p. This can be expressed as the expenditure or cost function

$$e(u,p) = \min_{q_1, \ldots, q_n} \sum_{i=1}^{n} p_i q_i \text{ subject to } u(q_1, \ldots, q_n) = u, \tag{1}$$

where the q_is are quantities of the n goods. The solution to this problem is a set of first order conditions that can be written as

$$q_i = q_i^c(u,p), \qquad \forall i = 1, \ldots, n, \tag{2}$$

which are the compensated demand equations which have a number of specific properties such as *symmetry*, *negativity*, and *adding-up* so that

$$\frac{\partial q_i^c}{\partial p_j} = \frac{\partial q_j^c}{\partial p_i}, \quad \frac{\partial q_i^c}{\partial p_i} \leq 0, \quad \sum_{i=1}^{n} p_i q_i^c = e(u,p), \tag{3}$$

where $e(u,p)$ is known as the consumer's expenditure function, i.e., the minimised expenditure when demands are given by (2). The expenditure function has a number of useful properties: it is homogeneous of degree zero, increasing and concave in p, and it satifies *Shephard's Lemma* which states that

$$\frac{\partial e(u,p)}{\partial p_i} = q_i^c(u,p), \tag{4}$$

so that the compensated demands can be derived easily from the consumer's *cost* (or expenditure) function and vice versa. Finally, the cost function can be inverted to yield the *indirect utility function*, $u = v(x,p)$ where x is the consumer's total expenditure (or income), which shows how the *maximum* level of utility achievable depends on the nature of the budget constraint.

The substitution of $v(x,p)$ for u into the compensated demands in (2) yields the standard uncompensated demand equations $q = q(x,p)$. Since the expenditure function, $e(u,p)$, can be thought of as the *cost* of achieving level of utility u at prices p, it also acts as a *money metric* measure of utility and an indicator of the household's living standard (for fixed p). It is thus frequently applied to measure the welfare change associated with a change of prices, perhaps induced by a policy reform or simply reflecting changes in relative prices over time or across countries. Thus, if a consumer has an income of x^0 and faces a change in prices from p^0 to p^1, then the change in their welfare could be measured by the difference in the cost evaluated, say, at prices p^1, of achieving the consumer's utilities in the two situations. This is the same as the change in the cost of achieving original utility $u^0 = v(x^0,p^0)$ associated with the change in prices and is known as the *compensating variation*, which is given by

$$CV \equiv e(u^0,p^0) - e(u^0,p^1) = e(u_1,p^1) - e(u^0,p^1) = x^0 - e(u^0,p^1) \tag{5}$$

$$= \sum_{i=1}^{n} \int_{p_i^0}^{p_i^1} q_i^c(u^0,p)\,dp_i$$

where the final equality arises because of Shephard's Lemma. Similarly, the change in welfare could be measured by the difference in the cost evaluated at original prices p^0. This is the same as the change in the cost of achieving the level of utility $u_1 = v(x^0,p^1)$ associated with the change in prices and is known as the *equivalent variation*, which is written as

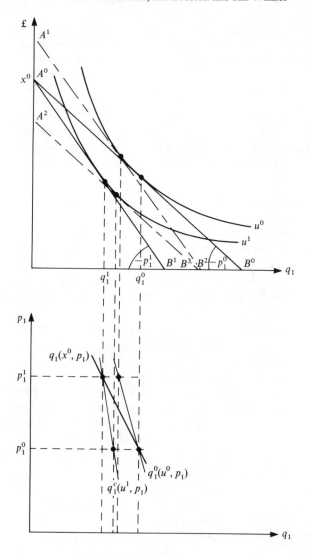

Figure 1.1 Compensating and equivalent variations

$$EV \equiv e(u^1, \boldsymbol{p}^0) - e(u^1, \boldsymbol{p}^1) = e(u^1, \boldsymbol{p}^0) - e(u^0, \boldsymbol{p}^0) = e(u^1, \boldsymbol{p}^0) - x^0 \qquad (6)$$

$$= \sum_{i=1}^{n} \int_{p_i^0}^{p_i^1} q_i^c(u^1, \boldsymbol{p}) \, dp_i.$$

These equalities hold because we have assumed that income remains at x^0; otherwise we would have needed to add a change in lump sum income to the above expressions.

In the case of just a single price change, say for p_1, we can treat all other goods as a composite commodity whose price can be normalised at unity, so that these measures can be illustrated as in figure 1.1. The budget constraint is originally given by A^0B^0 (where OA^0 is x^0 and p_1^0 is the original price of good 1), which supports utility level of u^0 at demand level q_1^0; the price of good 1 rises so that the constraint becomes A^0B^1, demand falls to q_1^1 and utility to u_1. The budget constraint A^1B^2 would support the original utility level at the new price, while the constraint A^2B^3 would support the new utility level at the original price. The CV is thus given by the distance A^0A^1 and EV is given by A^2A^0. Similarly, by Shephard's Lemma, the area below the compensated demand curve, $q_i^c(u^0,p_1)$, is the CV, while the area below $q_i^c(u^1,p_1)$ is the EV.

There is a considerable literature that points out that EV and CV rely on a knowledge of compensated demand curves or the utility function, neither of which are directly observable. What are directly observable are *ordinary* demand curves, such as $q_i(x_1,p^0)$ in figure 1.1. Thus, it has sometimes been argued that we cannot measure what we want to measure but we could measure the area underneath the ordinary demand curve (known as the *Marshallian surplus, MS*) as an approximation to it.[4] Work by Willig (1980) and others shows what the error in approximation depends on – obviously, from figure 1.1, the size of the income elasticity is important and it can be shown that in the one price change case a zero income elasticity is required to make the approximation exact.

When the price change occurs as a result of taxation then the above measures can be used as a basis for computing the *deadweight loss* or *excess burden* of the tax, i.e., the loss over and above the tax raised. Here aggregation is potentially involved since CV and EV are household concepts while tax revenue is usually regarded as a market concept. For the moment, suppose there is such a thing as a *representative* household so that we can effectively ignore the distinction and conduct the analysis on a *per capita* basis.[5] Thus, in figure 1.1 we could define DWL as EV-R where R is the tax revenue, defined as $(p_1^1-p_0^1)q_1^1$ (see Diamond and McFadden, 1975 and Kay, 1980 for the use of the cost function in computing DWL).

Hausman (1980) has pointed out that, even when the MS is a good approximation to the CV and EV, an approximation to the DWL based on MS would not, in general, be close.

A feature of Hausman's work is that, for computational purposes, he exploits the relationship between ordinary and compensated demand curves, given by the *Slutsky Equation*

$$\frac{\partial q_i}{\partial p_j} = s_{ij} - q_j \frac{\partial q_i}{\partial x}, \tag{7}$$

where $s_{ij} = \partial q_i^c(u,p)/\partial p_j = \partial^2 e(u,p)/\partial p_j \partial p_i$, to recover the *EV* and/or *CV* from the *ordinary* demand curve. The relationship between compensated and ordinary demand curves is also the cornerstone of nonparametric methods that have been suggested by Vartia (1983), Hausman and Newey (1993) and others (see Stoker, 1986, for example).

Equivalence scales and the cost of living

Equivalence scales are constructed so as to allow a comparison of welfare levels between households with different composition: in particular whether, and at what level, re-distribution may be required between households of different demographic type to ensure horizontal equity. Such scales are useful, for example, in assessing whether a tax or benefit reform reflects the differing needs of households with different com-position. If one ignores the fertility decision, then re-distribution based on such scales will not distort economic choices provided equivalence scales can be linked solely to demographic attributes. However, equivalence scales that are independent of the level of household income (or consump-tion) require strong restrictions on household preferences. Moreover, the ability to identify equivalence from expenditure (and labour supply) data, even when individuals can be followed over time, is severely limited. These limitations are developed formally in Blundell and Lewbel (1991). Here we follow their discussion closely. We also consider the issues involved in putting equivalence scales in an intertemporal setting.

Equivalence scales are defined as the proportionate increase (or decrease) in income necessary to maintain a certain level of household welfare in the face of some variation in demographic circumstances. They generally require statistical estimates of certain behavioural parameters relating to consumer choices by households of different type before they can be constructed. Unfortunately, as has been understood for some time (see Pollak and Wales, 1979, for example), behavioural models of con-sumer demand cannot identify all the parameters required for making welfare comparisons across households of different demographic type even where they contain demographic variables among the determinants of demand. As a result some prior restrictions on household behaviour are required before one can reach welfare conclusions on the basis of the empirical measurement of equivalence scales. Luckily, many popular forms of equivalence scales to be considered below impose restrictions that are more than sufficient to identify true welfare comparisons. Indeed, they generally impose testable restrictions. However, since the restrictions required to identify equivalence scales are only partially testable, welfare comparisons will always require prior assumptions or additional information not usually available in budget surveys.

An intertemporal setting for equivalence scale measurement would seem attractive but has been surprisingly uncommon in the empirical literature. Indeed, most consumer models that are used to recover equivalence scales are static or at least represent within-period allocations of goods ignoring choices over assets and savings. It seems reasonable to suggest that following a household's responses to changes in its demographic profile over its life-cycle and observing how total consumption (or savings) changes may provide some additional useful information on the consumption costs of children. It can certainly shed important light on the way in which the allocation of goods responds to demographic changes.

In general, the analysis of demand for goods by demographically different households identifies preferences conditional on household composition, i.e. conditional preference orderings. In contrast, a complete welfare comparison between households should depend on the joint distribution of preferences over goods and household composition (unconditional preference orderings). Even when the demographic attributes are not subject to choice (e.g., age), it is still the case that welfare comparisons depend on all the effects of demographics on utility, not just the effects that appear in the demands for goods. Consumer demand analysis can therefore identify only a subset of the parameters required for welfare comparisons in general and equivalence scales in particular.

Blackorby and Donaldson (chapter 2) in this volume provide a detailed theoretical analysis of various equivalence scales and their implied properties. For example, suppose that equivalence scales are independent of the base or reference utility level (see Lewbel, 1989a and Blackorby and Donaldson, 1990). In this case complete identification of equivalence scales is possible. While this assumption is commonly made in empirical demand work (see, for example, Jorgenson and Slesnick, 1983, 1987 and Ray, 1983), it does appear to be a strong restriction. Another popular class of equivalence scales introduced by Barten (1964), in which demographics enter simply as a scaling up of prices, also imply a unique 'natural' specification for equivalence scale structure.

Although complete identification of equivalence scales requires prior assumptions on utility function structure, these assumptions (like base independence or Barten scales) typically place some testable restrictions on the way demographic variables enter empirical demand systems. For example, it is possible to empirically reject the assumption of independence of base (IB). However, complete testing of IB is impossible. If the demand restrictions implied by IB are not empirically rejected, it remains impossible to infer that IB actually holds.

Cost functions and equivalence scales

We start by assuming households have total expenditure (income for short) x, and face a price vector p. Their demographic characteristics are denoted by z and we define the corresponding expenditure function $e(u,p;z)$ using (1) above. Given standard assumptions on the form of u, the demands q can be uniquely recovered from the expenditure or cost function $e(.)$. For any given price vector p, demographic characteristics z, and reference characteristics z^r, we define a schedule of equivalence scales

$$m(p;z,z^r) = \left\{ \left. \frac{e(u,p;z)}{e(u,p;z^r)} \right| \ u \text{ real} \right\}. \tag{8}$$

Each element of the set $m(p;z,z^r)$ equals the minimum cost for a household having characteristics z necessary to attain a given utility level u divided by the corresponding cost of attaining utility level u for a reference household with characteristics z^r.

As can be seen from (8) equivalence scales are independent of reference utility if, and only if, the cost function can be written in the form $g(p;z).G(p;u)$. This assumption that the *costs of children* are proportionate is clearly a restriction on preferences (see Blackorby and Donaldson, 1989). Alternatively we might assume that composition changes add linearly to costs so that the cost function is written $g(p;z) + G(p;u)$. This is also a restriction on preferences and defined as *translating* in Pollak and Wales (1981). In this case, however, equivalence scales remain dependent on the utility level at which they are evaluated.

The calculation of equivalence scales defined by (8) requires recovery of the cost function $e(.)$ from demands $q(.)$. However, there is a serious identification problem in doing so (see Pollak and Wales, 1979), since for any function $\phi(u, z)$ that is increasing monotonic in its first (scalar valued) element u, maximisation of the utility function $\phi(u(q;z),z)$ over q will, by ordinality, yield the same demands $q(x,p;z)$ that arise from $u(q;z)$. Hence the cost function $\tilde{e}(.)$ defined as $\tilde{e}(u,p;z) = \min[p'q \,|\, \phi(u(q;z),z) \geq u]$ will yield the same demands $q(p,x;z)$ that arise from $e(.)$. Let $\tilde{m}(p;z,z^r)$ be the schedule of equivalence scales defined using $\tilde{e}(.)$. If $\phi(.)$ is independent of z, then $\tilde{m}(.) = m(.)$, so no identification problem would arise (this corresponds to a simple renumbering of the indifference curves in q-z space).

However, when $\phi(.)$ depends on z, $\tilde{m} \neq m$, so the true schedule of equivalence scales is not identified from demand equations $q(.)$. This is because demands $q(.)$ represent preferences conditional on z and can only identify the indifference curves in q space, while equivalence scales depend on the indifference surfaces in q-z space. Changes in $\phi(.)$ correspond to changes in the shape of indifference surfaces in q-z space that do not change the q space slices of the surfaces.

As a result of this underidentification, Pollak and Wales (1979) argue that equivalence scales that are calculated from demand data cannot be used for welfare comparisons. This seems to be an overly negative assessment. Consumer demand data can be used to recover the cost of attaining each indifference curve in q space, i.e., conditional preferences, and hence contains some information on relative costs. In addition, this argument has no direct relationship to whether or not composition of z is jointly determined with q. It simply requires preferences to be defined over q and z.[6]

The usual approach to equivalence scale estimation is to assume a particular (conditional) cost function $e(.)$, and to calculate $m(.)$. As the above analysis shows, the resulting equivalence scale estimates depend on a subjective value judgement embodied in the implicit arbitrary choice of the function $\phi(.)$. Some empirical applications make the selection of $\phi(.)$ more or less explicit (e.g., Jorgenson and Slesnick, 1983, 1987 in their construction of inequality measures), but the results are no less subjective for that.

The question that needs to be addressed is: What information about equivalence scales can be identified from demand data on consumer budgets? This is the central focus of the Blundell and Lewbel (1991) paper in which it is shown that demands for goods provide no information about equivalence scales in a single price regime. That is, for any observed demand system, a cost function can be found that rationalises the demand system and yields any possible values for equivalence scales in any one given price regime p^r. However, it also shows that the cost function is unique[7] so that given the true values of equivalence scales in one price regime, Marshallian demands can be used to recover uniquely the true values of all equivalence scales in all other price regimes.

One implication of this result is that the standard practice of assuming a particular cardinalisation to calculate equivalence scales is identical to assuming an exact value of the equivalence scales in one price regime, then estimating the implied values of the equivalence scales in all others. Another implication is that if equivalence scales do not vary with prices then observed demands provide no information at all about true equivalence scales.

The relationship to cost of living indices

For any price regime p, any reference price regime p^r, and any demographic characteristics z, we can define a schedule of (Konus) cost of living indices $K(p, p^r; z)$ by

$$K(p, p^r; z) = \left\{ \left. \frac{e(u, p; z)}{e(u, p^r; z)} \right| \; u \text{ real} \right\} \tag{9}$$

(see Afriat, 1977). These indices represent the cost for a household having characteristics z and facing prices p to attain a given base utility level u, divided by the cost of the same household to attain the same utility level u when facing prices p^r. Unlike equivalence scales, the schedule of cost of living indices $K(p, p^r; z)$ are identical for all choices of the cost function $e(.)$ that yield observed demand equations $q(p, x; z)$, and so are uniquely determined by the demand data alone. For example, consider a specific equivalence scale given by:

$$\frac{e(u, p; z)}{e(u, p; z^r)} = \frac{e(u, p; z)/e(u, p^r; z)}{e(u, p; z^r)/e(u, p^r; z^r)} \cdot \frac{e(u, p^r; z)}{e(u, p^r; z^r)}$$

$$= \frac{K(p, p^r; z)}{K(p, p^r; z^r)} \cdot \frac{e(u, p^r; z)}{e(u, p^r; z^r)}. \tag{10}$$

It follows from this equation that the equivalence scale in price regime p equals the product of a ratio of household specific cost of living indices (the elements of $K(p, p^r; z)$ and $K(p, p^r; z^r)$), which are identified from demand data alone times the corresponding equivalence scale in the base price regime p^r. This simple decomposition, developed in Blundell and Lewbel (1991), shows that any equivalence scale that researchers report based on demand estimation is the product of relative cost of living indices uncovered by the data, multiplied by an arbitrary constant that the researcher has implicitly selected by his choice of $\phi(.)$.

Options for estimating equivalence scales

There appear to be only three options for estimating equivalence scales from empirical demand analysis. These are (i) report only what can be unambiguously calculated from consumers' expenditure data, i.e., results independent of the choice of $\phi(.)$ given u (where chosen utility $u^*(q, z) = \phi(u(q; z), z)$), or (ii) make some reasonable, though untestable, assumptions to arrive at a unique $u^*(q; z)$, i.e. choose a particular $\phi(.)$ given u, and report the equivalence scales that result, or (iii) augment demand equations $q = q(x, p; z)$ with additional data about preferences over z or psychometric data about attained utility levels to get more information about choice of $\phi(.)$ given u that corresponds to agents' actual welfare. Each of these options is discussed in turn before we move to an intertemporal or life-cycle setting for our equivalence scale analysis.

If we wish to have results that depend only on the observable demand equations $q = q(x,p;z)$ (and the assumption that the welfare of all agents be defined by the same unknown utility function $u(q;z)$), then the only component of equivalence scales that can be estimated is 'relative' equivalence scales, which are ratios of cost of living indices for different demographic groups (the first term on the right-hand side of equation (10)). From our discussion above we see that nothing can be inferred about the rest of equation (10) using demand data alone.

If actual equivalence scale estimates are required using only demand data $q = q(x,p;z)$, then an untestable choice of u^* (more specifically, an arbitrary choice of $\phi(.)$ given any u consistent with $q(.)$) must be made. This is not necessarily more offensive than the standard assumptions required for welfare analysis, such as interpersonal comparability, as long as one is explicit about the dependence of the resulting estimates on the untestable choice of $\phi(.)$.

In some cases, more specific structure in the demand equations may suggest a unique 'natural' choice for u^*. For example, suppose the demand equations have the form

$$\frac{q_i}{f_i} = x^* \left(\frac{p_1}{f_1}, \ldots, \frac{p_n}{f_n}, x \right) \tag{11}$$

where each f_i is some function of z. Barten (1964) labelled these *commodity specific* equivalence scales. It is clear that such specifications place testable restrictions on the empirical demand equations. If acceptable they uniquely identify the equivalence scales. Generalisations of this form have been proposed by Gorman (1976) and are a special case of the demand transformations considered by Lewbel (1985).

Another example of such demand structures is those consistent with the IB property, defined as the situation in which equivalence scales are independent of the base level of utility u at which the cost comparison is being made. IB can be viewed as a functional form property of the cost function, since equivalence scales are IB if and only if the cost function $e(.)$ equals $g(p;z)G(p,u)$. From (8) this yields equivalence scales of the form $g(p;z)/g(p;z')$. The IB property places testable restrictions on the (conditional) demand equations $q(.)$. In general, IB also implies a unique choice of equivalence scales.

Blackorby and Donaldson (1988b, and chapter 2 in this volume) and Lewbel (1989b) independently analysed the restrictions on demands and cost functions implied by the IB property (Blackorby and Donaldson call the IB property *Equivalence Scale Exactness*). Many empirical studies in equivalence scale estimation posit cost functions that possess the IB property (examples are Engel scales, homothetic demands, and the models of Jorgenson and Slesnick, 1983 and of Ray, 1983). However, the demographically translated Linear and Quadratic Expenditure Systems of Pollak and Wales (1981) do not necessarily satisfy the IB restriction. Moreover, the extensions of Deaton and Muellbauer's Almost Ideal model estimated in Blundell, Pashardes and Weber (1993) do not, in general, support the IB restriction.

It may be possible that additional data in the form of revealed preference for characteristics z (e.g., treating geographic location or household size as a choice variable) can be used to identify equivalence scales in a single price regime, or one may have opinions about equivalence scales arrived at by introspection. The extensive work by van Praag and his colleagues (see van Praag, chapter 4 in this volume; van Praag and Kapteyn, 1973; van Praag and van der Sar, 1988, for example) provides an important attempt to use psychometric data in the form of an Income Evaluation Question (see Tummers, chapter 11 in this volume) to overcome the identification problem. By asking households of different composition and income levels how they value an extra unit of income, one can attempt to identify the broad features of the monotonic transformation that cannot be recovered from Marshallian demand analysis. In either case, our discussion suggests how such information could be combined with estimates of relative equivalence scales to yield estimates of true equivalence scales. Of course, revealed preference over characteristics cannot be used for attributes that are not subject to choice, such as race or age.

An intertemporal setting for equivalence scale measurement

Some additional and potentially important information, omitted from standard demand analysis, can be expected to be revealed from intertemporal considerations. Modern models of intertemporal consumer behaviour seek to explain changes in consumption from one period to the next in terms of expected changes in prices, interest rates and other attributes and unexpected events that influence the path of consumption (see Hall, 1978). By working with individual household data over time, focus can be placed on the influence demographic variables, and their evolution, have on intertemporal consumption patterns, allowing an extension to the standard equivalence scale measures. Looking at the way consumption evolves as children arrive in a household and then grow older provides some useful information on the consumption costs of children. Indeed, this extension to the equivalence scale literature can be shown to contribute additional terms to the estimated equivalence scale, thereby highlighting the identification issues surrounding standard equivalence scale measurement discussed above.

In order to incorporate an intertemporal dimension we need to write down a life-cycle welfare function for the household. To do this, we define period specific indirect utilities $v_t(x_t, p_t, z_t)$ identifiable from within period demand analysis. Life-cycle utility is then the discounted sum of period specific utilities. Each period specific utility may be written

$$u_t = f_t(v_t(x_t, p_t; z_t); z_t) + d_t(z_t).$$ (12)

In the standard life-cycle model it is the discounted sum of these terms that is maximised (under expectation) subject to an asset accumulation constraint.

There are strong assumptions underlying the standard intertemporal model. First, life-cycle utility is explicitly additive in u_t. Secondly, preferences are separable over time, that is no $t - 1$ or $t + 1$ terms enter period t specific utility. This rules out habit persistence, for example. Finally, capital markets are assumed to operate efficiently such that the usual asset accumulation constraint (a fixed interest rate for limitless borrowing) can be assumed. Although strong, these assumptions are no more, or no less, than is typically assumed in standard intertemporal analysis. Borrowing constraints and/or habits would not harm the overall arguments of this section, but they would complicate estimation.

With this model in place the optimal path for consumption is one in which the (discounted) marginal utility of an extra unit of expenditure is 'smoothed' over time. In fact the consumer will act so as to equate the discounted marginal utility of income (or wealth) over time according to

$$E_t\left[(1 + r_{t+1})\frac{\partial u_{t+1}}{\partial x_{t+1}}\right] = \frac{\partial u_t}{\partial x_t}$$ (13)

where r_{t+1} is the real interest rate and E_t is a conditional expectation taken in period t to reflect uncertainty about the future.

From (12) we can see that (13) involves neither $d(z_t)$ nor $d(z_{t+1})$. These terms, which reflect the 'pure' lifetime value of children, can never be identified from consumption data alone even in an intertemporal setting. However, from the equality (13) all parameters of f_t in (12) up to a scalar can be recovered.

These points are developed in detail in Banks, Blundell and Preston (1994, and chapter 8 in this volume). However, to see how this life-cycle intertemporal analysis highlights the problem of identifying equivalence scales, consider the simplest specification of preferences in which

$$u_t = \frac{1}{\delta(z_t)} v_t \tag{14}$$

where $\delta(z)$ may be interpreted as a deflator of household utility that reflects changes in composition. If we consider the Almost Ideal cost function with the independence of base assumption (IB), we may write

$$\ln e(v_t, p_t; z_t) = \ln a(p_t; z_t) + b(p_t) v_t. \tag{15}$$

From (15) we can solve for v_t directly as

$$v_t = \frac{\ln x_t - \ln a(p_t; z_t)}{b(p_t)} \tag{16}$$

using the identity $x_t = e(v_t, p_t; z_t)$. From (16) the equivalence scale as estimated from Marshallian demand analysis may be written

$$\ln m_t = \ln a(p_t; z_t) - \ln a(p_t; z_t^r). \tag{17}$$

However, the equivalence scale recovered from the intertemporal model would use the following cost function in terms of u_t not v_t

$$\ln e_t = \ln a(p_t; z_t) + b(p_t) . \delta(z_t) u_t \tag{18}$$

resulting in the equivalence scale

$$\ln m_t = \ln a(p_t; z_t) - \ln a(p_t; z_t^r) + (\delta(z_t) - \delta(z_t^r)) b(p_t) u_t \tag{19}$$

which would equal (17) only if the factor $\delta(z_t)$ was independent of z_t. Chapter 8 in this volume provides empirical evidence on the size and importance of this feature for the allocation of expenditures over the life-cycle and for the estimation of equivalence scales. Using estimation results from standard demand analysis, it would be impossible to say anything about $\delta(z_t)$. An intertemporal analysis, however, identifies differences in $\delta(z_t)$ by taking an individual through time during which the z_t characteristics change. It should be pointed out that the equivalence scale (19) still relates to period specific costs and does not necessarily reflect all components of lifetime welfare in (12) unless $g_t(z_t)$ is independent of z_t (see Blackorby, Donaldson and Maloney, 1984; Keen, 1990). In chapter 8 in this volume, definitions of scales are extended to life-cycle welfare.

A critical requirement underlying this intertemporal analysis is to be able to follow households over time. Panel data is, therefore, all but essential for estimation, and may reflect why such analysis is so uncommon in the measurement of child costs. However, there is increasing availability of micro data on consumption which extends over time and a number of applications of this consumption model to panel data. For example, MaCurdy (1983) adopts such a procedure using the US Panel Study of Income Dynamics (PSID) which now covers in excess of 20 years.

Nevertheless the PSID only measures food expenditures, and most datasets that accurately record expenditures across a wide group of goods possess only a short panel element, as is the case for the Consumers Expenditure Survey in the USA, or no panel element at all, as is the case for the Family Expenditure Survey in the UK and the Budget de Famille in France, for example. Where a long panel dataset is not available, an alternative is possible where repeated cross-section data is available. Browning, Deaton and Irish (1985) utilise such data to form pseudo-panels of date of birth cohorts from the repeated cross-sections available through the Family Expenditure Surveys. This procedure, also adopted in the Blundell, Browning and Meghir (1994) study, is further analysed in chapter 8.

Within-household welfare distribution

Early approaches

Traditional approaches to the measurement of household welfare have taken the household as the level of decision making, modelling its behaviour as if it had a single objective function satisfying similar properties to individual utility functions, and then allocating the attained value of the objective (appropriately equivalised to adjust for economies of scale in the household) equally among its members.

Recent developments have questioned the assumption of a single objective function with properties in accord with traditional analysis of a single consumer, and the assumption of equal sharing of the outcome. Households are typically composed of many individuals with noncoincident preferences, unequal voices in decision making and unequal claims on resources. Significant recent advances have been made towards the development of improved models allowing the recovery of individual level preferences.

Samuelson (1956) was well aware of the problem in assuming families to behave as if they had the preferences of an individual, and recognised as unsatisfactory the convenient assumptions of either a dictator or consensus within the household. He noted, nonetheless, that a family would act as if maximising some family utility function, construed as some function of the individual members' utilities, if within the family there could be assumed to take place a permanent reallocation of income so as to keep each member's social marginal utility of expenditure equal. The mechanism for achieving such a 'utopian' outcome was not elaborated.

Becker's (1981b) famous Rotten Kid Theorem was another attempt to justify the single household utility function approach. In Becker's model there is a single composite consumption good to be split between the members of the household. Household behaviour which appears to obey a single household utility function is assured by the presence of a single caring member in the household, valuing the utility of other members and powerful enough to have the final say on how resources are allocated. Within-household transfers made by the altruist offset the selfish behaviour of nonaltruists – 'rotten kids' – and the rotten kid who realises this will see that he can best serve his own interests by himself behaving altruistically.

The implicit assumptions here are strong. Within-household conflict over the composition of spending, for instance, is ruled out by the assumption of a single composite commodity. Most importantly, the structure of decision making is left somewhat vague and, as several authors have pointed out (Manser and Brown, 1980; Ben-Porath, 1982), has to be such as to allow the carer (or carers) to have the last word, which is to say to adjust their spending freely to determine the collective outcome. The models discussed below suggest that this is only really likely if the carer controls a sufficiently large share of household resources to impose their preferences if decision making is noncooperative or is persuasive enough to enforce dictatorship as a cooperative outcome.

Noncooperative models

An early example of a noncooperative model is Leuthold's (1968) model of household labour supply as a Nash equilibrium in spouse's labour supplies, empirically applied in Ashworth and Ulph (1981). Each partner chooses in this model to work as long as suits them best given the hours of work chosen by their partner. Ulph (1988) develops in some detail a similar model of household consumption behaviour. Spouses are allowed to care about each other's consumption and choose to allocate private incomes optimally from their own point of view given the purchases of their partner. Provided that there is some good which both partners spend on then household spending will be locally independent of the within household distribution of income. This reult is closely related to results on

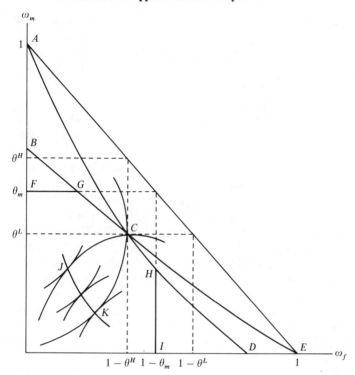

Figure 1.2   Equilibrium in a noncooperative model of household behaviour

private provision of public goods derived by Warr (1983), Kemp (1984) and Bergstrom *et al.* (1986).

It is only if income shares are so unequal that partners spend on mutually exclusive sets of goods that the division of income then matters.

Figure 1.2 illustrates a very crude special case. Say that a married couple spend a fixed household budget on three goods only – one public good, one good consumed exclusively by the husband and one consumed exclusively by the wife. Denote the respective shares in the total household budget by ω_0, ω_m and ω_f. Say, furthermore, that both partners are egoistic in the sense that they seek to maximise utilities dependent only on consumption of the public good and their own private good. Given a proportion ω_f of the household budget spent on the wife's good, the husband will have preferences over the way the remainder is split between the public good and his own private good, and since higher ω_f leaves less to be spent on both normality of the private good would suffice to ensure that the husband's desired ω_m will be a decreasing function of ω_f. The line

$BGCE$ represents such a relationship (and the line $ACHD$ the corresponding relationship for the wife). If, for instance, nothing were spent on the wife's private good then the husband would split the budget between the public good and his own private good in proportion as at B. For higher ω_f the proportion falls, until for obvious reasons it falls to zero as everything is spent on the wife's private good.

The most, however, that the husband can actually cause to be spent on his own privately consumed good is his own share of household income, θ_m, so the husband's ability to spend on himself in response to his wife's spending will be curtailed from above and will keep the household on the line $FGCE$ (just as the wife's reactions will keep it on $ACHI$ given that the share under her control is $1 - \theta_m$). The actual outcome will be at the intersection of these two lines. As illustrated, this is at C and one can see that this would be true for any θ_m between θ^H and θ^L. This is exactly Ulph's local invariance result – there is a large range of income shares over which the within-household distribution of income does not matter to the collective outcome. If $\theta_m < \theta^L$ then the outcome lies somewhere on CD with the husband spending all his income on his own private consumption and the share of the budget going to all goods depending upon his share of household income. If, alternatively $\theta_m > \theta^H$ then the solution lies on BC with the husband alone purchasing the public good.[8]

Chapter 5 in this volume, by Del Boca and Flinn, develops from earlier work using a noncooperative model of this sort in which the 'partners' are divorced parents and the public good is expenditure on their child.

The outcome in noncooperative games will typically be Pareto inefficient, particularly if individual preferences are egoistic, and one would be surprised if households did not make some attempt to exploit the gains available from cooperation. In the case just discussed, for instance, one can see that there is a free-rider problem with regard to spending on the public good and both partners would gain from an agreement to spend more on it. Utility contours passing through the equilibrium at C are CK for the husband and CJ for the wife, and it is clear that points of tangency along the locus JK leave both partners better off than at the noncooperative outcome[9].

Cooperative models

Authors such as Chiappori (1988a, 1991) and Apps and Rees (1988) have sought to explore the implications of assuming only that household collective decisions are Pareto efficient, or 'collectively rational' in

Chiappori's phrase. The directions of this research are well summarised in chapter 3 in this volume, by Bourguignon and Chiappori. In a model where all goods are private goods but partners may care about each other's well-being, collective rationality is equivalent to the existence of a sharing rule – partners behave as if unearned income is split between the two according to some rule and each then behaves as an isolated individual. The cooperative model is neither nested within nor nests the single household utility function approach, and the two are compatible if the household acts as if maximising some fixed function of the partner's utilities (Chiappori, 1988a).

The cooperative framework imposes a weak separability between consumption assignable to the two partners which is not required by the traditional model. The traditional model imposes an independence of outcomes from the division of incomes. What is most important to welfare measurement is that the sharing rule and individual preferences turn out in general to be recoverable from observation of demands, up to a level of indeterminacy which doesn't matter for identifying beneficiaries of reforms, provided that there is some good for which demand can be broken into components assignable to particular individuals. Leisure time is an obvious example of a good which may be assignable (Chiappori, 1992), though housework, being unobserved, may complicate matters. Clothing might be another example, though if either partner cares about the appearance of the other then the assumption of exclusive consumptions of male and female clothing clearly breaks down.

Other authors have sought to impose more structure on the nature of the bargains struck. Manser and Brown (1980), McElroy and Horney (1981) and McElroy (1990) have all investigated particular solutions, especially that due to Nash. McElroy and Horney, for instance, show that properties of individual consumer demands such as Engel aggregation and Slutsky symmetry may fail to hold for collective demands, because of the influence of price and income changes on either partner's opportunities outside the marriage, and they derive analogues for the Nash case. The Nash assumption would seem, however, difficult to test using demand data since the solution is not invariant to arbitrary monotonic transformation of utilities and one would therefore need to find some way of estimating cardinal utilities (Chiappori, 1988b, 1991) (see van Praag's chapter 4 in this volume, however, for a survey of one approach to estimating cardinal preferences from other information).

McElroy has pointed to some testable implications of the traditional model. For one thing, the effect of changes in either partner's income on demands should be indistinguishable, a conclusion which Thomas (1990), for example, empirically rejects. For another, influences on threat points will affect outcomes in a bargaining but not in the traditional framework (at least assuming no effect on preferences). If threat points are taken to be divorce (as McElroy assumes) then these might include legal rules, existence of supporting social networks, parental wealth, and so on. If, as Ulph (1988) argues, the threat points should be the noncooperative outcome then the determinants of this will matter; note also that since the noncooperative outcome may be locally invariant to the within-household income distribution so also therefore may be the bargained outcome. Note the implication that in a bargaining framework all of these have consequences for welfare conclusions – it could matter from an economic point of view, for instance, who governments pay benefits to, and what rules they set for divorce settlements.

Labour supply decisions and welfare

Leisure in the welfare function

Traditionally, the welfare of an individual is measured by real income or expenditure – often income deflated by some price index. However, such a measure ignores the contribution of 'leisure' to the standard of living. This is an important shortcoming, for two reasons. First leisure – or, more generally, non-market time – is a very important commodity in the sense that leisure's share in full income is likely to vary significantly across individuals and has also varied across time for significant groups in the labour market. Secondly, tax policy which changes income may be designed specifically to alter leisure's share by providing incentives (or disincentives) to work.

The literature to date has allowed for the additional complication of incorporating labour supply simply by treating leisure as an additional commodity. However the most important feature of the empirical literature which has distinguished the analysis of labour supply from that of commodity demands is the nonlinearity associated with the budget constraint – the econometric analysis of the determinants of labour supply in the face of such nonlinearities depends heavily on the interpretation given to the error term.[10] This section is concerned with the measurement of individual welfare in labour supply models which allow for the impact of income taxation and income support schemes on labour supply decisions and are motivated by the desire to develop welfare change measures which can be computed easily, can be interpreted readily, and which are directly comparable with net income – the measure of welfare often used in policy analysis.

In the existing literature the expenditure function is the classic money metric. This is exactly analogous to the full income expenditure function in the context of labour supply but a number of alternatives to the full income cost function can be derived, which we explore below.

Alternative measures of welfare

The real wage function, first proposed by Pencavel (1977), is an attractive option since it is readily interpretable and comparable with actual wages. However, for welfare measurement involving nonworkers the wage is not observed, and an alternative measure could be based on the consumption level at reference hours of zero. This is the intercept of the indifference curve with the vertical axis and we refer to it as the *intercept income function*. This measure is equal to actual income for nonworkers.

The individual is assumed to have preferences defined over goods and leisure with an ordinal representation $u(q,h;\gamma)$, where γ is a parameter reflecting tastes (which we suppress for the moment), q is consumption of a single composite commodity, taken as numeraire, and h is labour supply. Labour supply decisions are assumed to follow from optimisation subject to a budget constraint, which would in the simplest case be linear, i.e., $q = wh + \mu$ with a wage of w and unearned income μ, but in practice might be nonlinear because of taxation, discreteness in the availability of jobs, or nonnegativity in choice of hours of work, and so on.

Ordinality implies that any increasing function $\phi(.)$ of some chosen metric can serve as another equally valid measure. The choice of $\phi(.)$, which is just a matter of the numbering of indifference curves, might be motivated primarily in such a context by ease of interpretation.

One possible basis for a metric would be the consumption possibilities of a household at the given standard of living and a reference labour supply, h^r, which is given by

$$\phi_1(u;h^r) = q(u,h^r). \tag{20}$$

If h^r is chosen to be zero then one is effectively numbering each indifference curve according to its intersection with the vertical axis, a choice which has an appealing monetary interpretation. Under certain restrictions on preferences the gradient of the indifference curve at the point

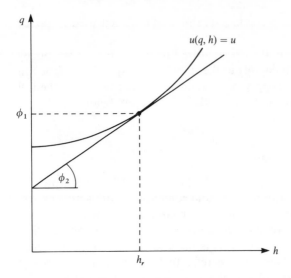

Figure 1.3   Welfare at reference hours

under discussion, which is to say the virtual wage at h^r, could also serve as a suitable, albeit less obvious, metric. This is given by

$$\phi_2(u;h^r) = \left[\frac{\partial q(u,h)}{\partial h}\right]_{h=h^r}. \tag{21}$$

For $h^r = 0$ this could be interpreted as a reservation wage metric. Since this essentially inverts the Hicksian labour supply function at reference hours, the appropriate restriction validating its use as a metric for welfare is simply normality of leisure at h^r across the range of living standards in question. Figure 1.3 illustrates $\phi_1(.)$ and $\phi_2(.)$ for $h^r > 0$.

The notion of the money metric, i.e., the lowest level of unearned income that allows the given utility to be attained at reference wage, is a familiar one (see King, 1983; Blackorby and Donaldson, 1988a; Donaldson, 1990). This can be written as

$$\phi_3(u;w^r) = e(u,w^r) = \min_{h\geq0} q(u,h) + w^r h \tag{22}$$

or, put more succinctly, the value of the unearned income expenditure function[11] at w^r.

The idea of inverting the indirect utility function in the wage at a reference level of unearned income μ^r is suggested by the work of Pencavel (1977, 1979). This yields the real wage function

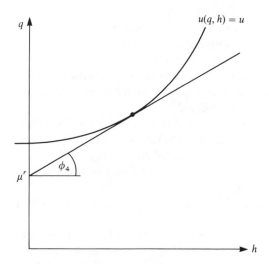

Figure 1.4   Welfare at reference unearned income

$$\phi_4(u;\mu^r) = r(u,\mu^r) = \min_{h \geq 0} \left[(q(u,h) - \mu^r)/h \right] \tag{23}$$

which is illustrated in figure 1.4.

If the optimal level of labour supply is in the interior of a linear budget constraint, it is possible to bound indices of welfare change based on certain of these metrics by fixed weight indices according to conventional Paasche and Laspeyre's inequalities. In particular this is true of indices based on the unearned income metric, $e(u,w)$, or real wage metric, $\phi_4(u,\mu^r)$, evaluated at pre-reform or post-reform reference wages or unearned incomes (see Cleeton, 1982).

Empirical illustration with nonlinear budget constraints

In much empirical work, labour supply models feature a random parameter which forms the error term in the estimated equation and this is invariably assumed to be normally distributed. We thus assume here that γ has a random component as well as systematically describing the observable characteristics. Typically, labour supply is found to depend strongly on demographic composition and as a result welfare measures become sensitive to the specification of demographic effects and the chosen equivalence scale (see Blundell, Meghir, Symons and Walker, 1988).

An important feature of empirical work on labour supply is the non-linearity associated with the budget constraint. The estimated preference parameters and an estimate of the variance of the random preference term then allow us to complete the probability of being on each and every facet of the constraint. Since the welfare of the household will depend on the location of the household on the budget constraint, and since economic models tell us only the probability of being at a particular point on the constraint, it is natural to take the expected value of welfare as a measure of the well-being of the household.

Small and Rosen (1981) construct aggregate measures of welfare when individual behaviour is subject to discrete choice. However, that analysis did not consider how this could be implemented empirically and it is clear that empirical analysis tells us only about the probability of being at each discrete point (or on each facet of a continuous, but nonlinear, constraint) so aggregation from individual data should clearly be on the basis of individual expected values.

Taking expectations over the unobservable characteristic enables us to compute expected welfare levels. One could do this at the level of any particular cardinalisation of the direct utility function and then compute the metrics as transformations of that expected level of utility. Clearly the choice of cardinalisation will make a difference to the expected welfare level. A sensible choice of cardinalisation, on grounds of interpretability, might be one of the metrics discussed above. However, since our measures, $\phi_1(.)$, etc. are all (different) transformations of $u(.)$ then applying the expectation operator to any one will, in general, produce a different result to applying it to any other.

As an example of this kind of work consider a model of discrete choice labour supply which corresponds to an extreme form of nonlinear budget constraint. In Preston and Walker (1992) a discrete choice model was derived from the preferences corresponding to a linear labour supply equation $h = aw + \beta\mu + \gamma(z)$. The analysis here is based on data on lone mothers drawn from the 1988 Family Expenditure Survey. The alternative values of hours of work were assumed to be 0 for nonparticipants, 25 for part-timers (those working less than 31), and 40 for full-timers (those working 31 or more).

The estimates (and t values) are $\beta = -0.264$ (1.97), $a = 10.636$ (2.14), and a constant of 29.924 (5.59), and dummy variables indicating that the youngest child was pre-school and primary school were -61.77 (4.60) and -13.24 (1.61) respectively. These results are entirely conventional: children, especially young ones, have a large negative impact on labour supply; the wage effect is positive and the unearned income effect negative – satisfying integrability conditions everywhere. Elasticities should be calculated by simulating the impact of wage and income changes on the labour force status probabilities. However, an approximate idea can be had by substituting the estimates into a linear equation. At average hours

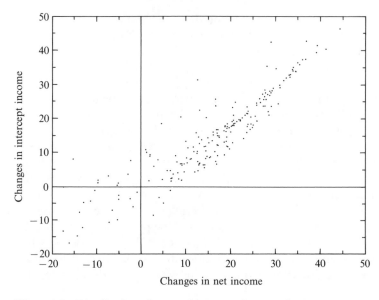

Figure 1.5   Distribution of net and intercept income changes

and wage, the wage elasticity is close to two-thirds and the income elasticity is close to minus one-quarter.

To illustrate the welfare significance of these results we simulate the impact of a reform to the UK system of child support which would increase the net incomes of many lone mothers who currently receive no child support but decrease the amount received by a few.[12] Chapter 5 considers child support issues in more detail and relates them to intra-household welfare measurement.

Figure 1.5 shows the distribution of net income changes and changes in $\phi_1(u, 0)$ which we think of as *intercept income* (i.e., ϕ_1 at reference hours zero) under the existing maintenance arrangements. This figure gives one a feel for the importance of taking account of behavioural changes in computing gains and losses. While the figure shows that the two measures of welfare change are likely to be positively related, the relationship is far from being a close one and there are a significant number of individuals who gain under one definition but lose under the other.

Social welfare, inequality and poverty

Social choice

Suppose the considerations of earlier sections have allowed the calculation of individual welfare measurement for some population. This section considers the aggregation of these individual judgements into some social judgement on collective welfare. The most immediate question regards the sufficiency and relevance of individual welfares to judgement on the desirability of social states. Many economists seem to have accepted the view labelled as 'welfarism', holding that social judgements, insofar as they can be made at all, should be based only on information on individual utilities. This is nonetheless far from uncontroversial and indeed the view that social arrangements should be judged solely on their consequences has been widely denied. Many would see utility-centred social judgements as blind, for instance, to notions of rights, entitlements and obligations. Note, though, that admitting the relevance of nonutility information need not imply the irrelevance of social welfare measurement, which may still be accepted as offering one among other inconclusive considerations. A variety of views on these points can be found, for instance, in the essays in Sen and Williams (1982). These issues, while conceptually important, have not been central to the applied literature and an adequate discussion would take us well beyond the scope of this book.

The nature of judgements which can be reached obviously depends on the nature of the utility information available, and in particular on assumptions made about measurability and interpersonal comparability. Does a comparison of an individual's utility in two situations tell us only in which situation they are better off, or does it tell us in some numerical sense by how much they are better off or even how well off they are in each situation? These sorts of issues are issues which we refer to as involving measurability. Does a comparison of two individuals' utilities in any situation or situations tell us anything about which of them is better off or which has benefited more from some change in their collective circumstances? We refer to these issues as issues involving comparability.

A convenient way to think of these questions is to put the issue (following, say, Roberts, 1980b) in terms of the implications of transforming utilities. Under what transformations of welfare functions should social judgements be unchanged? The most restrictive view requires that social judgements be unaffected by any monotone increasing transformation of any individual's utility function. Since transformations of this kind carry no implications for consumption or labour supply behaviour, economists of a positivist leaning have often been drawn to this opinion of utilities as both noncomparable and no more than ordinally measurable. It is a view which admits judgements based on the Pareto partial order, approving social reforms only if no-one loses and condemning them only if no-one gains, but which severely restricts the possible social choice rules for cases where the gains of some need to be weighed against the losses of others. Arrow (1951) formalised the problem of making social judgements in such a framework in his highly influential General Possibility Theorem. This showed that the only possible rule for social judgement giving a complete ordering for all possible configurations of individual preferences, compatible with the Pareto principle and requiring that the social ranking of any two states depends only upon the ordinal non-comparable utility information about these states,[13] would have to be a dictatorship, in the sense of simply following the preferences of one named individual. The apparent innocuousness of Arrow's assumptions, the strength of his result and its apparent robustness to further inquiry have seemed to many to undermine the whole idea of measuring social welfare.

Sen (1979), however, has drawn attention to the extraordinary restrictiveness of simultaneously allowing social judgements to depend on utility information only while so impoverishing the content of that information. Assessment of any proposed social reform could not, for instance, in this framework take any account of whether beneficiaries were among the rich or the poor. We cannot identify the less well off by their low utility because interpersonal comparisons of utility are not allowed and we cannot identify them by, say, their low incomes since Arrow's assumptions allow us only to use utility information. If taking from Peter to give to Paul is regarded as socially desirable when Peter is better off than Paul then one must also regard it as socially desirable when Peter is worse off if individuals' preferences with regard to the change are the same in both cases, since that is all the ordinal noncomparable utility information that there is to consider.

Relaxing noncomparability might allow one at least to identify the better off, even without relaxing ordinality and, therefore, to implement something like Rawls' (1971) concern for the well-being of the least well off.[14] More technically, requiring social judgements to be unaffected by arbitrary monotonic transformations of utility *provided* the same transformation be applied to everyone, while still leaving some sort of dictatorship as the only acceptable option, might at least allow one to identify the dictator by relative welfare rather than by name (see Roberts, 1980b). In the example of the previous paragraph, this would give a legitimate reason for approving the income transfer from Peter to Paul only when Peter was the better off of the two. Sen (1970) follows another route, developing ideas of 'partial comparability' allowing the possibility that the degree of ambiguity in interpersonal welfare comparisons, while real, may be limited.

Relaxing noncomparability *and* ordinality extends the variety of possible rules even further. For example, if social judgements are required to be unaffected only by identical positive affine transformations[15] to individual utilities then classical 'Benthamite' utilitarianism becomes a viable option. That is to say, one could then compare social states, if so inclined, by simply adding up utilities. Under different requirements still, it would be possible to evaluate social welfare by, say, adding up concave transformations of utilities.

The view of cardinal utility as not only a meaningful concept but also as amenable to practical measurement is defended by Bernard van Praag in chapter 4. He summarises his own work and that of various co-authors on the use of income evaluation questionnaires as a means to the recovery of cardinal information.

Social welfare and income inequality

To simplify things, this subsection turns to consider social judgements for a more tightly specified set of circumstances. To reduce the salience of issues of interpersonal comparison and within-household distribution, suppose we are considering a population of single individual households with identical tastes. To abstract also from problems of price variation assume that there is only a single good, the price of which is the same for all individuals and is normalised to unity. Dispersion in the vector of incomes, $\mathbf{x}$, is to be taken as the sole source of dispersion in household welfare levels. There is a well-developed literature on criteria for comparison in this heavily restricted context which constitutes the inevitable starting point for a consideration of more complex cases.

Let us suppose sufficiently rich utility information to permit social preferences giving a complete ordering over all possible vectors of economic entitlements, summarisable as a single function of the associated vector of household utilities $\mathbf{u} = u(\mathbf{x})$. Denote this function $W^*(\mathbf{u})$ and call its value the level of social welfare. Obviously this can also be written as a function of the vector of household incomes $\mathbf{x}$, $W(\mathbf{x}) = W^*u(\mathbf{x})$.

A common first argument is that impersonality requires that social evaluation be indifferent to permutations of the utility vector and, given identical utility functions, that $W(\mathbf{x})$ must therefore be symmetric in $\mathbf{x}$. Requiring $W(\mathbf{x})$ also to be increasing in all arguments seems unlikely to be contentious, corresponding merely to the assumption that Pareto improvements should be regarded as favourable. A change from one income vector to another will be preferred by all social welfare functions satisfying these two properties if it raises (or does not lower) all quantiles of the income vector.[16]

A possibly more interesting set of social welfare-improving changes

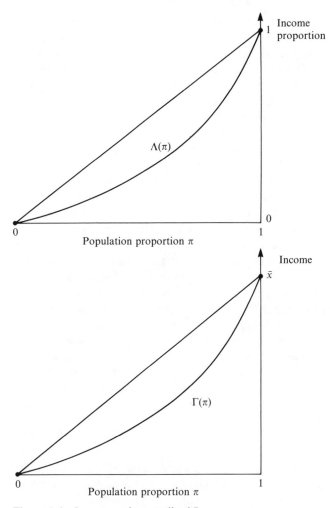

Figure 1.6 Lorenz and generalised Lorenz curves

might be that of lump sum progressive income transfers, which is to say transfers of income from richer to poorer households with an unchanging mean. There is a principle, usually attributed to Pigou (1912) and Dalton (1920), which holds that such transfers should be regarded as reducing inequality. A famous result (proved originally by Hardy, Littlewood and Pòlya, 1934 but only more recently applied in the present context by Atkinson, 1970; Dasgupta, Sen and Starrett, 1973; and Rothschild and Stiglitz, 1973) establishes a link between such changes and a familiar graphical analysis introduced by Lorenz (1905).

To understand the result and its relevance we need to define a device known as the Lorenz curve. This is a curve plotting proportions of the population from the poorest upward (on the horizontal axis) against the cumulative shares of income which they collectively hold (on the vertical axis). Figure 1.6 illustrates such a curve, labelled $\Lambda(\pi)$, where π is the population proportion. It is convex by construction – its slope at any point is the ratio of the income at that point in the distribution to the mean income – and the degree of 'bowed-outness' has long been regarded as an indicator of inequality. If one Lorenz curve lies everywhere above another – a situation in which the former is said to Lorenz dominate the latter – then the idea is that the former should be seen as unambiguously more equal. The Hardy *et al.* result reinforces this view by establishing that Lorenz dominance can be shown to be equivalent, if mean incomes are the same, to the existence of some series of progressive transfers linking the two distributions.

Another result of the same authors, rediscovered by Atkinson (1970), gives further reason for directing attention towards such changes. Say that one wished to evaluate social welfare as the sum of identical, concave and increasing individual utility functions, $W(\mathbf{x}) = \Sigma u(x_i)$. They establish a result equivalent to saying that those changes, among all those preserving mean incomes, which increase any such social welfare function are exactly those which can be represented as a series of progressive transfers. The key to understanding this is simple: under such assumptions about social welfare, taking income from a richer household has less effect on social welfare than giving the same amount to a poorer one, whatever the vector of incomes, i.e.,

$$\left(\frac{\partial W}{\partial x_i} - \frac{\partial W}{\partial x_j}\right)(x_i - x_j) \leq 0 \qquad \forall \mathbf{x}. \tag{24}$$

This condition characterises a more general class of (not necessarily additive) social welfare functions which increase given any mean-preserving progressive transfer. Functions with this property are known as Schur-concave.

Consideration only of changes which preserve means is clearly restrictive. Shorrocks (1983) considers the class of all changes which will increase any symmetric and increasing Schur-concave social welfare function. In order to describe the class, first define the generalised Lorenz curve as the Lorenz curve vertically multiplied by the mean income. It is a curve plotting proportions of the population from the poorest upward against their cumulative mean incomes multiplied by their population share, and an example is illustrated in figure 1.6, labelled $\Gamma(\pi)$. Then the class of changes in question are those raising (or not lowering) the generalised Lorenz curve everywhere.[17]

One would like to say something about inequality as well as social welfare in cases of changing mean incomes. Disagreement exists here as to the sort of changes which leave inequality unaffected. The Lorenz curve as defined above is unchanged by scale changes in the income vector (i.e., equal proportional changes in all incomes) and continuing to believe that inequality judgements can be based on its movements even when means are not fixed must imply the view (sometimes labelled 'relative') that such changes also leave inequality unaffected. An alternative view (sometimes labelled 'absolute') holds that it is translations of the income vector (i.e., equal additions to all incomes) which are inequality preserving, and Moyes (1987) and Shorrocks (1983) have suggested a form for an 'absolute' Lorenz curve and associated inequality ordering compatible with this idea. The curve in question is constructed as the vertical distance between the generalised Lorenz curve and the generalised Lorenz curve as it would be if everyone had mean income. Of course, the view may be held that neither of these changes preserves inequality and Kolm (1976a, 1976b) and others have sought to define and explore intermediate positions, though the rationale for so doing has been questioned by Broome (1989).

Indices of inequality

Inequality relations discussed so far have all been partial orderings. It has often been felt desirable to construct a single index to summarise the inequality in an income vector, and an obvious first requirement for any such index is that it preserve the appropriate partial orderings discussed above. Any homogeneous of degree zero Schur-convex[18] function of incomes is invariant to scale changes and decreased by progressive transfers, and can, therefore, be interpreted as a 'relative' inequality index. Examples abound, including the popular Gini coefficient, Theil entropy index or coefficient of variation. Likewise, any translatable of degree zero[19] Schur-convex function of incomes, such as the variance, can be interpreted as an 'absolute' inequality index (on both types of index see Blackorby and Donaldson, 1978, 1980).

One enduring and illuminating idea for the construction of an inequality index is owed to Atkinson (1970) and Kolm (1969). Define an 'equally distributed equivalent income', x^e, for any given income vector $\mathbf{x}$ by the identity $W(x^e.\mathbf{1}) \equiv W(\mathbf{x})$. It is, as the name suggests, that income which, if enjoyed by all, would give the same value of the social welfare function as does the actual income vector. Given $W(.)$ increasing in all arguments, it is unique and itself an indicator of social welfare. If the social welfare function is homothetic and Schur-concave then x^e is a linear homogeneous function of incomes and $I(\mathbf{x}) = 1 - x^e/\bar{x}$, where $\bar{x}$ is mean income, is homogeneous of degree zero, Schur-convex, and lies in the unit interval. This is, therefore, a relative inequality index[20] and is the measure proposed by Atkinson, in his case for a particular additive specification for the social welfare function[21]

$$W(\mathbf{x}) = \sum \frac{1}{1 - \epsilon} x_i^{1 - \epsilon}, \qquad \epsilon \geq 0, \ \epsilon \neq 1 \tag{25}$$

$$\Rightarrow I(\mathbf{x}) = 1 - \frac{x^e}{\bar{x}} = 1 - \left[\frac{1}{n} \sum \left(\frac{x_i}{\bar{x}}\right)^{1 - \epsilon}\right]^{\frac{1}{1 - \epsilon}}.$$

The index has a ready interpretation as the proportion of income wasted, from the viewpoint of maximising social welfare, as a result of the inequality.[22] The parameter ϵ in the Atkinson specification is indicative of the concavity in individual utility functions and is interpreted as a measure of 'aversion to inequality'.[23]

The separability of the social welfare function into terms involving mean income and inequality, $W(\mathbf{x}) = W(x^e.\mathbf{1})$ where $x^e = \bar{x}(1 - I(\mathbf{x}))$, has considerable interpretative value, seeming as it does to capture the frequent informal distinction drawn between the 'efficiency' and 'equity' issues raised by the evaluation of economic change. It can seem superficially to clarify what is informative and what is missing in judgements based solely on what has happened to mean income. Chapter 9 by Coulter, Cowell and Jenkins in this volume is a thorough investigation of changes in mean incomes of different population groups in a particular country over the last 10 years.

A number of proposals have been made for narrowing down the number of inequality indices admitted by the considerations so far detailed. Among them have been the suggestion of Shorrocks and Foster (1987; see also Foster and Shorrocks, 1987) that transfers of income should, in a sense which they make precise, be weighted more heavily if between those with lower incomes.[24] This turns out to have some interesting implications. Firstly it suggests that comparison in cases of single-crossing Lorenz curves can be effected simply by an additional comparison of variances, and secondly it appears to rule out several well-known indices including the Gini coefficient.

Another possible route, explored by Bourguignon (1979), Shorrocks (1980, 1984, 1988) and Blackorby, Donaldson and Auersperg (1981) among others, has been to require strong forms of decomposability across population subgroups. It is only, for instance, for a limited class of indices known as the Generalised Entropy class that the difference between overall inequality and the inequality which would pertain if inequality within subgroups were eliminated (by setting every income to its sub-group mean) can be expressed as a weighted sum of within-group inequal-ities with weights depending only on subgroup mean incomes and sizes. This is a class which contains increasing transformations of all the Atkinson indices and also of the coefficient of variation and Theil entropy indices. Blackorby, Donaldson and Auersperg (1981) propose an alter-native decomposition formula for the Atkinson index relying on the idea that between-group inequality should be measured as that which would hold if everyone in each subgroup were at the subgroup equally distribu-ted equivalent income rather than at the subgroup mean.[25]

Poverty

Concern with poverty has been widely construed as involving concern only with the incomes (or utilities) of those with incomes below a cut-off point or 'poverty line', say ξ. The factors determining the location of this cut-off point for any particular household have not often been a subject upon which economists have been ready to comment, though Callan and Nolan (1991) have drawn attention to an 'upsurge of interest' in the topic.

It is perhaps useful to separate out the issues involved in choosing ξ. One can distinguish, for instance, between the initial conceptual issue in deciding what aspects of a household's situation qualify it as being poor, and the secondary one of identifying at what income a household typi-cally falls into such a state. The oldest approach, evident for instance in Rowntree (1901), identifies poverty with inability to afford certain basic commodities and answers the second question by simply costing that bundle of commodities. The idea due to Engel (1895) that the share of the household budget spent on basic commodities, particularly food, can be a suitable indicator of household welfare in comparison of households of different type, see Blackorby and Donaldson (this volume). The associated idea that a household is poor if needing to spend too great a share of its budget on basic commodities is appealing in itself, and can be thought of as a second separate, and widely used, approach. Identification of a poverty line can, on this basis, proceed through the estimation of a demand system involving such goods.

A wider conception of a household's needs underlies a view seeing households as poor if unable to engage in a broader range of socially sanctioned activities. Townsend (1979) has claimed that empirical evi-dence points to the existence of an income threshold below which 'partici-pation in the national style of living' diminishes sharply, though this is a claim which has generated considerable debate (see Callan and Nolan, 1991, for references). Note that the fact that material requirements for full social participation are likely to vary with average incomes provides a reason for adopting a poverty line which also does so – a point which Sen (1983) has done much to clarify.

Other approaches look outward towards some social consensus on who can be regarded as poor, a consensus either supposedly embodied in government decisions on social assistance or to be deduced from public survey responses. Chapter 11 in this volume, by Tummers, is a development of the work by Kapteyn and von Herwaarden (1981) calculating 'subjective poverty lines' on the basis of households' answers to questions on how much they would need to 'make ends meet'.

Many of the ideas in the literature on measuring poverty can be best understood by considering censored income vectors derived from actual income vectors by censoring from above at the poverty line, which is to say replacing incomes above ξ with incomes of ξ. Atkinson (1987) and Foster and Shorrocks (1987, 1988) have looked at the possibility of basing poverty comparisons on restricted stochastic dominance relations, essentially involving the application of stochastic dominance concepts to censored income vectors. These are methods explicitly motivated by the recognition that the appropriate location of the poverty line is far from certain or uncontroversial and that judgements on poverty ought, therefore, to be robust to different decisions on where to fix ξ, at least over some reasonable range of values.

Still overwhelmingly the most common single index of poverty in practical applications is the simple headcount, i.e., the proportion of households with incomes below ξ. This is despite its obvious weaknesses with regard to its sensitivity to choice of cut-off point and insensitivity to depth of poverty of those below the line. Note incidentally that any policy maker using the headcount as a guide to success in reducing poverty would have an incentive to concentrate resources on the least poor amongst the poor, since it is they who could be got across the line most cheaply and moving people across the line would be all that would matter. A better index would be the total shortfall, suitably normalised, though even this can be criticised for its insensitivity to income transfers between poor households (which means it gives policy makers no more incentive to direct resources towards the very poor than towards the not-so-poor). Sen's (1976) pioneering inquiry into the possibility of a better index – one that acknowledges the possibility that deeper poverty may be in more urgent need of alleviation – has generated a large literature. Among interesting ideas have been that of Clark, Hemming and Ulph (1981) of comparing the equally distributed-equivalent income of the censored distribution to the cut-off point, and that of Foster, Greer and Thorbecke (1984) of basing an index on some sum of convex transformations of individual income gaps. The Foster, Greer and Thorbecke measure, $\Pi(\mathbf{x}) = \Sigma[\max(0, 1 - x_i/\xi)]^a$ where $a \geq 0$, has been particularly popular.

Extensions

By assuming a single good, it has been possible in preceding sections to ignore prices. Roberts (1980a) has investigated what is required for it to be legitimate to neglect prices in social evaluation in the case in which there are many goods.

Let prices $\mathbf{p}$ be the same in situations to be compared. Indirect utilities are $\mathbf{u} = v(\mathbf{x}, \mathbf{p})$ and social welfare is a function of the vector of incomes $\mathbf{x}$ and of prices $\mathbf{p}$, $\tilde{W}(\mathbf{x}, \mathbf{p}) = W^*(v(\mathbf{x}, \mathbf{p}))$. For it to be valid to reach conclusions about social welfare simply by observing changes in household incomes, irrespective of prices, requires that it be possible to separate the income vector $\mathbf{x}$ from prices $\mathbf{p}$ in the social welfare function $\tilde{W}(.)$.

To be precise, Roberts shows that we require that it be possible to write social welfare as a function of the price vector $\mathbf{p}$ and of a homothetic function of incomes, $g(\mathbf{x})$:

$$\tilde{W}(\mathbf{x}, \mathbf{p}) = G(g(\mathbf{x}), \mathbf{p}).$$

We can think of $g(.)$ as defining an equally distributed-equivalent income which is independent of prices. These circumstances are referred to by Roberts as admitting 'price-independent welfare prescriptions' (or PIWP) and by Slivinski (1983) as involving 'income separability'. Study of conditions admitting PIWP is particularly interesting since, as Roberts states, it 'requires an investigation of the interplay between individuals' and society's preferences'. Roberts shows, for instance, how requiring the aggregator function $W^*(.)$ to be additively separable in individual utilities restricts the possible forms for consumer demand if PIWP is to be retained, and likewise how requiring demands to take particular forms restricts admissible forms for the aggregator function. Slivinski (1983) extends Roberts' analysis to the case in which different households face different prices – conditions for PIWP become even more restrictive, requiring both homothetic individual preferences and a Cobb–Douglas social welfare aggregator.

If social welfare needs to be assessed as a function of individual utilities, taking account of prices and incomes, then one attractive metric in which to measure utilities might seem to be the money metric. That is to say, one could measure individuals' utilities by the minimum expenditure needed to leave them as well off at a reference set of prices. This looks attractive since the resulting money metric utilities are measured in the same units as incomes and one might think of evaluating social welfare as some Schur-concave function of money metric utilities, in the same way as social welfare functions are customarily constructed from incomes when the role of prices is being ignored. Blackorby and Donaldson (1988a) have, however, cautioned against such a practice, pointing out that unless money metric utility is concave in incomes – and it is only under quasi-homothetic preferences that this is guaranteed – then one could end up recommending *prima facie* inegalitarian income transfers. If money metric utility is not everywhere concave in income then taking income from a better off individual and giving it to one worse off could decrease the sum of money metric utilities and other supposed measures of social welfare based on them. Chapter 10 by Blackorby, Laisney and Schmach-tenberg in this volume points to a further problem, discussed also by Donaldson (1990) – any conclusions drawn in such a way will typically depend on the reference price vector chosen to calculate money metric utility. Their chapter shows that the only conditions in which this is not so are conditions admitting PIWP. These sorts of considerations apply, of course, to any other metric that might be suggested, including those discussed above in the context of labour supply decisions.

Variation between households in demographic composition introduces further complications. Let us assume, to simplify discussion, that we are considering again the case of a single good. One frequently used attempt to overcome problems of interpersonal comparison is to use equivalence scales to adjust the incomes of the different types of households on to a common basis, as discussed in earlier sections, and then to calculate measures of social welfare, inequality and so on from the vector of equivalent incomes. That is to say, the utilities of members of a household are measured by the minimum expenditure needed by a household with reference to demographic composition in order to leave its members as well off as the household in question. Quite apart from the problems of identifying the information needed to make welfare comparisons between households of differing demographic type, as discussed in the earlier sections, there are serious problems with such a method. A straight-forward extension of the Blackorby and Donaldson (1988) results makes clear that it is only under restrictive assumptions on tastes over demographic composition that equivalent incomes will be concave functions of income,[26] so that egalitarian income transfers even within demographic groups could lower measures of social welfare based on equivalent incomes. Likewise, it is clear from the remarks of Donaldson (1990) and of Blackorby, Laisney and Shmachtenberg that choice of reference demographic characteristics is unlikely to be immaterial.

Atkinson and Bourguignon (1982, 1987) make use of the literature on multivariate stochastic dominance to extend the results discussed above –

those results connecting classes of income distribution changes to guaranteed improvements in social welfare – so as to allow for variation between households in dimensions other than income. Without knowing anything about the effect of differing demographic characteristics on individual welfare, an improvement in social welfare for all additive Schur-concave social welfare functions would require generalised Lorenz dominance within each demographic group. No possible favourable or adverse views could thus be offered at this level of generality on any changes involving intergroup transfers. However, if needier groups could be identified, in the sense that groups could be ranked by the social marginal utility of their incomes, then a striking weakening of the condition would become possible. All that would be needed would be generalised Lorenz dominance in each of the groups formed by sequentially aggregating from the neediest upward.

With demographic heterogeneity, methods for decomposing overall inequality or poverty into within- and between-group components acquire an added relevance. Measures of inequality or poverty within homogeneous demographic subgroups should, in a sense, be less subject to problems of interpersonal comparability than between-group measures. Where households consist of more than one individual, decomposition results also have a natural application. Overall inequality can be thought of as some function of between-household and within-household inequality, with conventional procedures neglecting the latter aspect. Haddad and Kanbur (1990) investigate conditions under which the neglect of within-family inequality implicit in traditional approaches leads to an understatement of inequality and poverty.

The measurement of inequality with individuals determining their earnings by choice of labour supply at diverse wage rates has attracted the attention of a number of authors, including Allingham (1972), Stiglitz (1976) and Ulph (1978, 1981). The standard Atkinson (1970) approach to construction of an inequality measure can no longer be supported since equality of incomes is no longer a persuasive point of comparison. If wage rates can differ then equality of incomes need not correspond to equality of well-being nor will it typically be a feature of an optimal allocation of resources.

The idea behind the index may, nonetheless, be fruitfully developed. Ulph (1978), for instance, offering one possible extension of the idea, points out that the Atkinson index can be interpreted as the mean lump sum tax, expressed as a proportion of mean income, necessary to secure equality of utilities at the same level of social welfare as actually prevailing. Such an idea translates readily to the context in which labour supplies are flexible, though it becomes more sensible to express the hypothetical tax as a proportion of, say, mean wage since this, unlike mean income, will be unchanged by changes in taxes. However, this is still problematic. It is well known (from the optimal tax literature – see Mirrlees, 1971, for instance) that at the socially optimum division of resources, utilities will not be equal, since those with higher wages will be required to work harder. It is quite possible, therefore, to start with a distribution of resources such that equalising redistribution could reduce social welfare. If inequality can enhance social welfare then trying to measure inequality by social welfare loss can yield negative values and this is indeed a feature of the Ulph (1978) measure,[27] and of the proposals in the two earlier papers mentioned. Ulph's later paper (1981) suggests another generalisation of Atkinson's ideas, this time yielding a measure which is always positive.

Assessment of reforms

Complete modelling of demand is not always necessary to welfare assessment of reform proposals, particularly when the reforms in question are small. Ahmad and Stern, for instance, have shown in several recent practical applications (see, for example, Stern, 1987a, 1987b; Ahmad and Stern, 1987, 1991; and related papers) the possibility of using fairly limited information in offering informed recommendations on tax reform.

To see how these sorts of arguments work, consider the optimum tax problem of setting commodity taxes (and thereby prices) so as to maximise social welfare subject to an aggregate revenue constraint

$$\max_{\mathbf{p}} \tilde{W}(\mathbf{x}, \mathbf{p}) \quad \text{s.t.} \quad T(\mathbf{x}, \mathbf{p}) \geq \bar{T} \tag{26}$$

where $T(\mathbf{x}, \mathbf{p})$ is the function determining tax revenue and $\bar{T}$ is the revenue requirement. Note that the possibility of lump sum taxes is being excluded. At the optimum

$$\frac{\partial \tilde{W}}{\partial \mathbf{p}} + \chi \frac{\partial T}{\partial \mathbf{p}} = \frac{\partial W^*}{\partial \mathbf{u}'} \frac{\partial \mathbf{v}}{\partial \mathbf{p}} + \chi \frac{\partial T}{\partial \mathbf{p}} = 0 \tag{27}$$

where χ denotes the Lagrange multiplier on the revenue constraint and can be interpreted at the optimum as the marginal social cost of public funds.

Using Roy's identity we can convert this to the more useful form,

$$\chi_k \equiv \frac{\Sigma_i \gamma_i q_k^i}{\partial T / \partial \mathbf{p}} = \chi \tag{28}$$

where $\gamma_i \equiv (\partial W^*/\partial u_i)(\partial v(x_i, \mathbf{p})/\partial x_i)$ is the marginal social utility of income accruing to the ith household, sometimes called the ith household's welfare weight. What this equation captures is the simple point that if the marginal social costs of raising revenue through each tax is not the same, then the tax-setter cannot have achieved an optimum. In such a case, marginal shifts in the tax burden from goods with higher χ_k to those with lower values must enhance social welfare.[28] Provided one is prepared to stipulate values for welfare weights, one need only know expenditure levels of different households to calculate the social welfare effect of raising the tax on the kth good, which is to say the numerator in χ_k, and one need only know aggregate price elasticities in order to calculate the revenue effect, which is to say the denominator. Conclusions about socially advantageous directions for reform can, therefore, be drawn with fairly restricted information. The welfare weights, γ_i, are to be regarded as 'essentially value judgements'. Note that, given Schur-concavity of $\tilde{W}(\mathbf{x}, \mathbf{p})$ in incomes, we know at least that $(\gamma_i - \gamma_j)(x_i - x_j) \leq 0$. In practice the weights are usually set as some simple function of household expenditure. Questions of demographic heterogeneity, within-household distribution and so on can only complicate things and the sorts of issues raised in this volume ought to contribute to an informed choice of weights, particularly when the purpose of policy reforms under consideration involves a degree of redistribution between households of different demographic type.

The main problem with this type of analysis is perhaps that it applies only to small changes in linear taxes. It needs considerable amendment if it is to say anything interesting, except under restrictive assumptions, when there is a possibility of nonlinear direct taxes and where reforms under consideration may be large.

Conclusions and directions for future research

A wide variety of empirical work has attempted to measure the impact of policy changes on the behaviour and/or living standards of individuals. This kind of work has flourished in recent years with the increased availability of large micro datasets and significant decreases in the costs of analysing them using microeconometric methods. The aim of this chapter has been to complement the existing literature by concentrating on the issues that are highlighted in empirical applications.

A number of important issues have characterised the recent literature on the measurement of welfare: how to incorporate differences in household characteristics into welfare evaluations; how to evaluate the welfare of individuals when they live in households; how to incorporate intertemporal and labour market dimensions; the potential for using subjective survey data for measuring welfare; and how to measure social welfare, inequality and poverty from individual welfare measures.

Recent advances in the theoretical research on these topics have made it much clearer precisely what assumptions are required to conduct welfare analysis. The discussion in this volume makes it clear what can be achieved with the data we now have at hand. The objective is to encourage the use of microeconomic data in conducting welfare analyses.

The majority of the research that has been carried out by economists has not always reflected the priorities of those outside the profession. For example, there remains relatively little work being done on within-household distribution questions. Also, there is little work being done on the usefulness of questionnaire information. One objective of the volume is to stress the contributions that applied economists can make in such areas. In some cases existing datasets severely limit what can be learned about important welfare issues, and it seems evident that welfare economists will become more closely involved in data collection. In any event, with the increasing availability of better household databases, we can expect more emphasis on these issues in the future.

NOTES

Financial support for the research, from the ESRC Research Centre at the Institute for Fiscal Studies, is gratefully acknowledged. We would also like to thank James Banks, Pierre-André Chiappori, Ian Crawford, Michael Keen and Arthur Lewbel for many helpful comments.

1 Even favouring Pareto improvements could be controversial, involving normative judgements that conflict with certain ethical viewpoints.
2 See, for example, Blundell (1980).
3 See Kreps (1991) for a textbook description.
4 Note that there is a path dependency problem for MS. See Dixit and Weller (1979) for a clear statement of the path dependency problem.
5 The restrictions required for this are strong. Blackorby and Donaldson (1990), for instance, make a strong case against summing compensating variations in general applied welfare analysis.
6 However, in the labour supply literature it has become more common to analyse fertility decisions jointly (see Ermisch, 1989).
7 Up to the normalisation $e(u, p; z^r) = u$, that is, which is harmless because it only corresponds to the numbering of indifference curves.
8 Note, incidentally, that the equilibrium as illustrated is stable in the sense that one would expect both partners to react in ways such as to bring the household towards equilibrium from outside it.
9 By the very fact that everywhere on $BGCE$ the husband is maximising his own well-being subject to ω_f, his utility contours must be vertical as they cross $BGCE$. Likewise the wife's must be horizontal as they cross $ACHD$. The possibility of mutual improvement follows straightforwardly.
10 See Moffitt (1986) for a survey which emphasises the importance of the interpretation of the error for the estimation of models with nonlinear budget constraints.

11 One could, of course, use the full income cost function, although this would require an assumption to be made about the value of the time endowment.

12 Further details of the reform, the econometrics and the expressions for the welfare measures used for the linear labour supply case can be found in Preston and Walker (1992).

13 This follows Sen's (1979) interpretation of Arrow's 'Independence of Irrelevant Alternatives' axiom.

14 Rawls himself is unsympathetic to exclusive concentration on utility information, preferring to place emphasis on what he calls primary goods – 'social background conditions and all purpose means generally necessary for forming and rationally pursuing a conception of the good'.

15 This is often referred to as cardinal full comparability. It is not the weakest comparability assumption to admit utilitarianism as an option since it would not matter if the affine transformations mentioned had different origins for different individuals.

16 The relation between two such income distributions is referred to as first order stochastic dominance (or 'rank dominance' in the phrase used by Saposnik, 1981).

17 This is equivalent to saying those which lead to second order stochastic dominance.

18 A function $I(\mathbf{x})$ is said to be Schur-convex if $-I(\mathbf{x})$ is Schur-concave.

19 A function $I(\mathbf{x})$ is said to be translatable of degree λ if $I(\mathbf{x} + \kappa) = I(\mathbf{x}) + \lambda\kappa$.

20 If $W(.)$ is an increasing function of a function translatable of degree one then x^e is translatable of degree zero and $\bar{x} - x^e$ is an absolute inequality index.

21 In fact this is the only symmetric additive homothetic specification.

22 Sen (1978) has pointed to the danger in not keeping a clear conceptual distinction between inequality and the social welfare loss to which it gives rise. The Atkinson index is an index of inequality in incomes and is far from bearing interpretation as an index of inequality in *welfare levels*. Indeed from a utilitarian point of view there is nothing untoward in inequality of welfare levels – something which has often prompted criticism of the position.

23 The connection between the notion of inequality aversion and notions of risk aversion in the literature on economic uncertainty should be obvious to anyone familiar with that topic, as should that between the inequality index and a proportional risk premium. The relevant risk is that which would be borne by someone with an equal chance of enjoying the standard of living given by any income in $\mathbf{x}$.

24 The suggestion amounts to requiring that mean-preserving changes leading to third order stochastic dominance be regarded as inequality-reducing.

25 There is an argument for seeing this as more satisfying. The approach of Bourguignon and Shorrocks seems to imply that a decrease in inequality within any subgroup should not affect judgements on between-group inequality, even though the logic of the social welfare method would suggest that collective welfare in that subgroup had risen relative to all others.

26 Equivalence scale exactness is frequently assumed and is sufficient, though not necessary, for concavity.

27 One can make assumptions which eliminate the possibility, such as ruling out unearned income and thereby ensuring that the higher waged are better off in the absence of the equalising tax, but one cannot rule out the possibility in general.
28 Note that we are looking for favourable reforms rather than trying to advance in one leap to the global optimum.

REFERENCES

Afriat, S.N. (1977) *The Price Index*, Cambridge, Cambridge University Press
Ahmad, E. and N.H. Stern (1987) 'Alternative sources of government revenue for India, 1979–80', in D.M.G. Newbery and N.H. Stern (eds.), *The Theory of Taxation for Developing Countries*, Oxford, Oxford University Press, for the World Bank
  (1991) *The Theory and Practice of Tax Reform in Developing Countries*, Cambridge University Press, Cambridge
Allingham, M.G. (1972) 'The measurement of inequality', *Journal of Economic Theory*, 5, 163–196
Apps, P.F. and R. Rees (1988) 'Taxation and the household', *Journal of Public Economics*, 39, 335–364
Arrow, K.J. (1951) *Social Choice and Individual Values*, New York, Wiley
Ashworth, J. and D.T. Ulph (1981) 'Household models', in C.V. Brown (ed.), *Taxation and Labour Supply*, London, Allen & Unwin
Atkinson, A.B. (1970) 'On the measurement of inequality', *Journal of Economic Theory*, 2, 244–263
  (1987) 'On the measurement of poverty', *Econometrica*, 55, 749–764
Atkinson, A.B. and F. Bourguignon (1982) 'The comparison of multi-dimensioned distributions of economic status', *Review of Economic Studies*, 49, 183–201
  (1987) 'Income distribution and differences in needs', in G.R. Feigel (ed.), *Arrow and the Foundations of the Theory of Economic Policy*, London, Macmillan
Banks, J.W., R.W. Blundell and I.P. Preston (1994) 'Life-cycle expenditure allocations and the consumption costs of children', *European Economic Review*, forthcoming
Becker, G.S. (1981a) *A Treatise on the Family*, Cambridge, MA, Harvard University Press
  (1981b) 'Altruism in the family and selfishness in the market-place', *Economica*, 48, 1–15
Ben-Porath, Y. (1982) 'Economics and the family – match or mismatch? A review of Becker's "A Treatise on the Family"', *Journal of Economic Literature*, 20, 52–64
Bergstrom, T. C., L. Blume and H. Varian (1986) 'On the private provision of public goods', *Journal of Public Economics*, 29, 25–59
Blackorby, C. and D. Donaldson (1978) 'Measures of relative equality and their meaning in terms of social welfare', *Journal of Economic Theory*, 18, 59–80
  (1980) 'A theoretical treatment of indices of absolute inequality', *International Economic Review*, 21, 107–136

(1988a) 'Money metric utility: a harmless normalization?', *Journal of Economic Theory*, 46, 120–129

(1988b) 'Adult-equivalence scales and the economic implementation of interpersonal comparisons of well-being', University of British Columbia, *Discussion Paper*, 88–27

(1989) 'Adult-equivalence scales, interpersonal comparisons of well-being, and applied welfare economics', University of British Columbia, *Discussion Paper*, 89–24

(1990) 'A review article: the case against the use of the sum of compensating variations in cost benefit analysis', *Canadian Journal of Economics*, 23, 471–494

Blackorby, C., D. Donaldson and M. Auersperg (1981) 'A new procedure for the measurement of inequality within and among population subgroups', *Canadian Journal of Economics*, 14, 665–685

Blackorby, C., D. Donaldson and D. Maloney (1984) 'Consumer's surplus and welfare change in a simple dynamic model', *Review of Economic Studies*, 51, 171–176

Blundell, R.W. (1980) 'Estimating continuous consumer equivalence scales in an expenditure model with labour supply', *European Economic Review*, 14, 145–157

Blundell, R.W. and Lewbel, A. (1991) 'The information content of equivalence scales', *Journal of Econometrics*, 50, 49–68

Blundell, R.W., M.A. Browning and C. Meghir (1994) 'Consumer demand and the lifecycle allocation of household expenditures', *Review of Economic Studies*, 61, 57–80

Blundell, R.W., P. Pashardes and G. Weber (1993) 'What do we learn about consumer demand patterns from micro data?', *American Economic Review*, 83, 570–579

Blundell, R.W., C. Meghir, E. Symons and I. Walker (1988) 'Labour supply specification and the evaluation of tax reforms', *Journal of Public Economics*, 36, 23–52

Bourguignon, F. (1979) 'Decomposable inequality measures', *Econometrica*, 47, 901–920

Broome, J. (1989) 'What's the good of equality?', in J.D. Hey (ed.), *Current Issues in Microeconomics*, London, Macmillan

Browning, M.A. (1992) 'Modelling the effects of children on household economic behaviour', *Journal of Economic Literature*, 30, 1434–1475

Browning, M.A., A.S. Deaton and M. Irish (1985) 'A profitable approach to life-cycle labour supply', *Econometrica*, 53, 503–543

Callan, T. and B. Nolan (1991) 'Concepts of poverty and the poverty line', *Journal of Economic Surveys*, 5, 243–261

Chiappori, P.-A. (1988a) 'Rational household labour supply', *Econometrica*, 56, 63–89

(1988b) 'Nash-bargained household decisions: a comment', *International Economic Review*, 29, 791–796

(1991) 'Nash-bargained household decisions: a rejoinder', *International Economic Review*, 32, 761–762

(1992) 'Collective labour supply and welfare', *Journal of Political Economy*, 100, 437–467

Clark, S., R. Hemming and D.T. Ulph (1981) 'On indices for the measurement of poverty', *Economic Journal*, 91, 515–526

Cleeton, D.L. (1982) 'The theory of real wage indices', *American Economic Review*, 72, 214–225

Dalton, H. (1920) 'The measurement of the inequality of incomes', *Economic Journal*, 30, 343–361

Dasgupta, P., A.K. Sen and D. Starrett (1973) 'Notes on the measurement of inequality', *Journal of Economic Theory*, 6, 180–187

Deaton, A.S. and J. Muellbauer (1980a) *Economics and Consumer Behaviour*, Cambridge, Cambridge University Press

(1980b) 'An almost ideal demand system', *American Economic Review*, 70, 312–326

(1986) 'On measuring child costs: with applications to poor countries', *Journal of Political Economy*, 94, 720–744

Deaton, A.S., J. Ruiz-Castillo and D. Thomas (1989) 'The influence of household composition on household expenditure patterns: theory and Spanish evidence', *Journal of Political Economy*, 97, 179–200

Diamond, P.A. and D. McFadden (1974) 'Some uses of the expenditure function in measuring public finance', *Journal of Public Economics*, 3, 3–21

Dixit, A. and P.A. Weller (1979) 'The three consumer surpluses', *Economica*, 46, 125–135

Donaldson, D. (1992) 'On the aggregation of money measures of well-being in applied welfare economics', *Journal of Agricultural and Resource Economics*, 17, 88–102

Engel, E. (1895) 'Die Lebenskosten Belgischer Arbeiter-Familien früher und jetzt', *International Statistical Institute Bulletin*, 9, 1–74

Ermisch, J. (1989) 'Purchased child care, optimal family size and mother's employment', *Journal of Population Economics*, 2, 79–102

Fisher, F.M. (1987) 'Household equivalence scales and interpersonal comparisons', *Review of Economic Studies*, 54, 519–524

Foster, J. and A.F. Shorrocks (1987) 'Inequality and poverty orderings', *European Economic Review*, 32, 654–662

(1988) 'Poverty orderings', *Econometrica*, 56, 173–177

Foster, J., J. Greer and E. Thorbecke (1984) 'A class of decomposable poverty measures', *Econometrica*, 52, 761–766

Gorman, W.M. (1953) 'Community preference fields', *Econometrica*, 21, 63–80

(1976) 'Tricks with utility functions', in M. Artis and R. Nobay (eds.), *Essays in Economic Analysis*, Cambridge, Cambridge University Press

(1981) 'Some Engel curves', in A.S. Deaton (ed.), *Essays in the Theory and Measurement of Consumer Behaviour in Honour of Sir Richard Stone*, Cambridge, Cambridge University Press

Haddad, L. and R. Kanbur (1990) 'How serious is the neglect of intra-household inequality?', *Economic Journal*, 100, 866–881

Hall, R. (1978) 'The stochastic implications of the life-cycle permanent income hypothesis', *Journal of Political Economy*, 86, 971–987

Hardy, G.H., J.E. Littlewood and G. Pòlya (1934) *Inequalities*, London and New York, Cambridge University Press

Hausman, J.A. (1981) 'Exact consumer surplus and deadweight loss', *American Economic Review*, 71, 589–597

Hausman, J.A. and W.K. Newey (1993) 'Nonparametric estimation of exact consumer surplus and deadweight loss', *MIT Economics Working Paper*

Hurd, M.D. and J.H. Pencavel (1981) 'A utility based analysis of the wage subsidy programme', *Journal of Public Economics*, 15, 185–201

Jorgenson, D.W. (1990) 'Aggregate consumer behaviour and the measurement of social welfare', *Econometrica*, 58, 1007–1040

Jorgenson, D.W. and D.T.S. Slesnick (1983) 'Individual and social cost-of-living indices', in W.E. Diewert and C. Montmarquette (eds.), *Price Level Measurement*, Ottawa, Statistics Canada

(1987) 'Aggregate consumer behaviour and household equivalence scales', *Journal of Business and Economic Statistics*, 5, 219–232

Jorgenson, D.W., L.J. Lau and T.M. Stoker (1980) 'Welfare comparisons and exact aggregation', *American Economic Review*, 70, 268–272

Kapteyn, A. and G.R. van Herwaarden (1981) 'Empirical comparisons of the shape of welfare functions', *European Economic Review*, 15, 261–286

Kapteyn, A. and P. Kooreman (1992) 'On the empirical implementation of some game theoretic models of household labour supply', *Journal of Human Resources*, 25, 584–598

Kapteyn, A., P. Kooreman and R. Willemse (1988) 'Some methodological issues in the implementation of subjective poverty definitions', *Journal of Human Resources*, 23, 222–242

Kay, J. (1980) 'The deadweight loss from a tax system' *Journal of Public Economics*, 13, 111–120

Keen, M.J. (1990) 'Welfare analysis and intertemporal substitution', *Journal of Public Economics*, 42, 47–66

Kemp, M. (1984) 'A note on the theory of international transfers', *Economics Letters*, 14, 259–262

King, M.A. (1983) 'Welfare analysis of tax reform using household data', *Journal of Public Economics*, 21, 183–214

Kolm, S.C. (1969) 'The optimal production of justice', in J. Margolis and H. Glutton (eds.), *Public Economics*, London, Macmillan

(1976a) 'Unequal inequalities I', *Journal of Economic Theory*, 12, 416–442

(1976b) 'Unequal inequalities II', *Journal of Economic Theory*, 13, 82–111

Kreps, D. (1990) *A Course in Microeconomic Theory*, Princeton, Princeton University Press

Lazear, E. and R. Michael (1980) 'Family size and the distribution of real *per capita* income', *American Economic Review*, 70, 91–107

Leuthold, J.H. (1968) 'An empirical study of formula income transfers and the work decision of the poor', *Journal of Human Resources*, 3, 312–323

Lewbel, A. (1985) 'A unified approach to incorporating demographic or other effects into demand systems', *Review of Economic Studies*, 52, 19–35

(1989a) 'Household-equivalence scales and welfare comparisons', *Journal of Public Economics*, 39, 377–391

(1989b) 'The cost and characteristics indices and household equivalence scales', Brandeis University, *Economics Discussion Paper*, 206

Lloyd, P.J. (1979) 'Constant-utility index numbers of real wages: comment', *American Economic Review*, 69, 682–685

Lorenz, M.O. (1905), 'Methods of measuring the concentration of wealth', *Quarterly Publications of the American Statistical Association*, 9, 209–219

McElroy, M.B. (1990) 'The empirical content of Nash-bargained household behaviour', *Journal of Human Resources*, 25, 559–583

McElroy, M.B. and M.J. Horney (1980) 'Nash bargained decisions: toward a generalization of the theory of demand', *International Economic Review*, 22, 333–349

(1981) 'Nash-bargained household decisions: toward a generalization of the theory of demand', *International Economic Review*, 22, 333–349

(1990) 'Nash bargained decisions: a reply', *International Economic Review*, 31, 237–242

MaCurdy, T. (1983) 'A simple scheme for estimating an intertemporal model of labour supply and taxation in the presence of taxes and uncertainty', *International Economic Review*, 24, 265–289

Manser, M. and M. Brown (1980) 'Marriage and household decision-making: a bargaining analysis', *International Economic Review*, 21, 31–44

Mirrlees, J.A. (1971) 'An exploration in the theory of optimum income taxation', *Review of Economic Studies*, 38, 175–208

Moffitt, R. (1983) 'An economic model of welfare stigma', *American Economic Review*, 73, 1023–1035

(1986) 'The econometrics of piecewise linear budget constraints', *Journal of Business and Economic Statistics*, 4, 317–328

Moyes, P. (1987) 'A new concept of Lorenz domination', *Economics Letters*, 23, 203–7

Muellbauer, J. (1974a), 'Household composition, Engel curves and welfare comparisons between households: a duality approach', *European Economic Review*, 5, 103–122

(1974b), 'Prices and inequality: the UK experience, *Economic Journal*, 84, 32–49

(1975) 'Aggregation, income distribution and consumer demand', *Review of Economic Studies*, 62, 555–573

(1976) 'Community preferences and the representative consumer', *Econometrica*, 44, 525–543

(1977) 'Testing the Barten model of household consumption effects and the cost of children', *Economic Journal*, 87, 460–487

(1980) 'The estimation of the Prais–Houthakker model of equivalence scales', *Econometrica*, 48, 153–176

Musgrave, R.A. (1987) 'Short of euphoria', *Journal of Economic Perspectives*, 1, 59–71

Nelson, J.A. (1988) 'Household economies of scale in consumption: theory and evidence', *Econometrica*, 56, 1301–1314

Pashardes, P. (1991) 'Contemporaneous and intertemporal child costs: equivalent expenditure vs equivalent income scales', *Journal of Public Economics*, 45, 191–213

Pencavel, J.H. (1977) 'Constant-utility index numbers of real wages', *American Economic Review*, 67, 91–100

Pigou, A.C. (1912) *Wealth and Welfare*, London, Macmillan

Pollak, R.A. (1983) 'The theory of the cost of living index', in W.E. Diewert and C. Montmarquette (eds.), *Price Level Measurement*, Ottawa, Statistics Canada

Pollak, R.A. and T.J. Wales (1979) 'Welfare comparisons and equivalence scales', *American Economic Review*, 69, 216–221

(1981) 'Demographic variables in demand analysis', *Econometrica*, 49, 1533–1552

Prais, S.J. and H.S. Houthakker (1955) *The Analysis of Family Budgets*, Cambridge, Cambridge University Press

Preston, I.P. and I. Walker (1992) 'Welfare measurement in labour supply models with nonlinear budget constraints', *IFS Working Paper*, 92/12

Rawls, J. (1971) *A Theory of Justice*, Oxford University Press, Oxford

Ray, R. (1983) 'Measuring the costs of children: an alternative approach', *Journal of Public Economics*, 22, 89–102

(1986) 'Demographic variables and equivalence scales in a flexible demand system: the case of AIDS', *Applied Economics*, 18, 265–278

Roberts, K.W.S. (1980a) 'Price-independent welfare prescriptions', *Journal of Public Economics*, 13, 277–297

(1980b) 'Interpersonal comparability and social choice theory', *Review of Economic Studies*, 47, 421–439

Rothschild, M. and J.E. Stiglitz (1973) 'Some further results on the measurement of inequality', *Journal of Economic Theory*, 6, 188–204

Rowntree, B.S. (1901) *Poverty: a Study of Town Life*, Longmans, London

Samuelson, P.A. (1956) 'Social indifference curves', *Quarterly Journal of Economics*, 70, 1–22

Saposnik, R. (1981) 'Rank dominance in income distributions', *Public Choice*, 36, 147–151

Sen, A.K. (1970) 'Interpersonal aggregation and partial comparability', *Econometrica*, 38, 393–409

(1976) 'Poverty: an ordinal approach to measurement', *Econometrica*, 44, 219–231

(1978) 'Ethical measurement of inequality: some difficulties', in W. Krelle and A.F. Shorrocks (eds.), *Personal Income Distribution*, Amsterdam, North-Holland

(1979) 'Personal utilities and public judgements: or what's wrong with welfare economics?', *Economic Journal*, 89, 537–558

(1983) 'Poor, relatively speaking', *Oxford Economic Papers*, 35, 153–169

Sen, A.K. and B.A.O. Williams (1982) *Utilitarianism and Beyond*, Cambridge, Cambridge University Press

Shorrocks, A.F. (1980) 'The class of additively decomposable inequality measures', *Econometrica*, 48, 613–625

(1983) 'Ranking income distributions', *Economica*, 50, 1–17

(1984) 'Inequality decomposition by population subgroups', *Econometrica*, 52, 1369–1385

(1988) 'Aggregation issues in inequality measurement', in W. Eichhorn (ed.), *Measurement in Economics: Theory and Application of Economic Indices*, Heidelberg, Physica-Verlag

Shorrocks, A.F. and J. Foster (1987) 'Transfer-sensitive inequality measures', *Review of Economic Studies*, 54, 485–497

Slivinski, A.D. (1983) 'Income distribution evaluation and the law of one price', *Journal of Public Economics*, 20, 103–112

Small, K.A. and H.S. Rosen (1981) 'Applied welfare economics with discrete choice models', *Econometrica*, 49, 105–130

Stern, N.H. (1987a) 'The theory of optimal commodity and income taxation: an introduction', in D.M.G. Newbery and N.H. Stern (eds.), *The Theory of Taxation for Developing Countries*, Oxford, Oxford University Press, for the World Bank

(1987b) 'Aspects of the general theory of tax reform', in D.M.G. Newbery and N.H. Stern (eds.), *The Theory of Taxation for Developing Countries*, Oxford, Oxford University Press, for the World Bank

Stiglitz, J.E. (1976) 'Simple formulae for optimal income taxation and the measurement of inequality', Stanford University, *IMSSS Technical Report*, 215

Stoker, T.M. (1986) 'The distributional welfare effects of rising prices in the United States', *American Economic Review*, 76, 335–349

Thomas, D. (1990) 'Intra-household resource allocation: an inferential approach', *Journal of Human Resources*, 25, 635–664

Townsend, P. (1979) *Poverty in the United Kingdom*, Harmondsworth, Penguin

Ulph, D.T. (1978) 'On labour supply and the measurement of inequality', *Journal of Economic Theory*, 19, 492–512

(1981) 'Labour supply, taxation and the measurement of inequality', in C.V. Brown (ed.), *Taxation and Labour Supply*, London, Allen & Unwin

(1988) 'A general non-cooperative Nash model of household consumption behaviour', University of Bristol, *Working Paper*, 88/205

van der Gaag, J. and E. Smolensky (1982) 'True household equivalence scales and characteristics of the poor in the United States', *Review of Income and Wealth*, 28, 17–28

van Praag, B.M.S. and A. Kapteyn (1973) 'Further evidence on the individual welfare function of income: an empirical investigation in the Netherlands', *European Economic Review*, 4, 33–62

van Praag, B.M.S. and N.L. van der Sar (1988) 'Household cost functions and equivalence scales', *Journal of Human Resources*, 23, 193–210

Vartia, Y. (1983) 'Efficient methods of measuring welfare change and compensated income in terms of ordinary demand functions', *Econometrica*, 51, 79–88

Warr, P. (1983) 'The private provision of a public good is independent of the distribution of income', *Economic Letters*, 13, 207–211

Willig, R. (1976) 'Consumer surplus without apology', *American Economic Review*, 66, 589–597

2 Measuring the cost of children: a theoretical framework

CHARLES BLACKORBY and DAVID DONALDSON

Introduction

Parenthood has costs as well as benefits. Children must be fed, clothed, housed, and educated, and the resulting expenditures leave parents with less to spend on themselves. In addition, because some governments attempt to compensate families for the costs of children, reasonable estimates of the costs of children are a prerequisite for sensible policies.

But how should the costs of children be measured? We might choose, for example, to assume that the costs of a first child are the same for all families, regardless of income, or we might choose to include or disregard the psychic benefits to parents. In addition, because parents cannot typically imagine the childless alternative, interpersonal comparisons of levels of well-being between individuals in different households are necessary for the construction of sensible indexes.[1]

This chapter presents a theoretical framework for indexes of the costs of children using a methodology that is closely related to household equivalence scale techniques (see, as an example, Blackorby and Donaldson, 1988, 1991). Households' demand behaviour is assumed to be rationalised by standard preferences, individuals in each household are assumed to be equally well off, and comparisons of levels of utility between individuals in different households are assumed to be possible (see p. 52 below).[2]

In this framework, we introduce general classes of cost-of-children indexes (p. 53). The first class – relative cost-of-children indexes – regards the cost as equal in *percentage* terms for all households, while the second class – absolute cost-of-children indexes – regards the cost as equal in absolute terms.

On p. 55, we compare these indexes with two methods for making interpersonal comparisons of well-being between individuals in different households – the iso-prop and Rothbarth methods – and show that, although the iso-prop method is related to relative indexes and the Rothbarth method to absolute indexes, neither method corresponds exactly to its counterpart.

Then, (p. 59) demographic separability – a suggestion for structuring the preferences of households with children – is investigated and contrasted with the other methods.

In each of the three cases – iso-prop, Rothbarth, and demographic separability – closed-form characterisations of the requisite utility functions are found in terms of the expenditure function. In addition, a condition related to demographic separability – adult goods separability – is characterised. These are compared on p. 63.

A discussion of estimation of demand functions and the possibility of using *a priori* conditions on the structure of utility functions together with demand behaviour to reveal the indexes without explicit interpersonal comparisons is given on pp. 64–66; p. 66 draws a brief conclusion.

A model of household preferences

We represent the preferences of a household with characteristics a by a utility function defined over the consumption bundles of the household. Households are assumed to maximise a Leontief household welfare function. This results in a utility function U, where

$$u = U(x, z, a) \tag{1}$$

is the level of well-being of each member of a household with characteristics a consuming x – a vector of adult goods (or, alternatively, necessities) – and z – a vector of all other commodities. The associated expenditure function E is given by[3]

$$E(u, p, q, a) = \min_{\{x, z\}} \{px + qz \,|\, U(x, z, a) \geq u\} \tag{2}$$

where p is the vector of adult good prices and q is all other prices. E is assumed to be strongly pseudo-concave in (p, q).

The indirect utility function V of the household is given by

$$V(p, q, y, a) = \max_{\{x, z\}} \{U(x, z, a) \,|\, px + qz \leq y\} \tag{3}$$

where y is household income or expenditure. V and E are related by

$$y = E(u, p, q, a) \leftrightarrow u = V(p, q, y, a). \tag{4}$$

We partition a into two subvectors so that $a = (\beta, \gamma)$ where $\gamma = (\gamma_1, \ldots, \gamma_M)$ describes the characteristics of children, if any, in the household, and β is all other household characteristics.[4] As reference household types, those without children are chosen; their characteristics are (β, γ^r), and their expenditure functions are E^r,

$$E^r(u,p,q,\beta): = E(u,p,q,\beta,\gamma^r).$$ (5)

Relative and absolute exact measures of the costs of children

In this section we consider both relative and absolute measures of the costs of children. We then ask these measures to be exact: that is, independent of the level of household *per capita* utility. This leads to different restrictions on preferences in the two cases.

In order for the idea of the cost of children used in these indexes to be well-defined, it must be possible to compare utility *levels* between individuals in different households, or, equivalently, to make comparisons of *per capita* utility between households of different types. Thus, comparisons such as

$$U(x^1, z^1, \alpha^1) > U(x^2, z^2, \alpha^2)$$ (6)

must be meaningful. This is ensured by ordinal measurability of the function U. If U is replaced by $\tilde{U}$, where

$$\tilde{U}(x, z, \alpha) = \phi(U(x, z, \alpha))$$ (7)

for all (x, z, α) with ϕ increasing, then household preferences, demand behaviour, and interpersonal comparisons such as (6) are unchanged. If, on the other hand, ϕ is allowed to depend on α, preferences and demand behaviour are unchanged, but interpersonal comparisons may change. Consequently, we restrict U to the ordinal measurability defined by (6); this corresponds to making household utilities ordinally measurable and fully comparable.

The relative cost of children

The relative cost of children, r, is given by

$$V\left(p, q, \frac{y}{r}, \beta, \gamma^r\right) = V(p, q, y, \beta, \gamma).$$ (8)

r is the amount by which household income could be deflated if children were not present, without changing the levels of parental well-being. That is, the adults in the household would be equally well off without children if household income were reduced to y/r. If V measures economic well-being only, then r is greater than one for all household types with children. Using (4) we can solve (8) for r to obtain

$$r = \frac{E(u,p,q,\beta,\gamma)}{E(u,p,q,\beta,\gamma^r)}. \tag{9}$$

r depends, in general, on the household's utility level u, which is unobservable. For that reason, we refer to the case in which r is independent of u as *exactness*. The index is exact if and only if the expenditure function can be written as

$$E(u,p,q,\beta,\gamma) = \bar{E}(u,p,q,\beta)\hat{E}(p,q,\beta,\gamma), \tag{10}$$

in which case the relative cost-of-children index can be written as[5]

$$r = R(p,q,\beta,\gamma): = \frac{\hat{E}(p,q,\beta,\gamma)}{\hat{E}(p,q,\beta,\gamma^r)}. \tag{11}$$

(10) and (11) imply that the expenditure function can be written as

$$E(u,p,q,\beta,\gamma) = E^r(u,p,q,\beta)R(p,q,\beta,\gamma). \tag{12}$$

By construction, R is homogeneous of degree zero in prices (p,q) and $R(p,q,\beta,\gamma^r)$, the relative cost of children for childless households is one for all (p,q,β).

A special case of an exact cost-of-children index is the one we call an *Engel exact* index. This is the case when R is independent of prices, and Engel exactness of a relative index is satisfied if and only if the expenditure function can be written as

$$E(u,p,q,\beta,\gamma) = E^r(u,p,q,\beta)\bar{R}(\beta,\gamma). \tag{13}$$

Note that Engel exactness implies that the share of every commodity is independent of the characteristics of children γ.

The absolute cost of children

The absolute cost of children a, is given by

$$V(p,q,y - a,\beta,\gamma^r) = V(p,q,y,\beta,\gamma). \tag{14}$$

It measures the amount by which household income could be reduced if children were not present, without affecting parental well-being. Using (8) and (14), $a = y(r - 1)/r$. In addition, the value of a that solves (14) is zero for any childless household.

(4) can be used to solve (14) for a, and

$$a = E(u,p,q,\beta,\gamma) - E(u,p,q,\beta,\gamma^r). \tag{15}$$

This measure is homogeneous of degree one in (p,q), and it depends, in general, on the household's unobservable utility level; we call the index *exact* if and only if it is independent of u, and, in that case, the expenditure function may be written as

$$E(u,p,q,\beta,\gamma) = \bar{E}(u,p,q,\beta) + \hat{E}(p,q,\beta,\gamma). \tag{16}$$

When exact, the abolute cost-of-children index is

$$a = A(p,q,\beta,\gamma): = \hat{E}(p,q,\beta,\gamma) - \hat{E}(p,q,\beta,\gamma') \tag{17}$$

which in turn permits us to write the expenditure function of the household in question as

$$E(u,p,q,\beta,\gamma) = E^r(u,p,q,\beta) + A(p,q,\beta,\gamma). \tag{18}$$

(12) and (18) make it clear that, although the absolute and relative indexes can be derived from each other, the conditions for exactness are quite different. This observation plays a role in our discussion of the iso-prop and Rothbarth methods.

The iso-prop and the Rothbarth methods

In this section we provide necessary and sufficient conditions for the *iso-prop* and the *Rothbarth* methods to be exact. In each of these cases, a maintained hypothesis has implications for preferences and demands, enabling interhousehold comparisons of utility. The iso-prop method suggests looking at expenditure shares on some subset of goods, and declares different household types to be at the same utility levels whenever the shares are equal.[6] In order for this procedure to work, a particular condition on both preferences and interhousehold comparisons is required. The Rothbarth method follows the iso-prop method in levels rather than in shares. Each of the subsections that follow is devoted to one of these notions and presents closed-form necessary and sufficient conditions for them to be exact welfare indicators.

The iso-prop method

The idea behind the iso-prop method was suggested by Engel. Because the share of household expenditures devoted to food increases with family size and decreases as income rises, the claim that members of households with equal food expenditure shares are equally well off has some plausibility. The iso-prop method applies Engel's method to any subset of commodities, sometimes chosen to be necessities such as food, shelter, and clothing. We use the vector x and call it the vector of adult goods. We require that, if any household's expenditure share on x matches the expenditure share of a reference (i.e. childless) household, then the

members of both households are equally well off, provided that they face
the same prices. Partitioning the commodity indices as $\{I^x, I^z\}$, the share
of expenditures on adult goods in a household with characteristics
$a = (\beta, \gamma)$ is given by

$$\frac{\Sigma_{i \in I^x} p_i x_i}{y} = \frac{\Sigma_{i \in I^x} p_i E_{p_i}(u, p, q, \beta, \gamma)}{E(u, p, q, \beta, \gamma)}. \tag{19}$$

The iso-prop method requires that the welfare of this household be equal
to that of the reference household if their expenditure shares on adult
goods are equal. Thus,

$$\frac{\Sigma_{i \in I^x} p_i E_{p_i}(u, p, q, \beta, \gamma)}{E(u, p, q, \beta, \gamma)} = \frac{\Sigma_{i \in I^x} p_i E_{p_i}(u, p, q, \beta, \gamma')}{E(u, p, q, \beta, \gamma')} \tag{20}$$

for every (u, p, q, β, γ). We refer to satisfaction of (20) as exactness of the
iso-prop method.

The following theorem provides a characterisation of exactness of the
iso-prop method in terms of the expenditure function.

Theorem 1: The iso-prop procedure is exact – (20) holds for all (u, p, q, β, γ)
– if and only if the expenditure function can be written as

$$E(u, p, q, \beta, \gamma) = C(u, p, q, \beta) D(u, p, q, \beta, \gamma) \tag{21}$$

where D is homogeneous of degree zero in p.[7]

Proof: First we show sufficiency. The demands for adult goods are given
by

$$x_i = C_{p_i}(u, p, q, \beta) D(u, p, q, \beta, \gamma) + C(u, p, q, \beta) D_{p_i}(u, p, q, \beta, \gamma) \tag{22}$$

for all $i \in I^x$. Total expenditure on group I^x is given by

$$\sum_{i \in I^x} p_i x_i = D(u, p, q, \beta, \gamma) \sum_{i \in I^x} p_i C_{p_i}(u, p, q, \beta)$$
$$+ C(u, p, q, \beta) \sum_{i \in I^x} p_i D_{p_i}(u, p, q, \beta, \gamma)$$
$$= D(u, p, q, \beta, \gamma) \sum_{i \in I^x} p_i C_{p_i}(u, p, q, \beta) \tag{23}$$

where the last equality follows from the fact that D is homogeneous of
degree zero in p. Dividing (23) by total expenditure given in (21) yields the
share of expenditure on adult goods,

$$\frac{D(u, p, q, \beta, \gamma) \Sigma_{i \in I^x} p_i C_{p_i}(u, p, q, \beta)}{C(u, p, q, \beta) D(u, p, q, \beta, \gamma)} = \frac{\Sigma_{i \in I^x} p_i C_{p_i}(u, p, q, \beta)}{C(u, p, q, \beta)}. \tag{24}$$

This share is independent of γ and (21) is therefore sufficient for (20). To show necessity, define

$$F(u, \pi, q, \beta, \gamma) := \ln E(u, p, q, \beta, \gamma) \tag{25}$$

where $\pi_i := \ln p_i$ for all $i \in I^x$. (20) can be rewritten as

$$\sum_{i \in I^x} F_{\pi_i}(u, \pi, q, \beta, \gamma) = \sum_{i \in I^x} F_{\pi_i}(u, \pi, q, \beta, \gamma'). \tag{26}$$

From this it is clear that

$$\sum_{i \in I^x} F_{\pi_i \gamma_m}(u, \pi, q, \beta, \gamma) = 0 \tag{27}$$

for all $m = 1, \ldots, M$. The latter is a partial differential equation whose solution is easily given by

$$F_{\gamma_m}(u, \pi, q, \beta, \gamma) = \bar{F}_{\gamma_m}(u, \{\pi_i - \pi_1\}_{i \in I^x, i \neq 1}, q, \beta, \gamma). \tag{28}$$

Integrating (28) yields

$$F(u, \pi, q, \beta, \gamma) = \bar{F}(u, \{\pi_i - \pi_1\}_{i \in I^x, i \neq 1}, q, \beta, \gamma) + G(u, \pi, q, \beta). \tag{29}$$

Undoing the transformations given in (25) yields the result.

To see that (28) is the solution to (27), consider a function $z = f(x)$ that satisfies the partial differential equation

$$\sum_i f_i(x) = 0. \tag{30}$$

The characteristic equations associated with (30) are given by

$$\frac{dx_2}{dx_1} = 1, \ldots, \frac{dx_N}{dx_1} = 1, \frac{dz}{dx_1} = 0. \tag{31}$$

This yields

$$x_n = x_1 + \phi^n(K_1, \ldots, K_N) \tag{32}$$

for $n = 2, \ldots, N$ and

$$z = \phi(K_1, \ldots, K_N) \tag{33}$$

where the $\{K_n\}$ are the constants of integration. Solving for these constants yields

$$K_n = \psi^n(x_2 - x_1, \ldots, x_N - x_1, z) \tag{34}$$

for $n = 2, \ldots, N$. The solution to (30) is given by an arbitrary function of these constants, (34). That is, f must satisfy

$$\psi(K_1, \ldots, K_N) = 0 \tag{35}$$

where (34) holds. Solving (35) yields

$$f(x) = z = Z(x_2 - x_1, \ldots, x_N - x_1) \tag{36}$$

which substantiates the claim made in (28). ■

If there is but one good, then the function D must be independent of p – the price of the adult good – as a result of being homogeneous of degree zero in a scalar. This is consistent with the claim made by Muellbauer (1974) and Browning (1988a).[8]

An issue not made clear by the theorem concerns the homogeneity properties of C and D. We know only that their product is homogeneous of degree one in (p, q). Any assignment of homogeneity properties that is consistent with this and with concavity is permissible. Of course, some such assignments seem more natural or interesting than others. Perhaps the most useful homogeneity assignment requires C to be homogeneous of degree one in (p, q). This forces D to be homogeneous of degree zero in (p, q). However, because D is homogeneous of degree zero in p, this implies that D is also homogeneous of degree zero in q. This in turn makes D look very much like the cost-of-children index in (11). Finally, note that if D is independent of u and (p, q), then this yields Engel exactness, (13).

It is important to note, however, that iso-prop exactness and exactness of the relative cost-of-children index, (11), are not special cases of each other. Both may be satisfied simultaneously, however, if (21) is satisfied with D independent of u and (12) is satisfied with R homogeneous of degree zero in p. In this case, the relative cost-of-children index is

$$R(p, q, \beta, \gamma) = \frac{\bar{D}(p, q, \beta, \gamma)}{\bar{D}(p, q, \beta, \gamma')}, \tag{37}$$

and it may be estimated using the iso-prop method.

The Rothbarth method

The method suggested by Rothbarth (1943) assumes that, when the absolute amount spent on adult goods is the same in a household with characteristics $\alpha = (\beta, \gamma)$ and in a reference household, members of these households have the same level of well-being. It is, therefore, the same as the iso-prop method except that it is in levels.

We thus say that a utility function is exact for the Rothbarth procedure if and only if

$$\sum_{i \in I^x} p_i E_{p_i}(u, p, q, \beta, \gamma) = \sum_{i \in I^x} p_i E_{p_i}(u, p, q, \beta, \gamma') \tag{38}$$

for all (u, p, q, β, γ). A characterisation of Rothbarth method exactness in terms of the expenditure function is provided by Theorem 2.

Theorem 2: The Rothbarth method is exact – (38) holds for all (u, p, q, β, γ) – if and only if the expenditure function can be written as

$$E(u, p, q, \beta, \gamma) = C(u, p, q, \beta) + D(u, p, q, \beta, \gamma) \tag{39}$$

where D is homogeneous of degree zero in p.

Proof: Proceed exactly as in the proof of Theorem 1, but define F as

$$F(u, \pi, q, \beta, \gamma) := E(u, p, q, \beta, \gamma) \tag{40}$$

where $\pi_i := \ln p_i$ for all $i \in I^x$. ∎

Again, if there is only one adult good, D must be independent of its price.[9] In addition, Rothbarth exactness and exactness of the absolute cost-of-children index are not nested. Satisfaction of both requires D in (39) to be independent of u. If the absolute cost-of-children index is exact with $\hat{E}$ in (17) homogeneous of degree zero in p, then the Rothbarth method may be used to estimate it.

Demographic and adult goods separability

The most recent suggestion for structuring utility functions and demand functions across households of different types was made by Deaton, Ruiz-Castillo and Thomas (1989); they call it *demographic separability*. Although it is related to the iso-prop and Rothbarth methods, it is of interest itself.

One effect of having children is that, if household income stays the same, less will be spent on adult goods. One might expect therefore, that, as far as adult goods are concerned, the arrival of children would be similar to an income effect. Deaton, Ruiz-Castillo and Thomas therefore compare demographic separability to the case where adult goods are separable from all other commodities in the direct utility function. We follow a similar procedure in this section. We first provide necessary and sufficient conditions – in terms of restrictions on the expenditure function – for preferences to exhibit demographic separability. We then do the same for direct separability of adult goods. This presents a reasonably clear picture of the difference between the two notions and, in addition, permits us to compare demographic separability to the iso-prop and Rothbarth methods.

To proceed, we need to distinguish between the compensated and uncompensated demand functions. The compensated demand for x_i by a household with characteristics $\boldsymbol{\alpha} = (\boldsymbol{\beta}, \boldsymbol{\gamma})$ is

$$x_i^c = X_i^c(u, \boldsymbol{p}, \boldsymbol{q}, \boldsymbol{\alpha}) = E_{p_i}(u, \boldsymbol{p}, \boldsymbol{q}, \boldsymbol{\alpha}) \tag{41}$$

and the uncompensated or ordinary demand for commodity x_i is

$$x_i^o = X_i^o(\boldsymbol{p}, \boldsymbol{q}, y, \boldsymbol{\alpha}) = -\frac{V_{p_i}(\boldsymbol{p}, \boldsymbol{q}, y, \boldsymbol{\alpha})}{V_y(\boldsymbol{p}, \boldsymbol{q}, y, \boldsymbol{\alpha})} . \tag{42}$$

Demographic separability

Formally the set of adult commodities (the goods in I^x) is demographically separable from the characteristics γ if

$$\frac{\partial x_i^o}{\partial \gamma_m} = \theta^m \frac{\partial x_i^o}{\partial y} \tag{43}$$

for all $i \in I^x$, for all $(\boldsymbol{p}, \boldsymbol{q}, y, \boldsymbol{\alpha}) = (\boldsymbol{p}, \boldsymbol{q}, y, \boldsymbol{\beta}, \boldsymbol{\gamma})$, and for some function Θ^m, where

$$\theta^m = \Theta^m(\boldsymbol{p}, \boldsymbol{q}, y, \boldsymbol{\beta}, \boldsymbol{\gamma}), \tag{44}$$

for $m = 1, \ldots, M$. (43) requires X_i^o (and therefore X_i^c) to be differentiable with respect to each child characteristic and with respect to household income, which we assume. In addition, we assume that there is some non-adult characteristic, γ_m, and some adult good, $j \in I^x$, such that the derivative of the compensated demand function for good j with respect to γ_m is nonzero for all $(u, \boldsymbol{p}, \boldsymbol{q}, \boldsymbol{\beta}, \boldsymbol{\gamma})$ (the j and m may be different for each point), *or* that the compensated demands for adult goods are independent of γ.

Of course, there must be at least two adult goods in order for this notion to be nontrivial. However, in that case it is easy to see how this definition implements the idea put forward by Deaton, Ruiz-Castillo and Thomas. For $i, j \in I^x$,

$$\frac{\partial x_i^o / \partial \gamma_m}{\partial x_j^o / \partial \gamma_m} = \frac{\partial x_i^o / \partial y}{\partial x_j^o / \partial y} . \tag{45}$$

That is, a child characteristic γ_m changes the relative demand for two adult goods in the same way an income change would affect this relative demand. Theorem 5.1 in Blackorby and Donaldson (1989) provides a characterisation of demographic separability in terms of the expenditure function.

Theorem 3: Demographic separability is satisfied – that is, (43) holds for all $(\boldsymbol{p}, \boldsymbol{q}, y, \boldsymbol{\beta}, \boldsymbol{\gamma})$, for all $i \in I^x$, and for all $m = 1, \ldots, M$ – if and only if the expenditure function can be written as

$$E(u,p,q,\beta,\gamma) = \min_{\xi}\{C(p,q,\beta,\xi) + D(u,q,\beta,\gamma,\xi)\}. \tag{46}$$

or

$$E(u,p,q,\beta,\gamma) = C(u,p,q,\beta) + D(u,q,\beta,\gamma). \tag{47}$$

Proof: Using the fact that

$$x_i^o = x_i^c \tag{48}$$

whenever $u = V(p,q,y,\alpha)$, we know (suppressing the arguments of functions for convenience) that

$$\frac{\partial x_i^c}{\partial u} V_{\gamma_m} + \frac{\partial x_i^c}{\partial \gamma_m} = \frac{\partial x_i^o}{\partial \gamma_m}, \tag{49}$$

and

$$\frac{\partial x_i^c}{\partial u} V_y = \frac{\partial x_i^o}{\partial y}. \tag{50}$$

From (4), we know that

$$E(V(p,q,y,\alpha), p,q,\alpha) = y, \tag{51}$$

so that

$$0 = E_u V_{\gamma_m} + E_{\gamma_m} \tag{52}$$

and

$$1 = E_u V_y. \tag{53}$$

Using (49)–(53) to convert (43) into a relationship between compensated demand functions yields

$$E_{p_i\gamma_m}(u,p,q,\beta,\gamma) = \frac{E_{p_iu}(u,p,q,\beta,\gamma)}{E_u(u,p,q,\beta,\gamma)}(\bar{\Theta}^m(u,p,q,\beta,\gamma) + E_{\gamma_m}(u,p,q,\beta,\gamma)) \tag{54}$$

for all $i \in I^x$ where

$$\bar{\Theta}^m(u,p,q,\alpha) := \Theta^m(p,q,E(u,p,q,\alpha),\alpha). \tag{55}$$

By assumption, either, at each (u,p,q,α), there is some j and m such that $E_{p_j\gamma_m}(u,p,q,\alpha)$ is not zero, or E_{p_i} is independent of γ for all i. If the former holds, then, at the point in question,

$$\frac{E_{p_i\gamma_m}(u,p,q,\beta,\gamma)}{E_{p_j\gamma_m}(u,p,q,\beta,\gamma)} = \frac{E_{p_iu}(u,p,q,\beta,\gamma)}{E_{p_ju}(u,p,q,\beta,\gamma)}. \tag{56}$$

Our assumptions imply that (56) holds in a neighbourhood of the point and, because the right side of (56) is independent of m, (56) must hold for all m. We know, therefore, that the submatrix of the Hessian of E between prices in sector I^x and the characteristics associated with children γ and the utility level u has rank one. By Theorem 2 in Blackorby, Davidson and Schworm (1990), this implies that the expenditure function can be written as (46) in a neighbourhood of each (u, p, q, α). Hence, (46) holds.

Alternatively, E_{p_i} is independent of γ, which implies that both sides of (54) are zero. In this case, (57) results.

To show that (46) is sufficient, write the first order condition for the minimum in (46) as

$$C_\xi(p, q, \beta, \overset{*}{\xi}) + D_\xi(u, q, \beta, \gamma, \overset{*}{\xi}) = 0 \tag{57}$$

where $\overset{*}{\xi}$ is the optimal value of ξ and is determined by (57). Suppressing the arguments of the functions, and using (57), we can write (54) as

$$C_{p_i\xi}\overset{*}{\xi}_{\gamma_m} = \frac{C_{p_i\xi}\overset{*}{\xi}_u}{D_u}(\bar{\theta}^m + D_{\gamma_m}). \tag{58}$$

Computing the derivatives of $\overset{*}{\xi}$ from (57) and substituting into (58) yields

$$\bar{\theta}^m = \frac{D_u D_{\xi\gamma_m}}{D_\xi} - D_{\gamma_m}. \tag{59}$$

This shows that (46) is sufficient. ∎

The nature of the solution given by (47) has been discussed by Deaton, Ruiz-Castillo and Thomas (1989), who call it cost-separability. Contrary to their claim, however, it is clear that the condition for the exactness of the Rothbarth method, (39), is not a special case of (47) and, hence, demographic separability is not a necessary condition for Rothbarth exactness.

To explain (46), use the envelope theorem to derive the compensated demands for adult goods; they are given by

$$x_i^c = C_i(p, q, \beta, \overset{*}{\xi}) \tag{60}$$

for all $i \in I^x$. Hence, these demands are affected by changes in utility and the characteristics γ only in so far as these affect the optimal value of $\overset{*}{\xi}$. Ratios of these changes are therefore proportional as required by (56).

Direct separability of adult goods

Next we characterise the circumstances under which adult goods are separable from the other goods z in the direct preference ordering, and then compare this result to demographic separability.

If the adult goods are separable from nonadult goods, conditional on all characteristics, the direct utility function can be written as

$$U(x, z, \alpha) = \bar{U}(U^x(x, \alpha), z, \alpha) \tag{61}$$

where $\bar{U}$ is increasing in its first argument. In order to compare this with demographic separability we construct the expenditure function dual to (61). The expenditure function dual to U^x is

$$E^x(p, \alpha, \xi) = \min_x \{px \mid U^x(x, \alpha) \geq \xi\} \tag{62}$$

and the conditional expenditure function dual to $\bar{U}$ is

$$\bar{E}(u, q, \alpha, \xi) = \min_z \{qz \mid \bar{U}(\xi, z, \alpha) \geq u\}. \tag{63}$$

Then by Lemma 6.1 in Blackorby, Davidson and Schworm (1990), adult goods are separable from nonadult goods in the direct utility function if and only if the expenditure function can be written as

$$E(u, p, q, \beta, \gamma) = \min_\xi \{E^x(p, \beta, \gamma, \xi) + \bar{E}(u, q, \beta, \gamma, \xi)\}. \tag{64}$$

Comparing (46) and (64) we see that, if C in (46) were independent of q, then we would have both demographic and adult goods separability. On the other hand if E^x were independent of γ then (64) would exhibit demographic separability as well as separability of adult goods. Comparing (57) and (64) yields the second special case. More specifically, demographic and adult goods separability hold simultaneously if and only if the expenditure function can be written as

$$E(u, p, q, \beta, \gamma) = \min_\xi \{\bar{C}(p, \beta, \xi) + D(u, q, \beta, \gamma, \xi)\} \tag{65}$$

or

$$E(u, p, q, \beta, \gamma) = C(p, \beta) + D(u, q, \beta, \gamma). \tag{66}$$

This makes it clear that, in general, neither of these forms of separability implies the other.

A comparison of the methods

In this section, we compare the above results and derive the conditions under which some of them coincide.[10] First we look at the exact relative costs and the iso-prop method. Then we compare the exact absolute cost and the Rothbarth method and demographic separability.

Equivalence of iso-prop and relative exactness

The conditions for exactness of the relative cost-of-children index, (12), and those for the exactness of the iso-prop method, (21), to coincide is that R in (12) must be homogeneous of degree zero in p and for D in (21) must be independent of u. Because R is homogeneous of degree zero in (p, q), this implies that it must be homogeneous of degree zero in q as well. Therefore, the expenditure function can be written as

$$E(u, p, q, \beta, \gamma) = E^r(u, p, q, \beta) \, \tilde{R}(p, q, \beta, \gamma) \qquad (67)$$

where $\tilde{R}$ is homogeneous of degree zero in each of its first two arguments. In this case the share of expenditure on adult goods is given by

$$\frac{\Sigma_{i \in I^x} p_i x_i}{y} = \frac{\Sigma_{i \in I^x} p_i E^r_{p_i}(u, p, q, \beta)}{E^r(u, p, q, \beta)} ; \qquad (68)$$

the term involving $\tilde{R}$ has disappeared because it is homogeneous of degree zero in p.

Equivalence of Rothbarth and absolute exactness

The conditions for exactness of the absolute cost-of-children index and for exactness of the Rothbarth method coincide if and only if the absolute cost-of-children index A in (18) is homogeneous of degree zero in p and D in (39) is independent of utility u. Because A is homogeneous of degree one in (p, q), it must, therefore, be homogeneous of degree one in q. Given this, the expenditure function can be written as

$$E(u, p, q, \beta, \gamma) = E^r(u, p, q, \beta) + \tilde{A}(p, q, \beta, \gamma) \qquad (69)$$

where $\tilde{A}$ is homogeneous of degree zero in p and homogeneous of degree one in q. Total expenditure on adult goods is given by

$$\sum_{i \in I^x} p_i x_i = \sum_{i \in I^x} p_i E^r_{p_i}(u, p, q, \beta). \qquad (70)$$

Equivalence of Rothbarth and demographic separability

Clearly neither the Rothbarth method nor demographic separability are special cases of each other. However, if D in (39) were independent of p (instead of being merely homogeneous of degree zero in p), then the Rothbarth procedure and one of the two cases of demographic separability, (47), would coincide. Hence, if adult goods were homothetically separable from other commodities in the direct utility function, then demographic separability would be a necessary condition for the Rothbarth procedure.

Revealing behaviour from cost-of-children indexes

In Blackorby and Donaldson (1988, 1989) we demonstrated that, in the case of relative household equivalence scales, if index exactness (called equivalence scale exactness or ESE) holds and if preferences are not piglog, then the equivalence scales are revealed by behaviour (that is, the indexes are uniquely determined by household preferences). We extend that result to the case of relative and absolute cost-of-children indexes.

The general model we employ can make no inferences about interpersonal comparisons from behaviour alone. Specifically, if the utility function U is replaced with $\tilde{U}$, where

$$\tilde{U}(x,z,\alpha) = \phi(U(x,z,\alpha),\alpha), \tag{71}$$

behaviour is the same for all households but interpersonal comparisons between people from households with different characteristics can be changed arbitrarily.

Once exactness conditions are imposed, however, this arbitrariness of interpersonal comparisons vanishes. The reason is that exactness imposes structure on preferences and on interhousehold comparisons.[11]

Relative cost-of-children indexes, exactness, and behaviour

Suppose that there are two different exact cost-of-children indexes – $R(p,q,\alpha)$ and $R'(p,q,\alpha)$, say – that are consistent with the same household behaviour. Then there exists a function ϕ, increasing in its first argument, such that, from (8) and (11), we obtain

$$V'\left(p,q,\frac{y}{R'(p,q,\beta,\gamma)},\beta,\gamma^r\right) = \phi\left[V\left(p,q,\frac{y}{R(p,q,\beta,\gamma)},\beta,\gamma^r\right),\beta,\gamma\right] \tag{72}$$

for all (p,q,β,γ). Theorems 5.1 and 5.2 in Blackorby and Donaldson (1988) give necessary and sufficient conditions for (72) to hold locally and globally respectively, given a range condition on the ratio $R'(p,q,\beta,\gamma)/R(p,q,\beta,\gamma)$.[12] We repeat the first of those theorems here as Theorem 4.

Theorem 4: Given exactness of the relative cost-of-children index, two different indexes, $R'(p,q,\beta,\gamma)$ and $R(p,q,\beta,\gamma)$, satisfying the range condition, are consistent locally with the same (utility-maximising) household behaviour, (72), if and only if

$$E(u,p,q,\beta,\gamma^r) = a(p,q,\beta)[\phi(u)]^{b(p,q,\beta)} \tag{73}$$

with

$$R'(p,q,\beta,\gamma) = [S(\beta,\gamma)]^{b(p,q,\beta)} R(p,q,\beta,\gamma) \tag{74}$$

for all (u,p,q,β,γ) where $S(\beta,\gamma)$ is positive and $S(\beta,\gamma^r) = 1$ for all β.

This means that, if reference preferences do not satisfy (73), then the cost-of-children index, R, can be identified from the data; that is, the indexes are recovered from behaviour, conditional on exactness of the index. But estimating the cost-of-children indexes permits comparisons of utility levels between households.

Absolute cost-of-children indexes, exactness, and behaviour

We can repeat the above question for those absolute cost-of-children indexes that are exact. Suppose that there are two different exact indexes $A(p,q,\alpha)$ and $A'(p,q,\alpha)$, that are consistent with the same household behaviour. Then, there exists a function ϕ, increasing in its first argument, such that

$$V'(p,q,y - A'(p,q,\beta,\gamma),\beta,\gamma') = \phi[V''(p,q,y - A(p,q,\beta,\gamma),\beta,\gamma'),\beta,\gamma] \quad (75)$$

for all (p,q,β,γ). Given a range condition on the difference $A'(p,q,\alpha) - A(p,q,\alpha)$, we can give necessary and sufficient conditions for (75) to hold.

Theorem 5: Given exactness of the absolute cost-of-children index, two different cost-of-children indexes, $A'(p,q,\alpha)$ and $A(p,q,\alpha)$ satisfying the range condition, are consistent locally with the same (utility-maximising) household behaviour, (75), if and only if

$$E(u,p,q,\beta,\gamma') = a(p,q,\beta)\phi(u) + b(p,q,\beta) \quad (76)$$

with

$$A'(p,q,\beta,\gamma) = a(p,q,\beta)S(\beta,\gamma) + A(p,q,\beta,\gamma) \quad (77)$$

for all (u,p,q,β,γ), where $S(\beta,\gamma') = 0$.

Proof: Simply repeat the argument used to prove Theorem 5.1 in Blackorby and Donaldson (1988) with obvious changes needed to deal with absolute rather than relative exactness. ■

Hence, if the absolute cost-of-children index is exact and reference preferences are not quasi-homothetic the cost-of-children index can be recovered from behaviour. Again, interpersonal comparisons of utilities are revealed.

Conclusion

It is tempting to suggest that, from a theoretical standpoint, absolute indexes are superior to relative or relative indexes to absolute. But such judgements are not possible without data, and, given the results of the previous section, demand data are sufficient to distinguish the two cases.

It is, of course, possible that neither set of restrictions on demand behaviour fits the data very well. The implications of such tests are, however, not always clear. Because the conditions for exactness of the absolute or relative cost-of-children indexes imply, but are not implied by, the demand restrictions, such tests are conclusive only in the case of rejection. Because of the identification results of the previous section, however, we suggest that such tests be undertaken by specifying a functional form for the reference expenditure or utility functions that is not piglog (relative) or quasi-homothetic (absolute) with functional forms for other household types generated through a specification of a functional form for the cost-of-children indexes. Then estimation using this structure may be compared to a more general specification where exactness is not imposed.

The iso-prop and Rothbarth methods may be used to estimate cost-of-children indexes and, given the results on pp. 55–59, direct tests of the preference restrictions they imply may be performed. Similar tests of demographic and adult-goods separability are possible, given the results on pp. 59–63.

These indexes may be used for policy purposes. If, for example, governments want to compensate parents completely for the cost of children, relative or absolute indexes – whichever class fits the data better – may be used. If, however, governments wish only to ensure that children do not fall below a target or poverty level of well-being, an estimate of the expenditure function using any method that works well provides sufficient information to calculate the appropriate transfers.

NOTES

Russell Davidson and an anonymous referee provided helpful comments, for which we thank them. We also thank the SSHRCC for partial support of this project.

1 For a discussion of interpersonal comparisons in general and further references see Sen (1977) or Blackorby, Donaldson and Weymark (1984); the relationship between notions of interpersonal comparability and equivalence scales is discussed at some length in Blackorby and Donaldson (1991).

2 We have dealt with these issues explicitly in Blackorby and Donaldson (1988, 1991).

3 The designation of x as adult goods or necessities is theoretically unimportant (but of real practical significance). Any subset of goods and services would suffice.

4 Calling these the characteristics associated with children is a convenience for the discussion at hand.

5 See Blackorby and Donaldson (1988, 1991) and Lewbel (1989, 1991) for proofs of exactness of a similar condition on household equivalence scales. Their use

in welfare analysis is discussed in Lewbel (1989), Blundell and Lewbel (1991), and Blackorby and Donaldson (1993).

6 This has been called the *Engel* method by Deaton and Muellbauer (1986) and Deaton, Ruiz-Castillo and Thomas (1989) and the iso-prop method by Espenshade (1984) and Browning (1990, 1992). We will use the latter terminology so as to reserve the former name for a more restrictive notion as suggested by Deaton and Muellbauer (1980) and also used by us.

7 Muellbauer (1974) and Browning (1988b) have suggested solutions to this problem; both permitted there to be only one adult good. (21) reduces to the solution found by Browning if there is only one good. Muellbauer was interested in the case where every good could be the adult good.

8 Browning (1990) claims that this result for a scalar extends to the case of multiple adult goods; the sufficiency of (21) demonstrates that this claim is not correct.

9 This too has been shown by Browning (1988a) for the case of a single adult good.

10 This is not an exhaustive set of comparisons. We have chosen only those that seemed most interesting in the current context. Given that there are closed-form solutions for each of the above notions, a complete set of comparisons would be possible but tedious.

11 This is discussed at some length in Blackorby and Donaldson (1988, 1991).

12 This range condition requires that this ratio can be moved through some interval.

REFERENCES

Blackorby, C. and D. Donaldson (1988) 'Welfare ratios and distributionally sensitive cost-benefit analysis', *Journal of Public Economics*, 34, 265–290
  (1988) 'Adult-equivalence scales and the economic implementation of inter-personal comparisons of well-being', University of British Columbia, *Discussion Paper*, 88–27, forthcoming in *Social Choice and Welfare*
  (1991) 'Adult-equivalence scales, interpersonal comparisons of well-being and applied welfare economics', in J. Elster and J. Roemer (eds.), *Interpersonal Comparisons and Distributive Justice*, Cambridge, Cambridge University Press, 164–199
  (1993) 'Household-equivalence scales and welfare comparisons: a comment', *Journal of Public Economics*, 50, 143–146
Blackorby, C., R. Davidson and W. Schworm (1991) 'Implicit separability: characterisation and implications for consumer demand', *Journal of Economic Theory*, 55, 364–399
Blackorby, C., D. Donaldson and J.A. Weymark (1984) 'Social choice with interpersonal utility comparisons: a diagrammatic introduction', *International Economic Review*, 25, 327–356
Blundell, R.W. and A. Lewbel (1991) 'The information content of equivalence scales', *Journal of Econometrics*, 50, 49–68

Browning, M.A. (1988a) 'The effects of household characteristics on behaviour and welfare', Department of Economics, McMaster University, mimeo

(1988b) 'The exact preferences associated with the Engel and Rothbarth methods for measuring the costs of children', Department of Economics, McMaster University, mimeo

(1990) 'Modelling the effects of children on household economic behaviour', Department of Economics, McMaster University, *Working Paper*, 90-11

(1993) 'Modelling the effects of children on household economic behaviour', *Journal of Economic Literature*, 30, 1434–1475

Deaton, A.S. and J. Muellbauer (1982) *Economics and Consumer Behaviour*, Cambridge, Cambridge University Press

(1986) 'On measuring child costs: with applications to poor countries', *Journal of Political Economy*, 94, 720–744

Deaton, A.S., J. Ruiz-Castillo and D. Thomas (1989) 'The influence of household composition on household expenditure patterns: theory and Spanish evidence', *Journal of Political Economy*, 97, 179–200

Espenshade, T. (1984) *Investing in Children*, Washington, DC, The Urban Institute

Lewbel, A. (1989) 'Household-equivalence scales and welfare comparisons', *Journal of Public Economics*, 39, 377–391

(1991) 'Cost of characteristics indices and household equivalence scales', *European Economic Review*, 35, 1277–1293

Muellbauer, J. (1974) 'Household composition, Engel curves and welfare comparisons between households: a duality approach', *European Economic Review*, 5, 103–122

Pollak, R.A. and T.J. Wales (1979) 'Welfare comparisons and equivalence scales', *American Economic Review*, 69, 216–221

(1981) 'Demographic variables in demand analysis', *Econometrica*, 49, 1533–1552

Rothbarth, E. (1942) 'Note on a method of determining equivalent income for families of different composition', Appendix 4 in C. Madge, *War-Time Pattern of Saving and Spending*, *Occasional Paper*, 4, Cambridge, Cambridge University Press for the National Institute of Economic and Social Research

Sen, A.K. (1977) 'On weights and measures: informational constraints in social welfare analysis', *Econometrica*, 45, 1539–1572

3　The collective approach to household behaviour

FRANÇOIS BOURGUIGNON and PIERRE-ANDRÉ
CHIAPPORI

Microeconomic theory essentially considers the household as the basic decision unit. The usual tools of consumer theory have been applied at the household level; in particular, the latter has been described by a single utility function which is maximised over a single budget constraint. This 'traditional' framework, however, has recently been challenged by several authors, who have developed so-called 'collective' models of household behaviour.[1] The various contributions belonging to the collective approach share a fundamental claim, namely that a household should be described as a group of individuals, each of whom is characterised by particular preferences, and among whom a collective decision process takes place. The first objective of this chapter is to discuss some basic methodological issues involved in the collective approaches. A second objective is to review a particular class of collective models, based upon the Pareto efficiency hypothesis, that have recently been developed. Finally, the collective approach has important consequences for the measurement – and, as a matter of fact, for the very definition – of household welfare. This issue will be discussed in the final section of the chapter.

Models of household behaviour: some methodological issues

'Collective' versus 'traditional' approaches

The advantages of the traditional approach are well known. Essentially, the traditional setting allows a direct utilisation of the consumer theory toolbox. This includes generating testable restrictions upon demand functions, recovering preferences from observed behaviour in an unambiguous way, and providing an interpretation to empirical results. It has become increasingly clear, however, that the single utility framework, attractive and convenient as it may be, still exhibits some serious shortcomings.

70

A first weakness – which, in our view, is also a major one – is methodological: the traditional approach simply falls short of meeting the basic rule of neoclassical microeconomic analysis, namely *individualism*. From an individualistic viewpoint, an individual must be characterised by his (her) own preferences, rather than being aggregated within the *ad hoc* fiction of a collective decision unit; modelling a group (even reduced to two participants) as if it were a single individual can only be seen as a mere holistic deviation.

A second problem is that the single utility approach is quite inadequate for the study of such demographic issues as marriage or divorce. Before household formation (or after dissolution), individuals are, in the traditional approach, represented by distinct preferences. Marriage is essentially described as merging the latter into the black box of a household utility function, but little – if anything – is said upon the underlying 'aggregation' process. As a result, it is hardly possible to relate household preferences to each agent's initial tastes. In contrast, a 'collective' approach can easily address this kind of issue, since it preserves the existence of individual preferences even within the household.

A final shortcoming concerns the analysis of *intra-household allocation* (of consumption, wealth, or welfare). Again, in the traditional setting, each household is a black box: while its relationships with the outside economy can be characterised, nothing can be said about its internal decision processes. In particular, such issues as the allocation of the household's resources among its members are simply ignored. Here, the problems with the single utility approach are twofold. Conceptually, the very notion of individual *welfare* is in contradiction with this setting, since welfare can only be defined at the (aggregate) household level. Technically, though individual *consumptions* could *a priori* be considered, the theory will typically face a *non-assignability* problem: most datasets contain information upon aggregate household consumption only, while one would also be interested in individual consumptions within the household. A natural question, then, is whether insights about nonobservable, individual consumption could be deduced, with the help of adequate theoretical assumptions, from data on some good, the consumption of which can be unambiguously assigned to one of the members. But it can be shown that traditional models perform quite poorly in this respect;[2] again, collective approaches may be more adequate for this purpose.

As a matter of fact, scientific curiosity is not the only motivation for analysing intra-household decision processes. Welfare considerations may also matter; they might even be crucial. When considering, for instance, policy issues involving individual welfare (such as optimal taxation or cost-benefit analysis), traditional models can be seriously inadequate and in some cases misleading. They rest upon the idea that only the distribution of income *across* households matters. The underlying, implicit assumption is that the allocation of consumption and/or welfare *within* the household is either irrelevant, or systematically optimal relative to the policy maker's preferences. Of course, this is a purely *ad hoc* hypothesis, the realism of which is dubious. There is no rationale, as well as no evidence, for assuming that the internal distribution of resources is equal in any sense. Actually, it becomes increasingly clear that taking into account intra-household inequality might well significantly alter a number of normative recommendations provided by the traditional approach. An illustration of this claim is provided by Apps' chapter 6 in this volume; see also the discussion in Haddad and Kanbur (1991).

What should we require from a collective theory of household behaviour?

The previous arguments emphasise the need for an alternative approach that takes into account the collective components involved in household decision processes. This, of course, does not mean that *any* model based upon a collective representation will do. On the contrary, a collective theoretical framework will not be acceptable unless it satisfies some basic requirements.

Specifically, the role of any theory of household behaviour, whatever its precise content, is twofold:

(1) it generates *testable restrictions*, that can be used both to facilitate empirical estimation, and to check *ex post* the adequacy of the theory for observed behaviour;

(2) it allows the *recovery of 'structural' components* (such as preferences) from observed behaviour, and hence suggests interpretations for empirical results and provides a formal basis for normative recommendations.

For instance, in the traditional approach, demand functions must satisfy homogeneity, Walras' law and Slutsky's equations (or revealed preference restrictions). Moreover, integrability results state that from any system of demand functions fulfilling these conditions, it is possible to recover (at least locally) the agent's preferences; and the corresponding utility function is *uniquely defined*, up to an increasing mapping. The second property guarantees, in particular, that normative conclusions can be drawn in an unambiguous way, provided that we accept the underlying theoretical framework; and a good reason for such an acceptance might be that the testable implications of the theory turn out to be empirically fulfilled.

Therefore, a basic requirement is that a 'good' collective theory of household behaviour must both generate falsifiable restrictions (*testability* requirement) and allow unique recovery of the members' preferences and the decision process (*integrability* requirement). Finally, in addition to these 'traditional' requirements, the collective approach should help in solving the 'assignability' problem; i.e., it should (ideally) be able to fulfil the above requirements even though, for most commodities, only aggregate household consumption can be observed.

'Collective' decision processes: a general framework

In order to discuss in more detail the properties of a collective approach, it is useful to define a general framework within which the issues can be conveniently addressed.

Preferences and consumption bundles

We consider a household of two members, A and B, with respective preferences U^A and U^B. The household can consume $n + N$ goods, among which n are consumed privately by each member, whereas N are public goods for the household; let $x^A = (x_1^A, \ldots, x_n^A)$, $x^B = (x_1^B, \ldots, x_n^B)$ denote the respective private consumption bundles of A and B, and $X = (X_1, \ldots, X_N)$ the household consumption of public goods. Hence, U^A and U^B map R^{n+N} to R, and can be written respectively $U^A(x^A, X)$, $U^B(x^B, X)$. A polar case, considered for instance by Chiappori (1992a), is $N = 0$, all goods are privately consumed, and preferences are said to be *egoistic*. At the other extreme, we might assume, as in McElroy and Horney (1981), that all consumptions of any member do enter both members' utility function; then the preferences will be said to be *altruistic*, and take the form $U^A(x^A, x^B, X)$, $U^B(x^A, x^B, X)$. Of course, the altruistic setting is the most general one: the price to pay for this generality being, unsurprisingly, that it is less testable, and that the uniqueness of the structural model underlying a given demand function is more difficult to guarantee.[3]

An intermediate case of interest is Becker's notion of *caring*. Here, each member is assumed to maximise a welfare index that depends on both his (her) 'egoistic' utility and his (her) companion's utility. Technically, the preferences are of the form $W^A[U^A(x^A, X), U^B(x^B, X)]$, $W^B[U^A(x^A, X), U^B(x^B, X)]$. Interestingly enough, the properties of the 'caring' framework are, at least under the assumption of Pareto efficient decisions, much closer to the egoistic than to the altruistic case. The basic reason is that both the egoistic and the caring settings exhibit a *separability* property that will be shown to play an important role in deriving the properties of the model.

In what follows, $p \in R^n$ and $P \in R^N$ will be the price vectors of the private and public goods, and y will denote the household's total income, so that the overall budget constraint is $p.(x^A + x^B) + P.X = y$. In some cases, each member's income can be independently observed, i.e., $y^A + y^B = y$.

A last distinction that is relevant for private consumptions is between *exclusive, assignable,* and *nonassignable* goods. A good is exclusive when it is consumed by one member only; a typical example is labour supply (or leisure), at least insofar as it is not a public good for the household. A nonexclusive good is assignable when each member's consumption can be observed independently; it is nonassignable otherwise. As we shall see later, the existence of either an assignable good or a pair of exclusive goods will be crucial for the integrability properties of the models. Also, note that the observation of two exclusive consumptions will in general bring more information than that of an assignable good; this is because the prices of the exclusive goods will be different, while the assignable good has a single price whatever the number of consumers.

The decision process

The next step is to define the assumptions made on the decision process. A first and basic distinction is between *cooperative* and *noncooperative* settings. While a majority of models assume that the procedure is cooperative, in the (broad) sense that only Pareto efficient outcomes can be reached, other works adopt a noncooperative framework, in which the process is described as a game between the participants; in the latter case, efficiency may not – and in most cases will not – obtain. In what follows, we shall essentially be interested in the cooperative approach. We shall assume that the decision taken by the household – i.e., the functions $x^A(p,P,y)$, $x^B(p,P,y)$, $X(p,P,y)$ – can be written as the solution of a problem of the form:

$$\max \lambda U^A + (1 - \lambda) U^B$$

subject to (1)

$$p.(x^A + x^B) + P.X = y \tag{1}$$

for some well-chosen nonnegative function $\lambda = \lambda(p,P,y)$.

Several remarks can be made about this problem. First, it is similar to standard utility maximisation under budget constraint, but the maximand depends on prices; in particular, the solution will not satisfy Slutsky conditions in general. Also, we know that, for any given (p, P, y), the set of solutions, when λ varies, coincides with the set of Pareto efficient outcomes; hence to any efficient decision rule corresponds some function $\lambda(p, P, y)$, and conversely. It must, however, be remembered that the latter will then depend on the cardinal representation of preferences; i.e., the same λ will generate different demand functions whenever U^X is replaced by $F[U^X]$, where F is some nondecreasing mapping and $X = A$ (or B).

One may wish to describe the decision process independently from the particular cardinal representation of preferences. This is especially easy in the case of private goods and egoistic preferences, since efficiency is then equivalent to the existence of a sharing rule for income. Indeed, when all goods are private, any efficient decision process can be interpreted as follows: agents first allocate total income between themselves, according to some sharing rule θ, so that A receives $\theta(p, y)$, B receives $y - \theta(p, y)$; then each agent maximises his (her) utility, subject to his (her) budget constraint. Technically, thus, the functions $x^A(p, P, y)$ and $x^B(p, P, y)$ are solutions of (1) for some $\lambda = \lambda(p, y)$ if and only if there exists a sharing rule $\theta(p, y)$ such that:

$x^A(p, y)$ is the solution of

$$\max U^A(x^A)$$

$$p^A . x^A = \theta(p, y)$$

and $x^B(p, y)$ is the solution of

$$\max U^B(x^B)$$

subject to

$$p^B . x^B = y - \theta(p, y).$$

A formal proof (together with a detailed discussion) can be found in Chiappori (1988) and Bourguignon, Browning, Chiappori and Lechène (1992a). The important point, here, is that there is a one-to-one correspondence between the decision process and the sharing rule. Note, furthermore, that the sharing rule is an ordinal concept, i.e., it is defined independently of the cardinal representation of preferences.

This result can be extended in several directions. Assume, first, that utilities are of the 'caring' (rather than 'egoistic') type; i.e., agents maximise $W^A[U^A(x^A, X), U^B(x^B, X)]$ and $W^B[U^A(x^A, X), U^B(x^B, X)]$. Then any allocation that is efficient for W^A and W^B is also efficient for U^A and U^B; this is because any change that ameliorates is valid for caring utilities as well.[4] Also, in the presence of public goods, the sharing rule approach must be defined *conditionally* on the level of public expenditures (see Bourguignon, Browning, Chiappori, Lechène, 1992a, for a precise statement).

Nash bargaining

Within the class of cooperative models, a particular subclass that has been considered by a number of authors relies upon equilibrium concepts borrowed from cooperative game theory, and especially Nash bargaining. The first step is to define for each member a 'reservation utility' or 'threat point' $H^X(p, P, y)$ (where $X = A, B$), representing the minimum welfare level X could obtain in any case (and especially if no collective agreement could be reached); of course, this will depend on the economic environment, i.e., prices (including wages) and incomes. Then the surplus arising from cooperation is shared geometrically between the members; i.e., the household maximises $[U^A - H^A].[U^B - H^B]$ over the household budget constraint.

Of course, several problems have to be solved. One is the choice of threat points; should one take utilities when divorced, as in McElroy (1990), or rather noncooperative equilibrium within the household, as argued by Ulph (1988)? Also, in both cases, estimating the model is by no means an easy task. Simultaneous estimation of preferences *and* threat points from data on married couples may be quite difficult (according to the present state of knowledge, it is an open question whether it is possible at all). A solution, advocated for instance by McElroy, might be to estimate threat points from data on the behaviour of divorced individuals. But the problem here, is that the concept of Nash bargaining equilibrium requires a *cardinal* representation of preferences; i.e., it is not invariant through an increasing transformation of utilities, threat points, or both. Since such a transformation will typically lead to the same behaviour (at least in the absence of uncertainty), it cannot be identified from individual data. One may thus have to choose arbitrarily a particular cardinal representation (among the infinity compatible with observed behaviour), and the conclusion will then crucially depend on this choice.[5]

Despite these technical difficulties, however, the Nash bargaining approach may (once adequately designed) provide very useful insights on the consequences of taking into account intra-household decision processes. For instance, Haddad and Kanbur (1991) emphasise the impact of intra-household allocation issues for the 'targeting' of welfare policies. The design of an optimal in kind benefit will crucially depend on who exactly in the household receives the benefits; 'targeting' a food supplement to, say, children between three and 10 is meaningless if the corresponding increase is compensated by a reduction of the child's share of food at home. Another consequence is that the scope of a given policy may be much broader than suggested by the number of people who actually receive it directly. A minimum wage, for instance, will typically modify the threat point for nonworking spouses, and thus, according to the bargaining ideas, influence the sharing rule.

It can also be noted that the spirit of bargaining processes can be captured, even in the absence of a specialised model, by introducing within the general Pareto framework some specific and testable assumptions. For instance, any variable that is likely to be positively correlated with the bargaining power of one spouse (say, wage or nonlabour income) should have a positive effect on the latter's share – a conclusion that can be empirically tested in the collective framework, as argued by Chiappori (1992a).

Testability and integrability

As we argued above, the collective theories that we want to develop should have two basic properties. They must, on the one hand, be testable, i.e., imply some consequences that can potentially be falsified by empirical results; and, on the other hand, they must enable unique recovery of preferences and decision processes from the available observations on agents' behaviour. The precise translation of these general properties will depend on the particular formalisation adopted. A model can start from a 'reduced' form, i.e., a functional form for demand functions (or labour supply). Then the theory must provide us with necessary conditions upon the parameters and, conversely, enable us to recover the underlying 'structural' framework (preferences, decision rule). Conversely, a model may be based upon a structural setting (typically, functional forms for utility functions plus assumptions upon the decision processes), from which agents' demand functions are derived; the latter will thus automatically fulfil the theoretical restrictions. Testability, here, requires that the derived demand functions can be embedded within a more general form. Also, the parameters of the structural model must be identifiable from the estimation of the reduced form.

Concerning the two requirements of testability and integrability, some remarks are, however, in order. For one thing, there seems to be some confusion on the exact meaning of the testability criteria. It has been argued that the collective approach (and, more specifically, Nash bargaining models) could be tested *against* the traditional setting by investigating whether some conditions, that were implied by the traditional framework but not by the collective one, turned out to be empirically fulfilled or not. For instance, 'traditional' demand functions must satisfy Slutsky conditions. Moreover, as is well known by now, the single utility approach implies income pooling: only total income, and not income composition, may matter. Empirical evidence against these properties have thus been interpreted, on some occasions, as supporting the collective approach in general and, even worse, the particular collective model currently at stake. This is a clear mistake. Undoubtedly, any evidence against income pooling suggests that the traditional approach is not valid, at least unless a specific explanation can be given. But this mere fact does *not* support any alternative model in particular. There are certainly many *ad hoc* assumptions that could explain the observed results within the traditional approach, as well as many more or less odd alternative models that could justify them outside this framework. The only way to empirically support the collective setting is to derive, *from the particular model under consideration*, conditions that can potentially be, but are actually not falsified by empirical observation.[6] This requirement should be kept in mind when constructing the model.

Integrability, on the other hand, requires that one and only one structural model can be associated to the reduced form (i.e., demand functions) that is empirically estimated. An immediate consequence is that the strutural model must be *identifiable* in the usual econometric sense. It must, however, be stressed that *integrability is a much stronger requirement than identifiability*. Indeed, identifiability means that, given the initial functional form, the parameters can uniquely be recovered. It could, however, be the case that a *functionally different* structural model (i.e., different functional forms for utilities, decision rules, or both) leads to the same functional form for demands, as illustrated by the following example. Take a two-member household, and assume there are two public goods; the model simply assumes that the household maximises $\lambda U^A + (1 - \lambda)U^B$, where

$$U^A = a \ln X_1 + (1 - a)\ln X_2$$
$$U^B = \beta \ln X_1 + (1 - \beta)\ln X_2$$

and

$$\lambda = \lambda_1 \frac{p_1}{y} + \lambda_2 \frac{p_2}{y}.$$

The resolution of this problem gives the following demand function for good 1 (consumption of good 2 being then derived from the budget constraint):

$$p_1.x_1 = \beta y + (a - \beta)\lambda_1 p_1 + (a - \beta)\lambda_2 p_2.$$

Provided we have some additional information (say, a is known), this 'initial' model is *exactly* identified. However, any conclusion drawn from the estimation of the demand function above is highly suspect, because *the integrability condition is not satisfied.* To see why, assume, rather, that

$$U^A = a \ln(X_1 - \gamma_1) + (1 - a)\ln(X_2 - \gamma_2)$$

$$U^B = \beta \ln(X_1 - \gamma_1) + (1 - \beta)\ln(X_2 - \gamma_2)$$

and

$$\lambda = \text{constant};$$

then the demand function is:

$$p_1.x_1 = [\lambda a + (1 - \lambda)\beta]y + \gamma_1[1 - \lambda a - (1 - \lambda)\beta]p_1 + \gamma_2[\lambda a + (1 - \lambda)\beta]p_2.$$

This is an example where we get identical functional forms for demand through totally different structural models. The problem, here, is that the interpretation will crucially depend on the structural model with which we started. For instance, empirical estimates might lead, in the first setting, to the conclusion that λ, member A's weight in the collective welfare, is increasing with p_1, while in the alternative structural model, λ is constant whatever the data.

An important – and sometimes forgotten – property of the traditional setting is that such a situation is ruled out. But this is due to a very strong integrability result of neoclassical consumer theory: for any given (vector) demand function satisfying homogeneity, Walras and Slutsky, there exists *exactly one* set of individual preferences from which it can be derived. This property, however, does not necessarily hold true in other frameworks. This is why a preliminary and careful investigation of the theoretical properties of the model is strongly recommended and, more fundamentally, why the integrability requirement must be emphasised: it is a necessary prerequisite for any welfare conclusion.

An example: collective labour supply

In this section, we review results that have recently been obtained in the collective approach. Interestingly enough, they are based solely upon the efficiency hypothesis; i.e., no assumption is made upon the decision process besides the fact that it always generates outcomes located on the Pareto frontier.

In what follows, we consider cross-sectional data; as a consequence, prices are assumed identical for all households, while wages and non-labour income vary across households. Also, utilities are either of the egoistic or of the caring type; and we assume for the moment that all goods are private. We shall present an elementary model of labour supply, in which each member's labour supply is supposed to be freely chosen and observable (in the previous terminology, each spouse's labour supply is an exclusive good); there is, in addition, a unique, private consumption good which is nonassignable. This setting[7] has been considered by Chiappori (1988, 1992a).

Formally, assume that each member maximises an egoistic utility function $U^i[C^i, L^i]$, where C^i and L^i denote i's private consumption and labour supply. The budget constraint is:

$$w_A L^A + w_B L^B + C^A + C^B = (w_A + w_B) T + y$$

where the consumption good is taken as numeraire ($p = 1$). As before, Pareto efficiency is equivalent to the existence of a sharing rule; hence, agent A's problem is:

$$\max U^i[C^i, L^i]$$

subject to

$$w_A L^A + C^A = w_A . T + \theta(w_A, w_B, y),$$

and b's problem is obtained by replacing θ by $y - \theta$.

Under these assumptions, the following results can be proved. Assume that we are able to empirically observe individual labour supplies, but only aggregate consumption. Then:

(1) testable restrictions upon the labour supply functions can be derived, from both the parametric (partial differential equations) and non-parametric ('revealed preferences' types of conditions) viewpoints; and

(2) the sharing rule can be recovered from labour supplies up to an additive constraint. Each member's utility can also be recovered, up to the same additive constraint.

A detailed proof can be found in Chiappori (1988, 1992a). The intuition, however, can be briefly summarised. The key point is that under the exclusive good assumption, each member's wage can only have an *income* effect upon the spouse's behaviour; e.g., both my wife's wage w_1 and our (common) nonlabour income y will influence my behaviour through their effect on the sharing rule. Imagine, in particular, that a 10% increase in w_1 is observed to have exactly the same effect as a 5% increase in y. Then it must be the case that both changes affect my share of total income in an equivalent way. This will provide us with an estimate of the 'marginal rate of substitution' between w_1 and y in the sharing rule. The same argument can of course be applied to my wife's behaviour; and the two shares must add up to one. This will allow exact recovery of the partials of the sharing rule. It must, however, be stressed that the rule itself will only be defined up to a constant. The deep reason for this inderminacy is that behaviour depends on preferences, not on income *per se*; and it will be impossible to distinguish between an individual with utility $U(C, L)$, receiving an income θ, and an individual with utility $U(C + k, L)$ receiving an income $\theta - k$.

Welfare issues

Let us come now to welfare issues. The important point, here, is that since preferences and the sharing rule can be recovered, *each member's* welfare can be estimated using exactly the same techniques as in the traditional approach. Specifically, we may define member i's collective indirect utility v^i by:[8]

$$v^i(w_A, w_B, y) = U^i[L^i, w_i(T - L^i) + \theta(w_A, w_B, y)].$$

In words, v^i is i's utility when wages are w_A and w_B and *household* nonlabour income is y – taking into account the share of labour income that i will receive.[9] The previous results essentially show that these collective indirect utilities can be recovered solely from observation of labour supplies. The consequences are worth emphasis.

Firstly, it is possible to estimate the effects of any policy reform upon *each household member*, with exactly the same kind of tools as for individuals in the traditional setting. We need not assume *a priori* any kind of household welfare or utility function, either for modelling behaviour and estimating labour supply functions, or for formulating normative judgements.

Secondly, the conceptual framework described above allows for situations in which a reform increases one member's welfare while decreasing the other member's; more generally, it enables consideration of *intrahousehold* inequality as well as inequality across households.

Finally, while one can always 'aggregate' the collective indirect utilities into a convenient household index, the choice of the latter is left to the planner – rather than being automatically identified with the 'household utility', as in the traditional approach.

In conclusion, let us emphasise the general spirit of the contribution, rather than the interesting but still quite partial results it has reached so far. It has become more and more apparent that the traditional approach, by choosing the household as the elementary decision unit, has in a sense betrayed the principles of individualism that lie at the foundation of microeconomic analysis. Some attempts to reconcile the single utility approach with individualism should be mentioned; among them are Samuelson's household welfare index (taken to be a fixed function of the members' utilities), and above all Becker's Rotten Kid theorem. Samuelson's solution relies upon a very restrictive *ad hoc* assumption, namely that the household decision process (as represented, for instance, by the respective weights within the collective index) does not depend on the economic environment, and especially on prices, wages and incomes. Becker's contribution, on the other hand, does introduce fundamental elements, including the concept of a sharing rule; but it does rely upon specific and rather strong assumptions, that are needed to avoid an inconsistency with the traditional results (see Chiappori, 1992a for a detailed discussion).

The basic claim of the new approach is that such an inconsistency should be accepted, rather than avoided through the accumulation of *ad hoc* hypotheses. The essence of the collective approach described above lies in a return to the basic grounds of micro theory – individualism, rationality, and efficiency. The important message that the previous results bring is that this strategy may turn out to be surprisingly fruitful. Of course, this approach is still at a very preliminary stage. We, however, believe that it constitutes a coherent and promising research programme, which is likely to be pursued in the forthcoming years.[10]

NOTES

We thank two anonymous referees for useful comments. The chapter draws upon Bourguignon and Chiappori (1991).

1 Among early contributors, one can mention Apps (1981, 1982), Apps and Jones (1988), Apps and Rees (1988) and Chiappori (1988, 1992a, 1992b), who introduced cooperative models, while Ashworth and Ulph (1981), Bourguignon (1985), Ulph (1988) and Kapteyn and Kooreman (1992a) refer to non-cooperative game theory, and Kooreman (1991) simultaneously considers both settings. Also, Brown and Manser (1978), Manser and Brown (1980), Brown and Chuang (1981), McElroy and Horney (1981) and more recently Haddad and Kanbur (1990, 1991) have developed models based upon bargaining theory.

2 See for instance Gronau (1988) and Chiappori (1992a, 1992b).

3 For a detailed discusson, see Chiappori (1988, 1992a).

4 However, the set of allocations that are efficient for the *W*s is strictly included within the set of allocations that are efficient for the *U*s; e.g., some 'very unequal' allocations may be efficient for egoistic preferences but not in the case

of caring. As a consequence, while an income sharing rule will always be associated to any efficient decision process with caring, the converse may fail to be true for 'unequal' sharing rules.

5 Assume, for instance, that member A's utility when divorced is of the form $U^A - s^A(p, P, Y)$ (i.e., that divorce has a cost *per se* – not an unrealistic assumption, after all). Then s^A cannot be identified from data on divorced individuals, but will clearly play a key role in the Nash bargaining procedure. Of course, the same is true, more generally, for preferences of the form $F[U^A, p, P, y]$; the argument is in fact very similar to the analysis of equivalence scales in Blundell and Lewbel (1991).

Another solution would be to use direct information on preferences, collected from interviews or experiments (see for instance Kapteyn and Kooreman, 1992b).

6 Specifically, the new approach should have 'unexpected' empirical implications, i.e., consequences that must be true under the new theory but should be false under the old one; see Popper (1968).

7 Another class of models supposes, on the contrary, that each member's income is exogenous, for instance because working time is fixed by demand constraints (which requires, in particular, considering a subsample of households in which both spouses work full time), and concentrate on consumption decisions. These models, analysed by Bourguignon, Browning, Chiappori and Lechène (1992a, 1992b), are however less interesting for the present purpose, since the welfare conclusions are much less clear.

8 The collective indirect utilities defined here should be distinguished from the *individual* indirect utilities V^i, defined as a function of i's wage and nonlabour income. Specifically, the relationship between the two concepts depends on the sharing rule:

$$v_A(w_A, w_B, y) = V^A[w_A, w_A T + \theta(w_A, w_B, y)]$$

9 It must be emphasised that, with the notation of the previous paragraph, collective indirect utilities do *not* depend on the parameter k; i.e., all pairs of utility and sharing rule that are compatible with observed behaviour will lead to the *same* indirect utility (up to an increasing transformation).

10 Bourguignon, Browning, Chiappori and Lechène (1992a) provide preliminary estimates of the consumption model on French data, while Bourguignon, Browning, Chiappori and Lechène (1992b) analyse Canadian data.

REFERENCES

Apps, P.F. (1981) *A Theory of Inequality and Taxation*, Cambridge, Cambridge University Press

(1982) 'Institutional inequality and tax incidence', *Journal of Public Economics*, 18, 217–242

Apps, P.F. and G.S. Jones (1988) 'Selective taxation of couples', *Zeitschrift für Nationalökonomie*, *Suppl.*, 5, 63–74

Apps, P.F. and R. Rees (1988) 'Taxation and the household', *Journal of Public Economics*, 39, 335–364

Ashworth, J. and D.T. Ulph (1981) 'Household models', in C.V. Brown (ed.) *Taxation and Labour Supply*, London, Allen & Unwin

Blundell, R.W. and A. Lewbel (1991) 'The information content of equivalence scales', *Journal of Econometrics*, 50, 49–68

Bourguignon, F. (1985) 'Rationalité individuelle ou nationalité stratégique: le cas de l'offre familiale de travail', *Revue Economique*, 35, 147–162

Bourguignon, F. and P.-A. Chiappori (1991) 'Collective models of household behaviour: an introduction', *European Economic Review*, 36, 355–364

Bourguignon, F., A.M. Browning, P.-A. Chiappori and V. Lechène (1992a) 'Intra-household allocation of consumption: a model and some evidence from French data', *Annales d'économie et de statistique*, 19, 137–156

(1992b) 'Incomes and outcomes: a structural model of intra-household allocation', McMaster University, *Working Paper*

Brown, M. and C.F. Chuang (1981) 'Theoretical constraints on a household bargaining model', Buffalo University, *Working Paper*

Brown, M. and M. Manser (1978) 'Neoclassical and bargaining approaches to household decision making', Buffalo University, *Working Paper*

Chiappori, P.-A. (1988) 'Rational household labour supply', *Econometrica*, 56, 63–89

(1992a) 'Collective labour supply and welfare', *Journal of Political Economy*, 100, 437–467

(1992b) 'The collective approach to household behaviour: a presentation', in *Intrahousehold Resource Allocation: Policy Issues and Research Methods*, Washington, DC, International Food Policy Research Institute and the World Bank

Gronau, R. (1988) 'Consumption technology and the intrafamily distribution of resources', *Journal of Political Economy*, 96, 1183–1205

Haddad, L. and R. Kanbur (1990) 'How serious is the neglect of intrahousehold inequality?', *Economic Journal*, 100, 866–881

(1991) 'Public employment schemes and intrahousehold inequality', International Food Policy Research Institute, mimeo

Kapteyn, A. and P. Kooreman (1992a) 'On the empirical implementation of some game theoretic models of household labour supply', *Journal of Human Resources*, 25, 584–598

(1992b) 'Household labor supply: what sort of data can tell us how many decision makers there are?', *European Economic Review*, 36, 365–374

Kooreman, P. (1991) 'Empirical models of some discrete games, with an application to household labor force participation', Wageningen University, mimeo

McElroy, M.B. (1990) 'The empirical content of Nash-bargained household behaviour', *Journal of Human Resources*, 25, 559–583

McElroy, M.B. and M.J. Horney (1981) 'Nash-bargained household decisions: towards a generalization of the theory of demand', *International Economic Review*, 22, 333–349

Manser, M. and M. Brown (1980) 'Marriage and household decision-making: a
   bargaining analysis', *International Economic Review*, 21, 31–44
Popper, K. (1968) *The Logic of Scientific Discovery*, London, Hutchinson
Ulph, D.T. (1988) 'A general non-cooperative Nash model of household consumption behaviour', University of Bristol, *Working Paper*, 88/205

4 Ordinal and cardinal utility: an integration of the two dimensions of the welfare concept

BERNARD M. S. VAN PRAAG

Introduction

One of the key concepts in economics is *utility* or *welfare*.[1] The first thorough introductions of the concept were those by Gossen (1854), Jevons (1871) and Edgeworth (1881). They assumed that a commodity bundle **x** in the commodity space (R^{+n}) contained an intrinsic utility value $U(\mathbf{x})$. The consumer problem could then be described as looking for the bundle with the highest utility value that could be bought at prices **p** and income y.

Such a model was able to describe and to predict purchase behaviour. This was the *behavioural* aspect. But the model was also to be used for *normative* purposes, where we compare utility differences between bundles $\mathbf{x}_1$, $\mathbf{x}_2$, $\mathbf{x}_3$ for a specific individual. This is called *intra*-personal comparison. The utility of income levels y_1, y_2, y_3 may be calculated by means of the *indirect utility* function $V(y, \mathbf{p})$ which is defined as the maximum utility to be derived from income y at given prices **p**.

This led to the progressive income taxation rules, suggested by Cohen Stuart (1889) among others. Actually the latter use implies also that utility differences are comparable between individuals. This is called *inter*-personal comparability.

It would then also be possible to define social welfare functions $W(U_1, \ldots, U_n)$ where social welfare is a function of individual utilities. The most obvious application of that concept is to compare distributions of social wealth and to devise policies which will lead to a better distribution.

Pareto (1909) gave a fierce blow to the utility concept by showing that demand behaviour was completely determined by the contour lines, defined by the equation

$$U(\mathbf{x}) = \text{constant}$$

carved out on (R^{+n}); they are called the (utility) indifference curves.

The result is that demand behaviour does not define the utility function uniquely, but rather that there is a whole equivalence class of utility functions which will yield the same demand behaviour. Those utility functions $\tilde{U}(x)$ have the property that $\tilde{U} = \varphi(U)$ where $\varphi(.)$ is any monotonical increasing function.

This eroded utility concept is called the *ordinal* concept. The original one of, for example, Edgeworth is called the *cardinal* utility concept. Samuelson (1947) remarked that Edgeworth thought utility to be 'as real as his morning jam'. Pareto (1909) did not state that cardinal utility was a nonsensical concept, (see also Kirman, 1987) but only that it was not necessary to know the utility function to explain demand behaviour, as knowledge of the contour lines of the utility surface on the commodity space are all that we need. Nevertheless, this was a very helpful finding for our science, as it proved very difficult to measure utility in practice.

Robbins (1932) made a fierce attack on cardinal utility and stated that it was an unmeasurable concept altogether. Hicks and Allen (1934) and later on Houthakker (1950) gave rigorous explanations of demand behaviour without applying the utility concept at all. Deaton and Muellbauer (1982) make similar observations in their authoritative survey. So the utility concept degenerated into just a handsome tool to describe choice behaviour.

Still there was an undercurrent of 'true believers' in the utility of cardinal utility, which included famous names like Tinbergen who uses and defends the log (income) as a utility function and Frisch (1932) (see also Sen, 1979).

Harsanyi (1987) writes on interpersonal utility comparisons in the *New Palgrave*:

It seems to me that economists and philosophers influenced by logical positivism have greatly exaggerated the difficulties we face in making interpersonal utility comparisons with respect to the utilities and the disutilities that people derive from ordinary commodities and, more generally, from the ordinary pleasures and commodities of human life.

See also Shubik (1982). Indeed the whole literature on income inequality and poverty would be reduced to a sterile exercise if we did not accept the implicit cardinal utility measurement and interpersonal comparability on which these concepts are based.[2]

In general the questions which are posed by reality (e.g., in physics, medicine, sociology or economics) are answered by the development of science. If reality poses questions to which science has no answers, only few people would doubt that the correct way for scientific researchers would be to dig into these questions and to develop an operational theory as an answer.

However, in the case of utility history seems to have taken a different course. Reality abounds of normative questions with respect to distribution issues, income inequality, poverty, equivalence scales, etc. which are clearly answered in an intuitive way by policy makers in such a way that at least groups of the population feel that they agree with the policies proposed and the underlying value judgements. Such a utility base is also nearly indispensable for the evaluation of equilibria and the application of game theoretic models (see also Shubik, 1984). Nevertheless, it seems as if many economists have declared those questions nonissues which cannot be solved scientifically except for looking for Pareto optimality. It is rather remarkable that mainstream economics for half a century since Robbins has followed a way which is so different from what is going on in the development of most sciences. Mostly science is *following* reality, instead of *ignoring* it.

In this chapter we will show that the cardinal dimension of the utility concept may and should be identified by the use of other data than those which can be derived from the observation of demand behaviour.

In the second section we consider the precise relation between the cardinal and ordinal utility concepts on the commodity space, and outline the way in which cardinal utility can be measured. It turns out that we need a combination of *two* measurement instruments, which we consider in the third section. The first measurement tool is the observation of consumer behaviour from household budgets as described in surveys; the second tool of measurement is the Income Evaluation Question (IEQ), as developed by, among others, van Praag (1968, 1971), van Praag and Kapteyn (1973) and van Praag and van der Sar (1988). In the fourth section we consider the possibilities of translating qualifying verbal labels into figures. In the fifth section we describe the IEQ method, and we consider its validity and results. In the sixth section we report on some empirically estimated relationships with respect to income evaluation. In the seventh section we present an integrated cardinal utility function on (R^{+n}) by merging the two types of information and we apply the method on two well-known demand models – the Almost Ideal Demand System and the Translog Demand System. The eighth section concludes with a summary and discussion.

Up to now the IEQ methodology has been used by practitioners but it has not been embedded in mainstream consumer theory, for two reasons. The first was the use of specific assumptions ('equal quantiles' and 'log-normality') in the measurement method, for which there was no independent empirical evidence. A second point was that it was unclear how price variations would influence the results. Both objections will be met in this chapter.

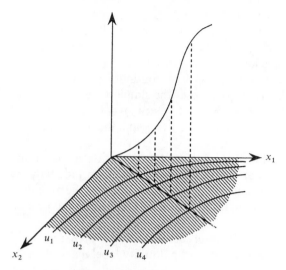

Figure 4.1 The utility hill

The behavioural and the normative aspects of utility

The utility hill in $(R^{+^{n+1}})$ described by the function U(x) on $(R^{+^{n}})$ may be sketched as in figure 4.1 (see Shubik, 1984, p. 43). The contour lines corresponding to the utility levels U_1, U_2 are projected into the (x_1, x_2) plane yielding the corresponding indifference curves, which we assume to be convex with respect to the origin. It is obvious that knowledge of the indifference curve implies knowledge of the demand curves, while knowledge of the demand behaviour implies that the net of indifference curves may be constructed. Demand behaviour says everything about 'the *horizontal* dimension of utility'. However, demand behaviour as such says nothing about 'the *vertical* dimension'.

The horizontal dimension defines an equivalence class of utility functions. Only if we put additional constraints to the functional specification such that in the equivalence class only one member satisfies the additional constraints, are we able to identify one member of the equivalence class as *the* utility function. We do not know of credible constraints.

A much better approach is to develop a measurement method to measure the vertical dimension. If we could succeed in identifying indifference curves with utility labels U_1, U_2, etc. which can be identified as expressions of a level of well-being attached to those indifference curves, we would have succeeded in the construction of a *cardinal* utility or welfare function.

Actually to succeed we need to know only the welfare evaluation U of *one* point at each indifference curve, as by definition the welfare evaluation of all other points on that indifference curve is then known as well. It follows that we will have identified the cardinal welfare function if we know the function $U(\mathbf{x}(t))$ where $\mathbf{x}(t)$ is a continuous and increasing vector function in $(\mathbf{R}^{+n})$ with respect to t. The simplest way is clearly to take prices as given and to consider $U(x_1(y), x_2(y)) = \tilde{U}(y)$ where $\mathbf{x}(y)$ stands for the demand vector when income y rises and the price vector $\mathbf{p}$ is constant.

Let us assume that we know the horizontal dimension of the utility function, either directly from the indifference curves or indirectly by knowing the household cost function $c(u, \mathbf{p})$, where $c(u, \mathbf{p})$ is the minimum cost (at prices $\mathbf{p}$) to reach the indifference curve labelled by the ordinal utility level u.

If $\tilde{U}(y)$ is the *true* cardinal utility level corresponding to $(y, \mathbf{p})$ for a fixed price vector, the relation between the ordinal utility label u and the true utility level $\tilde{U}$ is

$$\tilde{U}(y) = \tilde{U}(c(u, \mathbf{p})).$$

This relation describes the monotonically increasing function $\tilde{U} = \varphi(u)$, which links the ordinal utility label u to the (cardinal) height $\tilde{U}$ of the utility hill. The same procedure is possible with a variable price structure, as long as we have one $\tilde{U}$ value for each indifference curve u.

Using this transformation we may now shift to the cardinal utility definition by introducing the cardinal version of the household cost function

$$y = c(\varphi(u), \mathbf{p}) = \tilde{c}(\tilde{U}, \mathbf{p}).$$

In this latter case

$$\frac{dy}{dU} = \frac{d\tilde{c}}{dU} = \frac{1}{\lambda}$$

where λ is the well-known marginal (cardinal) utility of income. At the moment the estimation of the ordinal household cost function $c(u, \mathbf{p})$ is well-established in the literature. In the next two sections we shall concentrate on the empirical estimation of the function $U(y)$, the vertical dimension.

Measurement of the cardinal dimension

The fundamental problem is evidently how to measure the cardinal[3] welfare evaluation U corresponding to an income level y. The problem is very similar to the measurement problem met in other disciplines. The starting point is a pre-scientific notion like temperature, time, loudness, humidity, hunger or health. We all know from empirical experience whether it is 'warm' or 'cold', what is 'long ago' and what is 'recent', what sound is loud and what soft, whether it is 'dry' or 'wet', whether we are 'hungry' or not, whether we are feeling 'healthy' or not. Nevertheless, it took a long time for mankind to devise a method of measurement for temperature that was acceptable for most people. The same holds for time, where a reliable clock and calendar are relatively recent inventions. When such a measurement method and its unit of measurement is generally accepted, we face a process of convergence between the empirical notion and the measurable concept. It can still be observed when children learn to use the clock or the thermometer. Gradually 'early in the day' is replaced by eight o'clock and 'cold' by − 5 °C. The exact numerical descriptions get an emotional meaning as such, as they steadily refer to a situation which is considered to be the same. However, there are situations and people for whom eight o'clock is 'late'; in winter sports resorts − 5 °C may be rather hot; a temperature of − 5 °C may be very cold when a chilly wind is also blowing.

The adoption of a specific frame of reference implies that the rather simple mostly one-dimensional measurement result is sometimes felt to be an inadequate description of the real empirical notion, or rather the perception of it. It is an empirical question whether the measured counterpart of the empirical notion, as defined by the measurement method, is reflecting the empirical notion sufficiently. This of course depends on the degree of fit between the pre-scientific perceptions and the empirically measured observation results. The same caveats obviously hold, and to an even larger extent, when we try to measure feelings like 'hunger' or a situation like 'health' or the perception of brightness of light. The reason is clearly that those concepts are much more subject-related and much more subjective: that is, the same objective situation is perceived and evaluated differently by different individuals. The evaluation made by one individual of his situation probably even varies over time according to his mood, etc. Nevertheless, such types of feelings may also be made more objective in the sense that there are basic objective explanatory factors.

The same holds for the evaluation of income by individuals, which will be the subject of this chapter. How people evaluate their income is basically a feeling. If we want to know how an individual evaluates his own income or other levels of income, we have to ask about it. More precisely, can we extract information from the individual as to what he considers to be a 'good' income, a 'bad' income, etc.?

We started in 1969 by formulating the so-called Income Evaluation Question (IEQ) which runs as follows:

Please try to indicate what you consider to be an appropriate amount for each of the following cases? Under my (our) conditions I would call a net household income per week/month/year of

about	(250)	*very bad*
about	(350)	*bad*
about	(450)	*insufficient*
about	(700)	*sufficient*
about	(1,200)	*good*
about	(1,600)	*very good*

Please enter an answer on each line and underline the period you refer to.

The answers in parentheses represent an answer by an American respondent referring to monthly net household income. The idea of this question is that a verbal label sequence $i = 1, \ldots, 6$ is supplied to the respondent and that the respondent reacts to this stimulus by giving income levels $c_1, \ldots, c_6$. The respondent may select the payment period with which he is most familiar.

The use of this type of questioning is rather unfamiliar to mainstream economists. According to Sen's statement on empirical economic methodology (1982, p. 9), there is a strong predilection among economists for *observable behaviour*. Sen continues:

One reason for the tendency in economics to concentrate only on 'revealed preference' relations is a methodological suspicion regarding introspective concepts. Choice is seen as solid information, whereas introspection is not open to observation ... Even as behaviorism this is particularly limited since verbal behavior (or writing behavior, including response to questionnaires) should not lie outside the scope of the behaviorist approach.

Indeed, the IEQ may be considered as an example of the observation of *verbal* behaviour in Sen's sense.

We do not stick to the precise wording of those labels in the IEQ. They have to be distinguishable from each other and they have to suggest a specific order. Several different wordings have been used both in Europe and in the USA. Although most questionnaires have used a six-level question, in the earliest research (van Praag, 1971; van Praag and Kapteyn, 1973) we utilised versions with eight or nine levels. Those questions were well answered, although the nonresponse rate was higher. In mail-back questionnaires the valid response is about 50%. In oral surveys it is over 90%.

For quantitative analysis of the IEQ we need to translate those verbal levels into numerical figures. We devote the next section to this problem.

Translation of evaluative verbal labels in a context-free setting

The translation of verbal evaluations into numerical figures is a matter of routine in many rating procedures. For instance, in Dutch universities and schools results of exams are rated on a $[0, 10]$ scale where the significance of a 6 is 'sufficient', 7 is 'better than average' and so on. The same numerical rating is used for rather esoteric things like the quality of music performances, ice-skating, etc. As a matter of fact, people frequently become so used to numerical translations of evaluations that one forgets about the original verbal evaluations and takes the numerical figures themselves as evaluation: 'I got an eight for my exam' for instance.

Clearly the correspondence between labels and figures depends on the *number* of different levels. The first question is, then, whether such a translation of verbal labels into numerical values is unambiguous. That is, *is the meaning of such a sequence of verbal labels the same for all respondents?* The best way to study this question is to study it in a *context-free setting*, that is, without specification of what matter is evaluated.

In order to get an answer on this question we carried out the following survey experiment (see also van Doorn and van Praag, 1988). In a survey where the respondent could type in his responses on a desk computer we asked two questions:

1. assign *numbers* between one and 1,000 to 4 verbal labels, where one stands for the very worst and 1,000 for the very best.

   very bad   bad   not bad, not good,   good   very good

2. assign *line segments* to the five labels, where a line segment of one unit stands for the worst and a line segment of 40 units for the best.

Notice that these two questions do not make any reference to an evaluation context. There is no reference to a specific subject matter to be evaluated, e.g., income. The sample consists of 364 net observations.

The responses to the first question are denoted by $v_{i,n}$ ($i = 1, \ldots, 5$; $n = 1, \ldots, 364$) and the responses to the second question are denoted by $w_{i,n}$. Actually, the label sequence is intended to describe on a discrete scale a phenomenon which is evaluated 'in the mind' on a continuous scale. The continuous value scale is the real interval $[0, 1]$ which is divided into adjacent intervals $I_1, \ldots, I_5$, as sketched in figure 4.2.

The verbal scale is efficiently used if the underlying intervals have *equal length*.[4] That this is so may be seen as follows. Let us assume that a

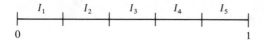

Figure 4.2   A discrete division of the evaluation scale

random phenomenon has to be evaluated by X and that the *a priori* distribution of values X offered is homogeneous on $[0, 1]$. We write $p_i = P[X \in I_i]$. Then the entropy $\Sigma p_i \ln p_i$ is a measure which describes the discriminatory power of the discrete scale. That entropy is maximal if $p_1 = p_2 = \ldots = p_5 = 1/5$. Hence, our prediction is that ideally v_i and w_i are situated at the mid-point of I_i, or that

$$v_i = w_i = (2i - 1)/10, \qquad i = 1, \ldots, 5.$$

We call this the 'equal-interval assumption' (EIA).

In table 4.1 we present the mean observations for both measurement methods with their corresponding sample standard deviations. In the last column we give our theoretical prediction $(2i - 1)/10$.

These results show that our predictions are not exactly verified. However, if we take account of the difficulty of the questions and the fact that there is an error term involved, we find the results quite satisfactory.

Table 4.1. *Translation into numbers and line-segments*

Numbers:	Empirical mean	St. dev.	Th. pred.
Very bad	$\bar{v}_1 = 0.0892$	0.0927	0.10
Bad	$\bar{v}_2 = 0.2013$	0.1234	0.30
Not bad, not good	$\bar{v}_3 = 0.4719$	0.1117	0.50
Good	$\bar{v}_4 = 0.6682$	0.1169	0.70
Very good	$\bar{v}_5 = 0.8655$	0.0941	0.90

Line-segments:	Empirical mean	St. dev.	Th. pred.
Very bad	$\bar{w}_1 = 0.0734$	0.0556	0.10
Bad	$\bar{w}_2 = 0.1799$	0.0934	0.30
Not bad, not good	$\bar{w}_3 = 0.4008$	0.1056	0.50
Good	$\bar{w}_4 = 0.5980$	0.1158	0.70
Very good	$\bar{w}_5 = 0.8230$	0.1195	0.90

In only one case ($\bar{w}_2$) does the estimate lie outside a one σ interval about the predicted value.

It appears that there is a downward bias of all ws and vs, which is perhaps a measurement effect. Every respondent takes care not to take too much room in the beginning, to keep space for the later scale values.

The two measurement results of what is claimed to be two different descriptions of the same basic rating phenomenon are also highly consistent. We regressed v on w and we found the following regression.

$$v_{i,n} = 0.0557 + 0.9737\ w_{it} \qquad R^2 = 0.848$$
$$\underset{(0.0049)}{\phantom{v_{i,n} = 0.0557}}\ \underset{(0.0097)}{}$$

for $364 \times 5 = 1{,}820$ observations, where we did not take into account that the level disturbances per individual will be strongly correlated.

On the basis of this exercise we conclude that

(1) A verbal label sequence is similarly understood by different respondents, irrespective of the context or the individual respondent.
(2) A verbal label sequence may be translated either on a numerical scale or on a line scale; in both cases the translations are uniform over individuals.
(3) Translations via various translation mechanisms (lines and figures) are consistent with each other. That is, we measure the same thing, irrespective of whether we use line segments or numbers.
(4) The verbal evaluations are translated on a bounded scale in accordance with the Equal Interval Assumption (EIA).

The interesting point is that these results have been found in a context-free setting – the respondents did not know what concept they were evaluating.

The evaluation of income by the IEQ

Let us now return to the IEQ introduced in the previous section. We are looking for the evaluation of c_i and we call that evaluation the *utility* or *welfare* derived from c_i. This is an empirical definition. If there is a 'natural' numerical translation of a verbal label sequence, following the previous section, then it stands to reason that the evaluations of the k income levels $c_1, \ldots, c_k$ are given by $v_1, \ldots, v_k$ or by $w_1, \ldots, w_k$ or by $(2i - 1)/2k$ $(i = 1, \ldots, k)$. This is now justified, as we showed in the previous section that verbal label sequences may be translated unambiguously to an interval scale.

It follows that we have to look for a functional specification $U_n(c)$, the

welfare function of individual n or the Individual Welfare Function (IWF)
such that

$$U_n(c_i) = (2i - 1)/2k \qquad (i = 1, \ldots, k)$$

where U_n is a distribution function after appropriate scaling. We call this
assumption of equal quantiles on the income axis the Equal Quantile
Assumption (EQA). Considering the response patterns of various
respondents it is seen that a rich man may quote \$50,000 as a good net
household income (c_5) while a poor man would call \$20,000 his c_5 level.
We have thus to recognise that different individuals n will evaluate income
levels on different scales. Therefore we indexed the function U by n.

More precisely we parameterise the function as

$$U_n(c_i) = U(c_i; \theta_n)$$

where θ_n stands for an individual parameter vector. The next problem we
are facing is *the specification of the function* U(.).

The evaluation of income and many other concepts is basically done by
situating the income into the perceived distribution of incomes. It is comparative evaluation.[5] As all income distributions have an approximately
log-normal shape, especially if we think about the smoothing regularising
perception of it by individuals, it stands to reason that we assume that

$$U_n(c) = \Lambda(c; \mu_n, \sigma_n) = N(\ln c; \mu_n, \sigma_n)$$

where Λ and N stand for the log-normal and normal distribution functions respectively. If the EQA is true, we will have per individual roughly
symmetrical answers about μ_n, and it follows that μ_n may be estimated by

$$m_n = \frac{1}{k} \sum_{i=1}^{k} \ln c_{i,n}.$$

In a similar way we estimate σ_n^2 by

$$s_n^2 = \frac{1}{(k-1)} \sum_{i=1}^{k} (\ln c_{i,n} - m_n)^2$$

(see also van der Sar, van Praag and Dubnoff, 1988 and van Praag, 1989).

Now we 'standardise' the answers $c_{i,n}$ by defining

$$u_{i,n} = \frac{\ln c_{i,n} - m_n}{s_n}.$$

Then the EQA combined with log-normality of U(.) implies that

$$N(u_{i,n}; 0, 1) = (2i - 1)/2k \qquad i = 1, \ldots, k$$

should hold.

In our experimental questionnaire where we asked for the translation of
the verbal *five*-label sequence into numbers v or the segments w we posed
the IEQ as a *five*-level question as well. It should then hold that the verbal

labels in the IEQ referring to income should give the same stimulus as when these labels are used in a subject-free context. Hence, we expect

$$N((\ln c_{in} - \mu_n)/\sigma_n; 0, 1) = v_{in} \qquad \begin{aligned} t &= 1, \ldots, 364 \\ i &= 1, \ldots, 5 \end{aligned}$$

and

$$N((\ln c_{in} - \mu_n)/\sigma_n; 0, 1) = w_{in}.$$

Here we do *not* assume that the EQA holds.

Estimating μ_n and σ_n as above from the five-level question we should approximately get

$$\ln c_{i,n} \approx \mu_n + \sigma_n N^{-1}(v_{in})$$

$$\ln c_{i,n} \approx \mu_n + \sigma_n N^{-1}(w_{in}).$$

OLS regression yields

$$\ln c_{in} = -0.0398 + 1.0136\,\mu_n + 0.6292\,\sigma_n N^{-1}(v_{in}) \qquad R^2 = 0.796$$
$$\phantom{\ln c_{in} = }\;{\scriptstyle(0.1605)}\qquad{\scriptstyle(0.0213)}\qquad{\scriptstyle(0.0090)}$$

$$\ln c_{in} = -0.3521 + 1.0634\,\mu_n + 0.8197\,\sigma_n N^{-1}(w_{in}) \qquad R^2 = 0.847$$
$$\phantom{\ln c_{in} = }\;{\scriptstyle(0.1392)}\qquad{\scriptstyle(0.0185)}\qquad{\scriptstyle(0.0097)}\qquad N = 364.$$

These results suggest that the hypothesis of log-normality holds approximately, even if we do not assume EQA. That it does not hold exactly seems to be due to random errors and inexperience of the respondents in answering the questions with respect to v and w.[6]

Table 4.2 shows that the assumptions of log-normality and equal quantiles are very reasonable indeed.

On the basis of this combined evidence it appears justified to assume that

$$U(c) = N((\ln c - \mu)/\sigma; 0, 1)$$

where μ and σ are estimated per individual from the IEQ by the formulae

$$m = \frac{1}{k} \sum_{i=1}^{k} \ln c_i, \qquad s^2 = \frac{1}{k-1} \sum_{i=1}^{k} (\ln c_i - m)^2.$$

Additional evidence on a six-level version of the IEQ confirms the previous evidence. We consider the hypothesis for a sample of 500 American respondents, created by Dubnoff for the Boston region. We present in table 4.2 the mean values of $u_{1,n}, \ldots, u_{6,n}$, the corresponding sample standard deviations $\sigma(u_i)$, the resulting average welfare values $N(u_i; 0, 1)$ and the predicted values according to the EQA. We see that the prediction is pretty well validated by table 4.2.

At this point we mention some important differences between this

Table 4.2. *Average u levels, sample st. dev., resulting welfare levels and prediction*

	$\bar{u}_i$	$\sigma(u_i)$	(u_i)	Pred.
1	− 1.291	0.236	0.09	0.083
2	− 0.778	0.190	0.22	0.250
3	− 0.260	0.241	0.40	0.417
4	0.259	0.239	0.60	0.583
5	0.760	0.190	0.78	0.750
6	1.311	0.229	0.90	0.917

result and the now usual[7] method described in van Praag (1971). In the 1971 approach we *a priori* postulated a log-normal function on the basis of theoretical arguments in van Praag (1968). Also we postulated the EQA without empirical evidence for it.

Then we *estimated* μ_n and σ_n per person by applying OLS on the equation

$$\ln c_{in} = \mu_n + \sigma_n u_i$$

per individual n, where u_i was based on the EQA postulate.

In the present approach, we reverse the line of reasoning. We estimate μ_n and σ_n^2 as the mean and the variance of the logarithmic IEQ responses.

Having defined the u_{in} we see that the u_{in}s may be interpreted as equal-quantile responses if $U(.)$ is a $\Lambda(.;\mu,\sigma^2)$ distribution function. Hence, we conclude that the log-normality assumption is acceptable.

It may be shown quite easily that the new μ definition and the old one according to OLS are identical.[8] For σ^2 this is not true except in the case of exact-normality.

At this point we notice that there are many other functions suggested and estimated by van Herwaarden and Kapteyn (1981). They concluded that the log-normal *and* the logarithmic function fitted best. As the logarithm is unbounded this does not conform with the usual everyday practice of a bounded evaluation interval.

Empirically estimated relationships

As already hinted, μ_n and σ_n^2 vary over individuals. The variance σ_n^2 (sometimes called the welfare sensitivity parameter) is very hard to explain by objective individual factors. It seems established that σ_n^2 is heavily dependent on the income inequality in a country as measured by the log variance. This is in accordance with the idea that the function $U(y)$

is a reflection of the objective income distribution function. Within a country we take the variable as constant, say σ. The individual μ_n is explainable to a large extent, as has been shown in many of the references. We refer to those papers for details. The basic relationship, first established by van Praag (1971) and van Praag and Kapteyn (1973) appears to be

$$\mu_n = \beta_0 + \beta_1 \ln fs_n + \beta_2 \ln y_{c,n}$$

where fs stands for family size (head count) and y_c for current net household income. The typical estimates are

$$\mu_n = \beta_0 + 0.10 \ln fs_n + 0.60 \ln y_{c,n} \qquad R^2 \approx 0.6.$$

The intuitively plausible result says that μ_n depends on the own *current* income level. It follows that the indirect utility function drifts with the level of current own income $y_{c,n}$. We may write

$$U_n(c) = N((\ln c - \mu_n)/\sigma; 0, 1)$$
$$= N((\ln c - \beta_0 - \beta_1 \ln fs_n - \beta_2 \ln y_{c,n})/\sigma; 0, 1).$$

We have called this effect *preference drift* and the parameter β_2 the *preference drift rate*.

Obviously this drift will not be immediately realised as a result of an income change. Let us assume that log income shifts from $\ln y_c^{(0)}$, to $\ln y_c^{(1)}$, the difference being Δy_c. Then we may define the *ex ante* $\mu_n^{(0)}$ and the *ex post* $\mu_n^{(1)} = \mu_n^{(0)} + \beta_2 \Delta y_c$ accordingly. It follows that people with different incomes will have different (cardinal) utility functions. This variation will increase if β_2 increases. If $\beta_2 = 1$ it would imply that everybody would evaluate his own income by

$$N((-\beta_0 - \beta_1 \ln fs)/\sigma; 0, 1)$$

irrespective of his income level. Fortunately β_2 is almost always estimated far below one.

The *ex ante* function with fixed μ_0 is called the *virtual* IWF. The function $N(\ln y_c - \mu(y_c); 0, \sigma)$ is called the *true* IWF. It describes the welfare evaluation of an individual for his own current income.

Similarly it is clear that family size has a (cost) effect on the evaluation of income. Family equivalence scales are derived by setting

$$\ln y_c - \beta_0 - \beta_1 \ln fs - \beta_2 \ln y_c = \text{constant}$$

which yields a constant welfare equation

$$\ln y_c = \frac{\beta_0 + \beta_1 \ln fs}{1 - \beta_2}.$$

We may also interpret it as the *true* household cost function.

We find the family size elasticity

$$\frac{d \ln y_c}{d \ln fs} = \frac{\beta_1}{1 - \beta_2}.$$

We refer to van Praag and van der Sar (1988) for similar findings in an ordinal setting.

Equivalence scales in practice

In this case welfare constant income follows the relationship

$$y_c = C \, fs^{\beta_1/(1 - \beta_2)}$$

where C depends on the base welfare level. Typically the exponent is about $0.10/0.40 = 0.25$. The corresponding family equivalence index, taking $fs = 2$ as the reference family, is

$$e(fs) = \left(\frac{fs}{2}\right)^{0.25}.$$

This index is not welfare-level specific. How far is this index dependent on the log-normal specification? It results as well from a utility specification

$$U(c) = \varphi(N((\ln c - \mu)/\sigma; 0, 1))$$

where $\varphi(.)$ is any monotonically increasing function.

It is also possible to go without a cardinal utility function at all, as is done in van Praag and van der Sar (1988). We consider the answers $\{c_{in}\}$ per level i, and we estimate

$$\ln c_{in} = a_{0i} + a_{1i} fs_n + a_{2i} \ln y_{c,n}.$$

Say, for instance that i corresponds to the verbal label *good*. If $\ln c_{in}$ is satisfactorily explained by the log-linear equation, then we find that y_c should vary with fs according to

$$y_c = C_i \, fs^{a_{1i}/(1 - a_{2i})}$$

in order to keep the individual for varying family size at an income level which he evaluates as *good*, i.e., equivalent with the reference income which a two-person family considers to be *good*.

In this case the equivalence index is *welfare-level specific*, that is,

$$e_i(fs) = \left(\frac{fs}{2}\right)^{a_{1i}/(1 - a_{2i})}.$$

Notice that this is a purely ordinal index. In van Praag and van der Sar (1988) such indices have been calculated for a number of countries.

Table 4.3. *Level equations and corresponding equivalence scales*

Level	Equations β_0	β_1	β_2	R^2	Equivalence scales $fs = 2$	$fs = 3$	$fs = 5$	$fs = 6$
The Netherlands ($N = 2160$)								
1	5.135 (0.325)	0.175 (0.016)	0.417 (0.033)	0.423	0.81	0.92	1.07	1.13
2	5.143 (0.546)	0.160 (0.020)	0.434 (0.055)	0.503	0.82	0.92	1.07	1.12
3	4.840 (0.587)	0.148 (0.020)	0.479 (0.060)	0.542	0.82	0.92	1.07	1.12
4	4.893 (0.791)	0.140 (0.026)	0.497 (0.080)	0.548	0.82	0.92	1.06	1.12
5	5.276 (1.157)	0.136 (0.036)	0.478 (0.118)	0.506	0.83	0.93	1.06	1.11
6	3.943 (0.431)	0.090 (0.018)	0.634 (0.044)	0.520	0.84	0.93	1.06	1.10
United Kingdom ($N = 1950$)								
1	5.578 (0.218)	0.247 (0.028)	0.218 (0.027)	0.186	0.80	0.91	1.07	1.14
2	5.566 (0.218)	0.237 (0.026)	0.247 (0.027)	0.234	0.80	0.91	1.07	1.14
3	5.388 (0.233)	0.213 (0.022)	0.293 (0.029)	0.263	0.81	0.92	1.07	1.13
4	5.662 (0.237)	0.186 (0.021)	0.300 (0.030)	0.292	0.83	0.93	1.06	1.11
5	5.915 (0.275)	0.173 (0.022)	0.294 (0.034)	0.260	0.84	0.93	1.06	1.10
6	5.406 (0.248)	0.121 (0.027)	0.389 (0.031)	0.238	0.87	0.94	1.05	1.08
France ($N = 2700$)								
1	4.520 (0.103)	0.157 (0.015)	0.381 (0.013)	0.357	0.84	0.93	1.06	1.11
2	4.707 (0.233)	0.152 (0.018)	0.387 (0.029)	0.391	0.84	0.93	1.06	1.11
3	4.720 (0.097)	0.149 (0.014)	0.410 (0.012)	0.418	0.85	0.94	1.05	1.10
4	5.003 (0.097)	0.137 (0.014)	0.410 (0.012)	0.401	0.85	0.94	1.05	1.10
5	5.252 (0.101)	0.115 (0.014)	0.409 (0.012)	0.369	0.87	0.95	1.04	1.08
6	5.463 (0.271)	0.079 (0.021)	0.416 (0.033)	0.298	0.91	0.96	1.03	1.06

In table 4.3 we find a typical example. The value of $a_1/(1 - a_2)$, and consequently of the index, do not change very much for the various utility levels, although a_1 and a_2 themselves vary quite considerably.

These indices are rather flat, which is contrary to conventional wisdom. A scale advocated in the OECD list of social indicators proposes to count the first adult by 1, the other adults by 0.7 each and children by 0.5 each. This corresponds to an exponent of about 0.7.

The question then arises which of the two types of indices should be given more credit. To answer this question, let us compensate a reference family, who is at the 'sufficient' level, for an additional child according to the OECD scale. The result is that they will evaluate their income by a higher label than 'sufficient', say 'good', because the OECD scale is steeper than the scale which keeps verbal evaluations constant. Hence, we conclude that the OECD scale *over*compensates. It is then hard to call the OECD proposal an *equivalence* scale. Actually, the IEQ and its resulting relationships for $c_1, \ldots, c_k$ serve as a litmus test for any family equivalence scale. If incomes y_1 and y_2 are evaluated by the same verbal label by two families of size fs_1 and fs_2 respectively, then y_2/y_1 reflects equivalence. This holds for all family equivalence scales. Obviously, this does not imply that the equivalence scale should be *derived* from IEQ answers. It may be any scale, for instance, derived from a complete demand system or based on food shares.

However, if it is a true equivalence scale, it should satisfy this equal *verbal* evaluation test. The reason that the IEQ scale is rather flat may be seen as evidence for Pollak and Wales' (1979) argument, repeated by Pollak (1991), that there is basically no reason why families with identical incomes but a different size should be at different welfare levels. If the family size is a matter of free decision just as buying a car or furniture, then there is indeed no reason why families of different size but equal purchasing power should experience different welfare levels. Nevertheless, in practice at the time of 'child-buying' one may have incorrectly predicted future conditions and/or preferences may change over a lifetime; both factors may cause welfare differences later on. Clearly this is nothing special for child-buying, but it may arise with the buying of any consumer durable.

An interesting example of a very steep scale based on the IEQ approach is given by Pódgorski (1990) for Poland. He found the exponent 0.51 for the level 'the minimum to make ends meet'. This demonstrates both that the resulting family equivalence scale may be quite steep and that Pollak's argument has validity, for in Poland during the last 20 years, as a strongly Catholic country, contraceptive devices were not generally available and for many Poles not permitted.

In general, we see that there is no scientific reason to assume a uniformly valid (family) equivalence scale to be applied to all societies. The method applied to derive *family* equivalence scales, may also be applied to derive other equivalence scales. We have to estimate

$$c_i = g(fs, y_c, x)$$

where x may stand for any vector of variables. In van Praag (1989) we estimated a *climate* equivalence scale for Europe. In van Praag and Flik (1991) we estimated a scale, depending on *fs*, age of the respondent, region of living and the labour participation degree of husband and spouse.

Those examples show that, even if we do not accept cardinality, the IEQ approach is most useful to derive general equivalence scales. It is easy, intuitively plausible and cheap as it does not require information on purchase behaviour, as gathered by household budget surveys.

The main other application of the IEQ approach thus far is on poverty analysis. We refer to Goedhart *et al.* (1977), van Praag, Hagenaars and van Weeren (1992) and Hagenaars (1986). The IEQ approach is used for a definition of *subjective* poverty. This can be done either by identifying the poverty line with a specific *verbal* label or by identifying it with a specific numerical value of the individual welfare function of income.

The first method may be illustrated as follows. Poverty is defined by that income level C_3 which corresponds to 'insufficient'. In that case we find from the equation

$$C_3 = a_{03} + a_{13}\ln fs + a_{23}\ln y_c$$

the family size-differentiated 'poverty line'

$$\ln y_3^* = \frac{a_{03} + a_{13}\ln fs}{1 - a_{23}}.$$

For the second method we specify

$$\Lambda(y_{0.4}^*; \mu(y_{0.4}^*, fs), \sigma) = 0.4$$

yielding

$$\ln y_{0.4}^* = \frac{\beta_0 - u_{0.4}\sigma + \beta_1\ln fs}{1 - \beta_2}.$$

In Goedhart *et al.* (1977) a third subjective poverty line is based on the outcome of a one-level question (MINQ), which specifies the verbal label: as 'the minimum income for your household to make ends meet'.

For this label the poverty line is called the Subjective Poverty Line (SPL).[9]

The integration into ordinal consumer behaviour models

In this section we shall link our results with the traditional neoclassical models. We shall show that the vertical dimension can be added in a fairly simple way to ordinal models. As examples, we shall consider the Almost Ideal Demand System, developed by Deaton and Muellbauer (1980) and the Translog Demand System, originally proposed by Christensen, Jorgenson and Lau (1975) in its version by Jorgenson and Slesnick (1984).

Both models are based on the simple cost function

$$\ln c = u\, b(\mathbf{p}) + a(\mathbf{p})$$

where u stands for an ordinal utility label. In this case we may write the ordinal utility index as an explicit (indirect utility) function of c and $\mathbf{p}$:

$$u = \frac{\ln c - a(\mathbf{p})}{b(\mathbf{p})}.$$

Let us assume we know the cardinal utility function $U_n(c; \mathbf{p}_0)$ for a specific $\mathbf{p}_0$ vector and there holds for a specific individual with $(\mu_0; \sigma_0)$

$$U_n(c; \mathbf{p}_0) = N\!\left(\frac{\ln c - \mu_0}{\sigma_0}; 0, 1\right).$$

It follows that we may write $\mu_0 = a(\mathbf{p}_0)$, $\sigma_0 = b(\mathbf{p}_0)$ in which case

$$u = \frac{\ln c - \mu_0}{\sigma_0}$$

and

$$U = \varphi(u) = N(u; 0, 1).$$

Now we extend this to arbitrary price vectors $\mathbf{p}$. We define $B(\mathbf{p}) = b(\mathbf{p})/b(\mathbf{p}_0)$ and $A(\mathbf{p}) = a(\mathbf{p})/a(\mathbf{p}_0)$.

Then we may write for general prices

$$u = \frac{\ln c - \mu_0 A(\mathbf{p})}{\sigma_0 B(\mathbf{p})}$$

and

$$U(c; \mathbf{p}) = N\!\left(\frac{\ln c - \mu_0 A(\mathbf{p})}{\sigma_0 B(\mathbf{p})}; 0; 1\right)$$

with $A(\mathbf{p}_0) = B(\mathbf{p}_0) = 1$.

The corresponding cost function is

$$\ln c = u\sigma_0 B(\mathbf{p}) + \mu_0 A(\mathbf{p})$$

where $u = N^{-1}(U; 0, 1)$.

The price-differentiated welfare parameters are then

$$\mu(\mathbf{p}) = \mu_0 . A(\mathbf{p})$$

$$\sigma(\mathbf{p}) = \sigma_0 . B(\mathbf{p}).$$

If the demand system is described by the Almost Ideal Demand System (Deaton and Muellbauer, 1980) we have

$$a(\mathbf{p}) = a_0 + \Sigma a_k \ln p_k + \tfrac{1}{2}(\ln(\mathbf{p})')\Gamma \ln \mathbf{p}$$

$$b(\mathbf{p}) = \beta_0 \Pi p_k^{\beta_k}.$$

If the demand system is of the Translog type we find the same (Jorgenson, Lau and Stoker, 1980, 1981) Gorman formula, where

$$b(\mathbf{p}) = 1/(1 - i' B_{pp} \ln \mathbf{p})$$

$$a(\mathbf{p}) = a_0 + \Sigma a_k \ln \mathbf{p} + \tfrac{1}{2}(\ln \mathbf{p})' \Gamma \ln \mathbf{p}.$$

Family size effects are now included by setting

$$\mu_0^{(1)} = \mu_0^{(0)} + \beta_1 \Delta \ln fs.$$

Notice that this introduces a term in $\Delta \ln fs . \beta_1 A(\mathbf{p})$. This implies that price effects may depend on family size via an interaction term. We may write

$$\ln c = u\sigma_0 B(\mathbf{p}) + (\mu_0^{(0)} + \beta_1 \Delta \ln fs) A(\mathbf{p}).$$

In a similar way we get dependence on own current income y_c by

$$\ln c = u\sigma_0 B(\mathbf{p}) + (\mu_0^{(0)} + \beta_1 \Delta \ln fs + \beta_2 \Delta \ln y_c) A(\mathbf{p}).$$

From this formula we may find a *true* household cost function, setting $\ln c = \ln y_c$. It follows that

$$\ln y_c = \frac{1}{1 - \beta_2 A(\mathbf{p})} \left[u\sigma_0 B(\mathbf{p}) + (\mu_0^{(0)} + \beta_1 \Delta \ln fs) A(\mathbf{p}) \right].$$

The family size elasticity becomes

$$\frac{d \ln y_c}{d \ln fs} = \frac{1}{1 - \beta_2 A(\mathbf{p})} \beta_1 A(\mathbf{p}).$$

Consider now the indirect utility of log-income. It equals

$$U(c) = N \left(\frac{\ln c - \mu}{\sigma} \right)$$

and hence

$$U'(c) = \frac{dU}{dc} = \frac{1}{c} \frac{1}{\sqrt{2\pi}} \exp\left[-\tfrac{1}{2}\left(\frac{\ln c - \mu}{\sigma}\right)^2 \right]$$

The relative risk aversion becomes (see also van Praag, 1971)

$$\frac{d \ln U}{d \ln c} = -1 - \frac{(\ln c - \mu)}{\sigma^2}.$$

Discussion and conclusion

In this chapter we argue that a cardinal welfare function is a measurable concept. It may be split up into an ordinal and a cardinal part. The ordinal part is estimated in the traditional way by studying consumer demand behaviour. The cardinal part, an indirect welfare function of income (IWF), is estimated from the IEQ, a specific type of an attitude question battery. It is argued on empirical evidence that this function is approximately a log-normal distribution function with welfare parameters μ and σ. The two dimensions are knitted together into the cardinal welfare function. It is shown how the welfare parameters take their place in the Almost Ideal Demand System or the Translog Demand System.

The main new results in this chapter are as follows:

(1) the log-normal form of the individual welfare function of income is derived from empirical evidence instead of being postulated on the basis of a theoretical argument, as in earlier studies;
(2) the assumption of equal quantiles is verified on empirical evidence;
(3) the IWF-concept is shown to be interpretable as an indirect utility or welfare function;
(4) it is found how μ and σ change when prices change;
(5) it is shown how any ordinal demand system can be combined with any cardinal welfare function.

In this chapter we did not attempt to evaluate social welfare or welfare inequality. It can be shown that most inequality indices may be based on the log-normal welfare function (see, e.g., van Praag, 1981). Also we do not make use of the empirically estimated welfare functions to evaluate market equilibria or to model games, based on utility functions. Clearly, here lies a wide field of applications.

Notes

A slightly different version of this chapter appeared in the *Journal of Econometrics*, 50 (1/2) (1991), 69–89.

I thank Robert Jan Flik for his invaluable support with the empirical part of this chapter.

1 We will use the words utility and welfare indiscriminately.
2 See also Atkinson (1970), Jorgenson, Lau and Stoker (1980, 1981) and Apps and Savage (1989) who are implicitly using a cardinal interpersonally comparable welfare concept. However their cardinal utility functions have no empirically-based welfare dimension, but they are based on implicit value judgements only.
3 We drop the tilde, when confusion is improbable.
4 Similar quantitative arguments may be found in van Praag (1971) and a generalization of it in Kapteyn (1977).
5 It is well-known that people, when faced with an unusual phenomenon, do not know how to evaluate it, as they have 'nothing to compare it with'. It is also well-known that students' performances are frequently evaluated on an explicitly comparative basis as one being in the top 5% or being in the top half, etc. This link was first made by Kapteyn, Wansbeek and Buyze (1980); see also van Praag (1981, 1989).
6 Finally we might consider the OLS equation where we assume that the EQA holds as well. We did this in the *Journal of Econometrics* (1991). It can be shown that due to the definition of m_n, s_n and the EQA assumption we end up with an artefact

$$\ln c_{in} h = m_n + s_n N^{-1} \left[\frac{2i - 1}{10} \right].$$

7 The IEQ is now experimentally used by EUROSTAT, most official statistical offices in the European Community and by Statistics Canada. It is especially used for the definition of the poverty line (see Goedhart, Halberstadt, Kapteyn and van Praag (1977), Hagenaars (1986), Ghiatis (1989)).
8 This was first brought to my attention by Reuben Gronau.
9 The poverty line defined by 0.4 is called by Hagenaars (1986) a *subjective* poverty line and by EUROSTAT a Leyden Poverty Line (LPL). Hagenaars (1986) called the MINQ-based poverty line a Leyden Poverty Line, but Kapteyn *et al.* (1985) call it the Subjective Poverty Line (SPL). Following EUROSTAT we shall follow the latter terminology. Preliminary results for EUROSTAT-commissioned research suggest that the SPL based on a *one*-level question (MINQ) leads to results which are not comparable over countries as 'make ends meet' seems to have different emotional connotations in different countries. The sequence of *five* or *six* (emotionally neutral) verbal labels in the IEQ wording gives the possibility to respondents to give the answers from a *relative* perspective.

The poverty lines are all subjective in the sense that they do not correspond to *absolute* material levels of 'command over goods and services' (Townsend,

1979), nor are they completely relative in the sense that they rise proportionally by x% when all incomes rise with x% (see Hagenaars and van Praag, 1985).

REFERENCES

Apps, P.F. and E.J. Savage (1989) 'Labour supply, welfare rankings and the measurement of inequality', *Journal of Public Economics*, 39, 335–364

Atkinson, A.B. (1970) 'On the measurement of inequality', *Journal of Economic Theory*, 2, 244–263

Christensen, L.R., D.W. Jorgenson and L.J. Lau (1975) 'Transcendental logarithmic utility functions', *American Economic Review*, 65, 367–385

Cohen Stuart, A.J. (1889) *Bijdrage tot de theorie der progressive inkomensbelastingen*, The Hague, Nijhoff

Deaton, A.S. and J. Muellbauer (1980) 'An almost ideal demand system', *American Economic Review*, 70, 312–326

(1980) *Economics and Consumer Behaviour*, Cambridge, Cambridge University Press

Edgeworth, F.Y. (1881) *Mathematical Psychics: an essay on the application of mathematics to the moral sciences*, London, C. Kegan Paul

Frisch, R. (1932) *New methods of measuring marginal utility*, Tübingen, Mohr

Ghiatis, A. (1989) 'Low income groups obtained by enhanced processing of the household budget surveys in the EC summary figures for Italy and The Netherlands', presented at the EUROSTAT seminar on poverty statistics in the European Community (Noordwijk)

Goedhart, T., V. Halberstadt, A. Kapteyn and B.M.S. van Praag (1977) 'The poverty line: concept and measurement', *Journal of Human Resources*, 12, 503–520

Gossen, H.H. (1854) *Entwicklung der gesetze des menschlichen verkehres und der daraus fliebenden regeln für menschliches handeln*, Braunschweig

Hagenaars, A.J.M. (1986) *The Perception of Poverty*, Amsterdam, North-Holland

Hagenaars, A.J.M. and B.M.S. van Praag (1985) 'A synthesis of poverty line definitions', *Review of Income and Wealth*, 31, 139–145

Harsanyi, J. (1987) 'Social welfare', in J. Eatwell *et al.* (eds.), *The New Palgrave: A Dictionary of Economics*, London, Macmillan

Hicks, J.R. and R.G.D. Allen (1934) 'A reconsideration of the theory of value', *Economica*, 1, 52–75, 196–219

Houthakker, H.S. (1950) 'Revealed preference and the utility function', *Economica*, 17, 159–174

Jevons, W.S. (1871) *The Theory of Political Economy*, London, Macmillan

Jorgenson, D.W. and D.T.S. Slesnick (1984) 'Aggregate consumer behaviour and the measurement of inequality', *Review of Economic Studies*, 51, 369–392

(1990) 'Inequality and the standard of living', *Journal of Econometrics*, 43, 103–121

Jorgenson, D.W., L.J. Lau and T.M. Stoker (1980) 'Welfare comparisons and exact aggregation', *American Economic Review*, 70, 268–272

(1981) 'Aggregate consumer behavior and individual welfare', in D. Currie, R.

Nobay and D. Peel (eds.), *Macroeconomic Analysis*, London, Croom Helm, 35–61

Kapteyn, A. (1977) *A Theory of Preference Formation*, Leyden University, unpublished Ph.D. thesis

Kapteyn, A., T.J. Wansbeek and J. Buyze (1980) 'The dynamics of preference formation', *Journal of Economic Behavior and Organization*, 1, 123–157

Kapteyn, A., S. van de Geer and H. van de Stadt (1985) 'The impact of changes in income and family composition on subjective measures of well-being', in M. David and T. Smeeding (eds.), *Horizontal Equity, Uncertainty, and Economic Well-Being*, Chicago, Chicago University Press, 35–64

Kirman, A.P. (1987) 'Pareto as an economist', in J. Eatwell *et al.* (eds.), *The New Palgrave: A Dictionary of Economics*, London, Macmillan

Moriani, C. (1989) 'Italian experience on poverty harmonized measures', presented at the EUROSTAT seminar on poverty statistics in the European Community (Noordwijk)

Pareto, V. (1909) *Manuel d'Economie Politique*, Paris, V. Giard et E. Brière

Pódgorski, J. (1990) 'Subjective poverty lines in Poland: an application of Leyden Poverty Line Definition', Central School of Statistics and Planning, Warsaw, *Working Paper*

Pollak, R.A. (1991) 'Welfare comparisons and situation comparisons', *Journal of Econometrics*, 50, 31–48

Pollak, R.A. and T.J. Wales (1979) 'Welfare comparisons and equivalence scales', *American Economic Review*, 69, 216–221

Robbins, L. (1932) *An Essay on the Nature and Significance of Economic Science*, London, Macmillan, 1st edn

Samuelson, P.A. (1947) *Foundations of Economic Analysis*, Cambridge, MA, Harvard University Press

Sen, A.K. (1979) 'Interpersonal comparisons of welfare', in M. Boskin (ed.), *Economics and Human Welfare: Essays in Honor of Tibor Scitovsky*, New York, Academic Press

(1982) *Choice, Welfare and Measurement*, Cambridge, MA, MIT Press

Shubik, M. (1982) *Game Theory in the Social Sciences*, Cambridge, MA, MIT Press

(1984) *A Game-theoretic Approach to Political Economy*, Cambridge, MA, MIT Press

Townsend, P. (1979) *Poverty in the United Kingdom*, Harmondsworth, Penguin

van der Sar, N.L., B.M.S. van Praag and S. Dubnoff (1988) 'Evaluation questions and income utility', in B. Munier (ed.), *Risk, Decision and Rationality*, Dordrecht, Reidel Publishing Co., 77–96

van Doorn, L. and B.M.S. van Praag (1988) 'On the measurement of income satisfaction', in W.E. Saris and J.N. Gallhofer (eds.), *Sociometric Research*, 1, London, Macmillan, 230–246

van Herwaarden, F.G. and A. Kapteyn (1981) 'Empirical comparison of the shape of welfare functions', *European Economic Review*, 15, 261–286

van Praag, B.M.S. (1968) *Individual Welfare Functions and Consumer Behavior: a theory of rational irrationality*, Amsterdam, North-Holland

(1971) 'The welfare function of income in Belgium: an empirical investigation', *European Economic Review*, 2, 337–369

(1978) 'The perception of income inequality', in W. Krelle and A.F. Shorrocks (eds.), *Personal Income Distribution*, Amsterdam, North-Holland

(1981) 'Reflections on the theory of individual welfare functions', *Report*, 81.14, Center for Research in Public Economics, Proceedings of the American Statistical Association, Leyden University

(1989) 'The relativity of the welfare concept', in M. Nussbaum and A. Sen (eds.), *Quality of Life*, Oxford, Clarendon Press

(1991) 'Ordinal and cardinal utility: an integration of the two dimensions of the welfare concept', *Journal of Econometrics*, 50 (1/2), 69–89

van Praag, B.M.S. and R.J. Flik (1991) 'Towards a European poverty concept', Third European Poverty Project, Brussels, *Working Paper*

van Praag, B.M.S., A.J.M. Hagenaars and H. van Weeren (1992), 'Poverty in Europe', *Review of Income and Wealth*, 28, 345–59

van Praag, B.M.S. and A. Kapteyn (1973) 'Further evidence on the individual welfare function of income: an empirical investigation in the Netherlands', *European Economic Review*, 4, 33–62

van Praag, B.M.S. and N.L. van der Sar (1988) 'Household cost functions and equivalence scales', *Journal of Human Resources*, 23, 193–210

5 The determination of welfare in nonintact families

DANIELA DEL BOCA and CHRISTOPHER FLINN

Introduction

Within both intact and nonintact families in which children are present, the allocation of resources to children is best viewed as the outcome of a complicated process in which love, altruism, investment motives, fairness, and self-interested behaviour on the part of parents all play a role. Except in extreme circumstances, such as child-neglect cases, official agents of the society like courts, social service agencies, and policing institutions interfere little in the intra-household resource allocation process.

In contrast, agents of societal institutions do intervene, at least indirectly, in the *inter*household consumption allocation decisions made by divorced parents. The principal instruments of intervention are the terms and enforcement of legally-stipulated divorce agreements as they relate to custody arrangements and wealth and income transfers between the ex-spouses. In our view, though parents and their legal representatives are able to shape the specifics of a divorce agreement, the environment wherein such agreements are concluded is sufficiently restrictive so as to necessitate our consideration of it as the main determinant of custody arrangements and child support orders (this approach was originally articulated by Mnookin and Kornhauser, 1979). Societal institutions only indirectly affect resource allocations in nonintact families because their interventions principally affect only the income distribution across households and, in the view taken below, the preferences of the parents. Presumably due to the existence of difficult monitoring problems and issues connected with rights to privacy, societal agents rarely prescribe interpersonal resource allocations directly to nonintact or intact families.

The rationale for societal agents to intervene in the interhousehold resource allocation process after marital dissolution stems from concern with the deleterious effects of the child's partial separation from the parents on each parent's motivation to spend resources (time and income)

111

on the child and on the overall dimunition in resources controlled by one
or both of the parents from the loss of economies of scale in household
production and consumption. Since most custody arrangements specify
that the majority of the child's time is to be spent with the mother, and
since the mother typically has a substantially lower income than the father
following a divorce, income transfers from the father to the mother are
often ordered because of income disparities between parents, and possibly
out of the concern that the motivation for noncustodial fathers to spend
resources on the child will be reduced due to the limited amount of time
the father will spend with the child following the dissolution of the
marriage.

The purpose of the analysis reported in Del Boca and Flinn (1990)
(hereafter DF) and continued in this chapter is to examine *both* compliance with child support orders *and* the nature of the orders and custody
arrangements themselves for the purpose of determining their cumulative
effects on expenditures on the child. There is some reason to believe that
the event of noncompliance with child support orders will become less
common with the passing of time as more states adopt payment procedures such as automatic withholding to eliminate the choice of noncompliance by a parent under orders.[1] The explanation of noncompliance *per
se* is not the focal point of either DF or the current chapter; rather, under
a highly structured model of parental preferences and the preferences of
institutional agents, we seek to use compliance data to estimate
behavioural parameters which will shed some light on the interpersonal
allocation of resources among nonintact households. In particular, using
the models and results reported in DF and in this chapter, we can
determine the amounts of parental income spent on the child in the event
of noncompliance or compliance for given divorce arrangements and
parental income distributions. Eventually, we hope to use these results to
characterise optimal divorce arrangements from the point of view of
societal agents with particular classes of preferences.

Because our ultimate goal is the performance of empirical work, a
number of strong assumptions regarding preferences will be made at the
outset. In addition, the analysis requires specification of the mode of
interaction between parents when it comes to making expenditure decisions on the public good, the child. In DF, we assumed that public good
expenditures were determined within a noncooperative (Nash) equilibrium; the primary analytic contribution of the present chapter is to
consider the case of cooperative expenditure decisions.

The analysis contained in DF and the present chapter relies heavily on
the seminal work of Becker in the area of economic analysis of intra-
household interactions (see Becker, 1981 for a summary of his contri-

butions in this area) and related contributions in the public economics literature. In analysing intra-household allocations, the standard device utilised by Becker is to postulate the existence of a utility function for the 'head' of the household which includes as arguments the amount of consumption of a single consumption good by each member of the household, $U(x_1, \ldots x_n)$, where x_i denotes the consumption level of household member i. Let the head of the household be household member number 1, and denote the income of household member i by I_i. When $I_1 > 0$ and $I_k = 0$ for $k \in \{2, \ldots n\}$, the household allocation problem is simply a standard utility maximisation problem with the consumption of member i reflecting the head's preferences and income.

This framework is easily extended to allow for nontrivial interactions between household members in the following way. Let $U_k(x_k)$ denote the utility function of household member k, $k \geq 2$, which is defined only with respect to his or her own consumption. Each household member controls his or her own income allocation, I_k. The Rotten Kid Theorem of Becker (1981) establishes that when the head makes positive income transfers to each household member, the allocation of household consumption is identical to that obtained when the head is given discretion to allocate *all* household income $[\Sigma I_k]$ in a manner consistent with maximisation of U. The basic idea behind the result is that for each dollar of own income a 'selfish' household member spends on his or herself, the head offsets the expenditure with a deduction in the income transfer to that member.

The result is subject to a number of qualifications, some of the more interesting of which are well summarised in Bergstrom (1989). The most important (and obvious) qualification of the result from the point of view of the application below is the condition that the head is making positive transfers to all members of the household. When this condition is not met, consumption allocations will depend on the distribution of incomes across members, not merely the sum.

Not surprisingly, a similar result obtains if we consider a situation in which household members all have preferences defined over some public good. For simplicity, consider the case in which $n = 2$, and define the utility functions of agent i as $U_i(x_i, z)$, where z denotes a public good. Once again taking incomes as exogenous and assuming appropriate concavity conditions on the U_i, we can define a unique Nash equilibrium level of expenditures on the public good by agent k of $z_k^*(I_1, I_2)$. Warr (1983) was the first to formally establish the result $z_1^*(I_1, I_2) + z_2^*(I_1, I_2) = \mathcal{Z}(I_1 + I_2)$ for all pairs (I_1, I_2) for which $z_k^*(I_1, I_2) > 0$ for $k = 1$ *and* 2. Thus, for all income distributions for which Nash equilibrium expenditures on the public good are strictly positive for both agents, the total level of expenditures on the public good is a function only of the total income of the two agents. The implication of this result is that the distribution of utilities of the two agents is also independent of the income distribution (holding the sum fixed) when both agents make positive expenditures on the public good. Kemp (1984) has extended this result to the case of several public goods, but only for the case in which all agents provide a positive amount of each good. Work by Bergstrom *et al.* (1986) extends and qualifies these results when the possibility of corner solutions exists; when one of the agents is not providing positive amounts of the public good, the level of provision of the good will of course depend on the distribution of income and not only the sum.

The analyses of Warr and Bergstrom *et al.* pertain to situations in which agents with preferences defined over some public good could not implement a Pareto improving cooperative solution to the public good expenditure problem. Within intact families, presumably 'good will' and close monitoring combine to make the selection of a cooperative solution to the expenditure coordination problem more likely. Manser and Brown (1980) and McElroy and Horney (1981) have provided innovative analyses of the division of resources within the household and even the decision of whether or not to form a household using axiomatic cooperative bargaining models. Both sets of authors examined Nash bargaining solutions to the division of household resources where the utilities of the two bargainers were defined over both private and public good consumption.[2] Recent contributions to this literature include Chiappori (1988a, 1988b) and McElroy (1990), both of whom explore the question of whether or not household bargaining models yield testable restrictions on estimable demand systems. For further discussion of some of these issues, the reader is referred to chapter 3 in this volume by Bourguignon and Chiappori.

In contrast to the literature on the allocation of resources within intact households, which consists almost exclusively of theoretical contributions, research on the behaviour of parents following marital dissolution is empirical for the most part (a notable exception is the work of Weiss and Willis, 1985, 1989, 1990). Moreover, empirical studies of the interactions between divorced parents typically focus exclusively on resource transfers between the households.

While the term 'cooperation' has a very specific meaning in the context of bargaining models, the term is used to represent a variety of characteristics of the interactions between divorced parents in the empirical work on compliance with child support orders. In some contexts, compliance with child support orders and 'cooperative' behaviour between the parents are treated as virtually synonymous. In the empirical literature on the post-divorce behaviour of parents, it is probably fair to say that cooperation is loosely used to signify the fact that *both* parents contribute resources (money and/or time) to the children.[3] In the modal post-divorce arrangement in which the mother has custody and the father is ordered to pay child support, satisfaction of his child support obligations satisfies this criterion for cooperative behaviour. As we show below, under the formal bargaining definition of cooperation, there exists no necessary connection between cooperation in expenditures on the children and the act of compliance.

Even under the rather weak implicit definition of cooperation present in the empirical work on post-divorce behaviour, compliance with child support orders has some severe limitations as an indicator of cooperation. One problem concerns the fact that a substantial number of couples do not have awards, because they negotiate their own financial and custodial arrangements within state law, that is they 'bargain in the shadow of the law' in the terminology of Mnookin and Kornhauser (1979). In this case, compliance is not a relevant indicator of the actual transfers, given that the implicit private negotiation with the ex-spouse is not observable.

Another issue regards whether the act of receiving or making a child support transfer alters parental behaviour in and of itself. For example, Del Boca and Flinn (1992) have found that divorced mothers' marginal propensity to purchase child specific goods is greater out of child support than out of other income. While such a result may be consistent with the existence of a 'moral imperative' to purchase more child specific goods the greater the share of child support receipts in total income or may indicate a misspecification of the demand system, it is also consistent with the existence of significant consumption externalities between parents even after divorce. While which interpretation is most consistent with reality is not at all clear, it is apparent that child support transfers should not be merely regarded as indicators of predetermined patterns of parental behaviour.

In the absence of direct measures of cooperation, the empirical work on compliance has tended to be descriptive in nature. Positing that compliance can be viewed as indicating cooperation (in some generic sense) between the parents, these studies essentially determine which of a set of empirical measures characterising the post-divorce characteristics of parents affect the probability of the parents behaving 'cooperatively'. A prototypical study is that of Peters *et al.* (1991), in which indicators such as custody arrangement, distance between parents' homes, and the level of conflict during negotiations were related to compliance.[4]

The empirical analysis of the behaviour of nonintact households is complicated by the presence of institutional actors (such as judges, lawyers, and social workers) who constrain and mediate the interactions between divorced parents. The effect of the institutional environment on the final divorce settlement is discussed in Mnookin and Kornhauser (1979) and Weitzman (1985). Albiston *et al.* (1990) and Mnookin *et al.* (1990) have examined the effect of parent characteristics and the nature of the relationship between the parents during divorce proceedings and the divorce settlement.[5] The effect of the (implicit) endowment of the custodial parent with rights concerning the *de facto* allocation of visitation time and the endowment of the parent under orders with control (via the compliance decision) over the consumption levels of the custodial parent on post-divorce behaviour has been investigated by Pearson and Thoennes (1988), Chambers (1979), Selzer *et al.* (1989), Furstenberg *et al.* (1983), and Weiss and Willis (1985), among others.

While difficult to summarise, this body of work taken as a whole demonstrates the complex manner in which parental characteristics determine post-divorce welfare after passing through the institutional 'filter'. One of our main goals for the simple model given below is to make the relationships between parents and institutional actors simple enough so that they are amenable to positive analysis.

The plan of the chapter is as follows. In the second section, under a set of assumptions regarding the form of parental utility functions, we show that the expenditures made by the parents on the child are unique given parental incomes and preferences (which are determined in part by the custody arrangement) whether the expenditure coordination problem is solved noncooperatively or cooperatively. The third section contains our specification of the econometric model of the compliance decision, as well as estimates of behavioural parameters generated under alternative assumptions regarding cooperation. The fourth section contains the conclusion, which includes a discussion of the problems faced by institutional agents in arriving at 'optimal' child support and custody arrangements.

Compliance with child support under alternative behavioural stategies

We begin by briefly laying out the model which formed the basis for the empirical analysis of compliance decisions in DF. As mentioned in the introduction, the behavioural strategies of divorced parents were assumed to be noncooperative in that paper. In this section, we extend that model of compliance decisions to include cooperative strategies, and show that by engaging in cooperative behaviour the utility levels of both parents can be increased (a standard result), *either* under compliance or noncompliance on the part of the parent under orders. Using standard models for choosing cooperative welfare levels from the literature on axiomatic bargaining theory, we show that both in the Nash bargaining (hereafter NB) and Kalai–Smorodinsky (hereafter KS) solutions to the bargaining problem, utility levels and child expenditure levels are uniquely determined. This uniqueness property means that it is feasible to incorporate cooperative bargaining solutions in an econometric model of compliance decisions. Note that compliance in the econometric model will refer only to whether the individual under orders transfers an amount of money to the other parent so as to satisfy his or her legally-prescribed obligations. We will have only a few words to say regarding the extremely interesting and important issue of the *implementability* of cooperative agreements between divorced parents. This issue is briefly considered at the end of this section.

Throughout our analysis, we will adhere to the functional-form assumptions utilised in DF. The divorced parents are assumed to have utility functions given by

$$u_p = U_p(c_p, z) = a_p \ln(c_p) + (1 - a_p)\tau_p \ln(z), \quad p \in \{m, f\} \qquad (1)$$

where c_p denotes the amount of consumption of a market good by p

z denotes the level of child quality

τ_p is the proportion of the time the child spends with parent p

and a_p is a parent specific preference parameter.

c_p is thus the amount of 'private' consumption of parent p; the price of the market good is normalised to unity. The public good which interconnects the utilities of the divorced parents are child specific goods z. Child specific goods are potentially purchased by both parents, and we define $z = e_m + e_f$, where e_p is the expenditure by parent p on child specific goods. Finally, and quite importantly, each parent p is assumed to have an exogenously determined level of income, I_p. In particular, the income level of parent p is *not* a function of the child support order and custody arrangement. It is also assumed that the incomes $\{I_m, I_f\}$ are perfectly observed by both parents m and f.

A child support order specifies both the proportion of time during which the father will have physical custody of the child and an income transfer from the father to the mother, denoted respectively by τ and T. We allow for the possibility that the mother may be ordered to transfer some of her income to the father; in this case, T will be negative. In both DF and this chapter, we assume that the custody order is faithfully complied with by both parents – thus $\tau_f \equiv \tau$ and $\tau_m \equiv 1 - \tau$ in (1). Since (i) compliance is assumed to be all-or-nothing (i.e., a parent under orders to transfer a positive amount of income to the other parent will either transfer exactly the amount ordered or transfer nothing) and (ii) for a given income distribution, expenditures by parents on the child specific good are independent of whether the parent under orders is complying with a child support order or not,[6] in constructing a formal model of the compliance decision it is only necessary to determine parental expenditures under the two income distributions which result from compliance and noncompliance. Under compliance, the *state variables* which determine parental expenditure levels take the values $\{I_m + T, I_f - T, \tau\}$; under noncompliance they assume the values $\{I_m, I_f, \tau\}$. We now turn to the problem of determining the equilibrium expenditure levels under any income distribution and for any given child support order.

The determination of expenditures in Nash equilibrium

In DF, we proved the following:

Proposition 1: For all triplets (I_m, I_f, τ) there exists a unique Nash equilibrium (NE) level of expenditures on child goods $(\bar{e}_m, \bar{e}_f)(I_m, I_f, \tau)$. The NE expenditures of the father (mother) are a nondecreasing (nonincreasing) function of the custody award τ.

An implication of Proposition 1 is that there exist two constants $\underline{\tau}(I_m, I_f)$ and $\bar{\tau}(I_m, I_f)$ such that for $\tau \leq \underline{\tau}(I_m, I_f)$ only the mother will make public good expenditures and for $\tau \geq \bar{\tau}(I_m, I_f)$ only the father will make expenditures on the children. For $\underline{\tau}(I_m, I_f) < \tau < \bar{\tau}(I_m, I_f)$, both parents will make public good expenditures. Neither $\underline{\tau}$ nor $\bar{\tau}$ is restricted to lie in the unit interval for all possible income distributions. For some income distributions there may thus exist no feasible custody arrangement (which is restricted to lie in the closed-unit interval) which will induce one of the parents to make expenditures on the children.

The effect of income redistribution on the NE described in Proposition 1 will be crucial in examining the behaviour of institutional actors whose objectives are to maximise expected expenditures on the public good, the child. For the preferences given in (1), it is well-known that when both parents are making positive expenditures on the public good, any redistribution of total parental income from one parent to the other results in exactly the same distribution of utility between the parents *as long as both parents continue to make positive expenditures on the public good after the income redistribution* (see Warr, 1983 and Bergstrom *et al.*, 1986). This result will have important implications for the child support orders and custody arrangements optimally set by courts.

In DF we attempt to characterise the optimal custody and child support orders of institutional agents attempting to maximise expected expenditures on the child, where uncertainty arises due to (possibly) imperfect compliance by parents under orders to pay child support. We show that when institutional agents only have the power to order custody arrangements, the optimal arrangement will be to give sole custody to one of the parents (which one depends on the preference parameters a_m and a_f and the income distribution) or to award 'joint custody', where the time sharing rule is only a function of the preference parameters (although the choice of joint custody itself is a function of both parental preferences and the parental income distribution). When the institutional agent can order both custody and child support, and when compliance with child support orders is perfect, the optimal arrangement is to give sole custody to the parent with the lower value of a_p, and to order the other parent to transfer all their income to him or her. It is much more difficult to characterise the optimal arrangement in the case of imperfect compliance. We are able to conclude that any optimal order will force that parent under orders to pay *not* to make additional expenditures on the child if he or she complies with the order (if a parent continues to spend on the child even after the child support transfer, then the total expenditures on the child will not have increased with respect to their pre-transfer levels by the argument given in the previous paragraph). The reader is referred to DF for further details.

Characterisations of bargaining solutions for divorced parents

In this chapter we initiate an investigation of the determination of equilibrium expenditures on the child specific good when the set of behavioural strategies available to the divorced parents is extended to include cooperative ones. In particular, we will show that cooperative behaviour in our model yields unique expenditures for the child specific good under two solutions to the standard two-person bargaining problem, those of Nash (1950) and Kalai and Smorodinsky (1975).

We will first briefly and generally describe the nature of the bargaining problem to which the NB and KS solutions apply.[7] A two-person bargaining game is described by a pair $(\delta, \mathcal{S})$ where $\delta \in \mathbb{R}^2$ and $\mathcal{S} \subseteq \mathbb{R}^2$. The point δ denotes the pair of utility levels realisable by the agents in the absence of a cooperative agreement. The set $\mathcal{S}$ contains all feasible utility pairs which the bargainers can attain under cooperation; definitionally, only points which are physically attainable given the resource constraints facing the individual agents and which result in no utility loss (with respect to the utilities associated with the disagreement outcome) to either agent are included in $\mathcal{S}$. It is assumed that the following conditions apply:

$\delta \in \mathcal{S}$. (2a)

$\mathcal{S}$ is compact and convex. (2b)

There exists at least one $u \in \mathcal{S}$ with $u > \delta$ ($\Rightarrow u_i > \delta_i$, $i = m, f$). (2c)

The set of all bargaining games satisfying (2) will be denoted $\mathcal{B}$.

Thus we have formally described the bargaining game in the space of the mother's and father's utility levels. The point δ represents the utility yields to the mother and father associated with *not* coming to a cooperative agreement. In our application, perhaps it is natural to associate the point δ with the utility yields to the mother and father in NE; let us denote these noncooperative utility levels by $\delta = (\delta_m, \delta_f)$. Condition (2c) states that at least one element of $\mathcal{S}$ must be strictly Pareto improving with respect to δ, that is, *both* parents must realise positive utility gains (with respect to δ) at such a point.

The two particular solutions to the bargaining game which we will examine are simply two elements of the class of functions $g^i: \mathcal{B} \rightarrow \mathbb{R}^2$ such that for all $(\delta, \mathcal{S})$, $g^i(\delta, \mathcal{S}) \in \mathcal{S}$. We will denote the two solutions to $\mathcal{B}$ considered here by g^{NB} and g^{KS}. Under (2), both solutions to $\mathcal{B}$ will be unique, but the solutions will in general be different due to the different objective functions utilised in determining which element of $\mathcal{S}$ is to be chosen. Under the Nash solution, the point of $\mathcal{S}$ selected as the agreement point is that which satisfies

$$[g_m^{NB}(\delta, \mathcal{S}) - \delta_m][g_f^{NB}(\delta, \mathcal{S}) - \delta_f] \geq [\mathcal{S}_m - \delta_m][\mathcal{S}_f - \delta_f] \quad \text{for all } \mathcal{S} \in \mathcal{S}. \quad (3)$$

Under the compactness and convexity assumption (2b) on $\mathcal{S}$, it necessarily follows that the NB solution is unique.

In order to state the point of $\mathcal{S}$ chosen to be the KS solution to $\mathcal{B}$, an additional concept must be introduced, one which will play an important role in proving some of the results presented below and in the empirical implementation of the model. Consider the problem faced by a member of the bargaining pair who is asked to choose *any* element of $\mathcal{S}$ he or she wishes subject to the condition that the other member's utility gain over the disagreement point is *no less than* ξ. Call this a quasi-dictatorial problem for parent p,[8] and express it formally as

$$S_p(\xi) = \max_{\mathcal{S}} u_p \quad (4)$$

$$\text{s.t.} \quad (u_{p'} - \delta_{p'}) \geq \xi.$$

We adopt the convention that if no element of $\mathcal{S}$ can be found which satisfies the constraint $u_{p'} - \delta_{p'} \geq \xi$, then $S_p(\xi) \equiv 0$. The 'ideal' point in $\mathcal{S}$ for the father is that for which the mother need not be given any surplus from agreement; the utility surplus for the father at this point is $S_f(0)$. Similarly, the ideal point in $\mathcal{S}$ for the mother yields a utility surplus for her given by $S_m(0)$. Now we can state the KS solution to $\mathcal{B}$ as the unique point satisfying

$$(g_m^{KS}(\delta, \mathcal{S}) - \delta_m) = \frac{(S_m(0) - \delta_m)}{(S_f(0) - \delta_f)} (g_f^{KS}(\delta, \mathcal{S}) - \delta_f). \quad (5)$$

In the literature on axiomatic models of cooperative decision making, there is considerable debate over the merits and demerits of the various solutions proposed to $\mathscr{B}$, which are derived under a set of desiderata regarding general properties which solutions to $\mathscr{B}$ should exhibit. We have neither the expertise nor the space to go into such matters here, and refer the interested reader to Roth (1979), Kalai (1985), and Moulin (1988) (and the numerous works referred to by these authors) for lucid discussions of the various axiomatic systems in existence. We merely note that there is no 'correct' solution g to the bargaining problem $\mathscr{B}$. In light of this indeterminacy, one of the motivations for the empirical work reported below was to assess the sensitivity of parameter estimates of parental preferences to variation in the bargaining solution utilised in determining expenditures on the public good.

From the point of view of using cooperative bargaining solutions in our analysis of the compliance decision, it will be important to establish several properties of g^{NB} and g^{KS}. First, it will be necessary to show that for our problem of optimal coordination of expenditures on the child specific goods the conditions in (2) are satisfied. Second, because we want to use the solution empirically, algorithms for computing the solutions are required.

Given the specific form of preferences in (1), the demonstration of uniqueness of NB and KS solutions is straightforward. Sufficient conditions for the uniqueness of these solutions (discussed in Manser and Brown, 1980) are for the parental utility functions to be strictly concave in the private and public good consumption levels of the parents and for the constraint in the quasi-dictatorial problem to be binding. The utility functions in (1) are strictly concave, and Result 1 below establishes that the second sufficient condition holds.

Result 1: The constraint involving the utility surplus of parent p' is always binding in the quasi-dictatorial problem of parent p.

Proof: In our application, (4) takes the specific form

$$S_p(\xi) = \max_{e_p, e_{p'}} a_p \ln(I_p - e_p) + (1 - a_p)\tau_p \ln(e_p + e_{p'}) \qquad (4')$$

$$\text{s.t.} \quad a_{p'} \ln(I_{p'} - e_{p'}) + (1 - a_{p'})\tau_{p'} \ln(e_p + e_{p'}) - \delta_{p'} \geq \xi.$$

Denote the expenditure solutions to (4') by the pair $\{\hat{e}_p^p(\xi), \hat{e}_{p'}^p(\xi)\}$. We will prove the result by contradiction. Assume that at the solution pair, the utility surplus of parent p' is greater than ξ. Construct an alternative expenditure pair $\{\hat{e}_p^p(\xi), \hat{e}_{p'}^p(\xi) + \Delta\}$, where $\Delta(>0)$ is defined by

$$a_{p'}\ln(I_{p'} - (\hat{e}^p_{p'}(\xi) + \varDelta)) + (1 - a_{p'})\tau_{p'}\ln(\hat{e}^p_p(\xi) + (\hat{e}^p_{p'}(\xi) + \varDelta)) - \delta_{p'} = \xi. \quad (6)$$

Since $u_p(\hat{e}^p_p(\xi), \hat{e}^p_{p'}(\xi) + \varDelta) > u_p(\hat{e}^p_p(\xi), \hat{e}^p_{p'}(\xi))$, no expenditure pair for which $\varDelta$ is positive can constitute a solution to the quasi-dictatorial problem of agent p. ■

By Result 1, we can use the constraint in the quasi-dictatorial problem to eliminate one of the choice variables for agent p. Any expenditure pair solution to (5') must satisfy

$$e_p(\xi, e_{p'}) = \exp\left\{\frac{\delta_{p'} + \xi - a_{p'}\ln(I_{p'} - e_{p'})}{(1 - a_{p'})\tau_{p'}}\right\} - e_{p'}, \quad (7)$$

so that (4') can be rewritten as

$$S_p(\xi) = \max_{e_{p'}} a_p\ln(I_p - e_p(\xi, e_{p'}))$$
$$+ (1 - a_p)\tau_p\ln(e_p(\xi, e_{p'}) + e_{p'}) - \delta_{p'}. \quad (4'')$$

The unique expenditure solution to the quasi-dictatorial problem (4'') will be denoted $\hat{e}^p_{p'}(\xi)$.

We are now in a position to verify that our model of expenditure decisions satisfies the conditions which define the bargaining problem $\mathscr{B}$.

Result 2: The Pareto frontier ($\mathscr{P}$) is continuous and differentiable with $d\mathscr{P}/d\xi < 0$ and $d^2\mathscr{P}/d\xi^2 <$, where $\mathscr{P}(\xi)$ gives the maximal utility surplus for agent p given a utility surplus for p' equal to $\xi \in [0, S_{p'}(0)]$.

Proof: By definition we have

$$S_p(\xi) = a_p\ln(I_p - e_p(\xi, \hat{e}_{p'}(\xi))) + (1 - a_p)\tau_p\ln(e_p(\xi, \hat{e}_{p'}(\xi)) + \hat{e}_{p'}(\xi)). \quad (8)$$

By Result 1, the utility pair $\{u_p = S_p(\xi), u_{p'} = \xi\}$ definitionally lies on the Pareto frontier $\mathscr{P}$. Since the function defining $S_p(\xi)$ is a continuously differentiable function of ξ, $\mathscr{P}$ is continuously differentiable. It is straightforward to show that the first and second partial derivatives of $S_p(\xi)$ are negative. ■

Besides establishing properties of the NB and KS solutions to our child expenditure game, the quasi-dictatorial functions $S_p(\xi)$ are useful for computational purposes. The nice differentiability properties of these functions simplify the characterisation of the solution. In determining the NB solution to the problem, we first compute the utility surplus to the parent p' at his or her 'ideal' point, which is given by $S_{p'}(0)$. Then NB utility levels are

$$\{u_{p'}^{NB} = \xi, u_p^{NB} = S_p(\xi)\} \quad \text{where } \xi = \arg\max_{\xi \in [0, S_{p'}(0)]} \xi \times S_p(\xi). \quad (9)$$

The arg max of the objective satisfies $S_p(\xi) + \xi dS_p(\xi)/d\xi = 0$, which is the condition utilised in our computational search for the solution.

The KS solution to the bargaining problem is given by

$$\{u_{p'}^{KS} = \xi, u_p^{KS} = S_p(\xi)\} \text{ where } \frac{S_p(\xi)}{\xi} = \frac{S_p(0) - \delta_p}{S_{p'}(0) - \delta_{p'}}, \, \xi \in [0, S_{p'}(0)]. \tag{10}$$

To compute this solution, we first must compute the dictatorial utility levels for both parents, which are $S_p(0)$ and $S_{p'}(0)$. Given these values, the right-hand side of the equality in (10) is a constant. The left-hand side of the equality in that equation has a derivative with respect to ξ which is everywhere strictly negative on the interval $[0, S_{p'}(0)]$, and by the boundary conditions we know there exists a unique value of ξ on this interval which satisfies the equality.

The implementation of cooperative agreements

Axiomatic bargaining theory is silent as to the manner in which cooperative agreements, unanimously approved, are to be implemented. While implementation of such agreements *ex post* may not be of interest to researchers interested in the *ex ante* properties of alternative axiomatic solutions to $\mathcal{B}$, such issues cannot be ignored in an analysis of compliance behaviour. As is well-known, for any cooperative solution to the static game described by $\mathcal{B}$, the welfare of either party can be increased by violating the stipulated agreement point *given* that the other party adheres to the agreement. In our application, this means that the maximum utility attainable for parent p given the expenditure of parent p' (*however* the other parent's expenditure level is determined) will always be that which is read off his or her reaction function. If the expenditures of parent p' correspond to some cooperative solution, the utility-maximising choice of p will be strictly less than the amount originally stipulated for this solution (since this amount is always positive). Both parents face the same incentive to spend less on the child good than was agreed to in the cooperative agreement, and the important question arises as to whether such cooperative agreements can be sustained. This question is particularly relevant in the present application, given the inherent difficulty of observing expenditures made by individuals living in different households.[9]

There are essentially two ways to sustain cooperative agreements associated with axiomatic solutions to the bargaining problem. The first and most obvious is to make the agreements binding in some manner, such as endowing them with the force of law. Such a mechanism will be most effective in situations in which the actions of both parties to the agreement are readily verifiable by a third party which has the exogenously given power to enforce the agreement, and in which possible deviations from the agreement are specifiable *ex ante*.

In the case of expenditures on the children by divorced parents, enforcement of cooperative agreements is problematic, and it seems unreasonable to expect that agents of legal institutions could possibly fulfil the third-party role referred to above. However, such cooperative agreements may be implementable if we look at the parents' expenditure decisions in a dynamic rather than a static context. Consider the case in which parental preferences are defined over some infinite or finite but random horizon, and where parental lifetime utility is equal to the discounted sum of contemporaneous utilities which are functions of period specific consumption levels of public and private goods. From 'folk theorem' results in the game theory literature,[10] it is known that cooperative behaviour can be achieved if each parent is sufficiently 'forward-looking', and if the punishment for deviating from cooperative expenditure levels is for the players to adopt noncooperative strategies. In this way, the short-term potential gains either parent can obtain by reducing expenditures from the cooperative level are more than offset by the loss in future utility due to the positive difference between cooperative and noncooperative utility yields (for specific applications and further general results, see Green and Porter, 1984 and Radner, 1985).

While we do not feel that it is reasonable to think that cooperative agreements regarding expenditure levels could ever be implemented through the threat of legal sanctions given cheating, we do think that it is eminently reasonable (and in fact preferable) to view the behaviour of divorced parents in a dynamic context. Even though our formal models of the compliance decision are static (primarily due to data limitations), looking at cooperative decisions in the context of repeated games gives credibility to the presumption that cooperative agreements between divorced parents are implementable. The specification and estimation of such models is one of the focuses of our current research.

An econometric model of the compliance decision

Given the results of the previous section, we are now in a position to develop an econometric model of the compliance decision which extends the one contained in DF. The principal extension relates to our consideration of alternative solutions to the parental expenditure game in addition to the noncooperative Nash outcome. After briefly developing our model, we will consider whether, to encourage compliance with child support orders, parents can credibly threaten each other with the possibility of noncooperative behaviour as a punishment strategy. We conclude with an empirical investigation of the effects of varying the expenditure game solution on the estimates of behavioural parameters.

An estimatable model of compliance

Because of our desire to build an econometric model of the compliance decision which would be estimable with the data available to us, we have kept the setup extremely simple. As mentioned earlier, legal orders are assumed to be characterised solely by the two parameters $\{\tau, T\}$. The parameter τ, which gives the proportion of time the child is to spend with the father after divorce, is assumed to exactly correspond to the actual amount of time which the child spends with the father. While it is an interesting and open question as to the extent of compliance with custody arrangements (see Albiston *et al.*, 1990), we simply do not have access to data which would allow us to consider this question. The parameter T gives the amount which the father has been ordered to transfer to the mother; because very few divorced mothers are ordered to pay child support to fathers, we will neglect such a possibility in the sequel and restrict T to be nonnegative.[11]

By compliance, we mean the extent to which the amount actually transferred by the father to the mother, denoted by $\mathcal{T}$, deviates from the amount ordered. Given a transfer of $\mathcal{T}$, the 'post-transfer' income distribution of the parents is $\{I_m + \mathcal{T}, I_f - \mathcal{T}\}$; the parents are assumed to make optimal expenditure decisions given the post-transfer income distribution, with expenditure levels being determined either in Nash equilibrium or according to the NB or KS solutions to the cooperative bargaining problem.

Operationally, compliance can be defined in many ways, and any given definition will be somewhat arbitrary. In the empirical exercise reported below, we define a father under orders to transfer an amount T to the mother as complying with the order if $\mathcal{T} \geq \theta T$, $\theta \in (0, 1]$. Using such a definition, compliance is a binary variable. Treating compliance as binary rather than continuous considerably simplifies the specification of behavioural models of the compliance decision.

Given that no parent has any absolute advantage in purchasing or producing child specific goods, under the preferences given in (1) there exists little motivation for a father under orders to pay child support to comply. Any mother who receives child support payments from the father can be no worse off in a utility sense than she is when no payments are received; therefore, mothers always (weakly) prefer compliance with orders to noncompliance. By the same token, fathers under orders to pay child support (weakly) prefer noncompliance to compliance. In this case, the only time in which compliance could occur is when fathers are indifferent as to making the income transfer or not. Such a situation occurs when both parents make positive expenditures on the public good in Nash equilibrium (under both the compliance and noncompliance income distributions). To generate a probabilistic compliance decision for purposes of empirical analysis, we modify the father's utility function specification to include a cost of noncompliance in the following manner:

$$u_f = U_f(c_f, z) - \chi\{\mathcal{T} < \theta T\}\lambda, \tag{11}$$

where λ is a random variable with support $\mathbb{R}$ and with cumulative distribution G, the U_f function is defined in (1), and $\chi\{A\}$ denotes the indicator function which takes the value one if statement A is true and zero otherwise. For technical reasons, we suppose that the utility 'cost' may be negative, thus implying that some fathers under orders gain positive utility from the act of noncompliance *per se*.[12]

Since U_f is a nonincreasing function of the transfer made from the father to the mother, under (11) it follows that the father's welfare can never be increased by transferring *more* than the amount ordered by the court.[13] The values of the compliance and noncompliance states to a father with custody arrangement τ, pre-transfer income distribution $\{I_m, I_f\}$, and noncompliance cost parameter λ are

$$V_c(S) = a_f \ln(I_f - T - \bar{e}_f^j(I_m + T, I_f - T, \tau))$$
$$+ (1 - a_f)\tau \ln(\bar{e}_m^j(I_m + T, I_f - T, \tau) + \bar{e}_f^j(I_m + T, I_f - T, \tau)); \tag{12a}$$

$$V_n(S, \lambda) = \bar{V}_n(S) + \lambda, \tag{12b}$$

$$\bar{V}_n(S) \equiv a_f \ln(I_f - \bar{e}_f^j(I_m, I_f, \tau)) + (1 - a_f)\tau \ln(\bar{e}_m^j(I_m, I_f, \tau) + \bar{e}_f^j(I_m, I_f, \tau)),$$

where $S = \{I_m, I_f, \tau, T, j\}$. Note that whether in the compliance state or the noncompliance state, the solution to the expenditure coordination problem between the spouses is assumed to be the same (i.e., the j superscript on the expenditure functions is constant across compliance states). In particular, we assume that the act of *noncompliance* by the parent under orders to make an income transfer does *not result in noncooperation* in the making of expenditure decisions. This point will be discussed and our position justified in the following subsection.

From (12), a father with state vector S and noncompliance cost parameter λ under orders to transfer the amount T will do so when $V_c(S) \geq V_n(S, \lambda)$. We observe all elements of the vector S; however, the parameter λ is unknown to us. This implies that we can only make a probabilistic statement concerning compliance, namely, that the probability of compliance given S is

$$p(\mathscr{C} \mid S) = p(V_c(S) \geq \bar{V}_n(S) - \lambda)$$
$$= - G(V_c(S) - \bar{V}_n(S)). \tag{13}$$

In the empirical work conducted below, we assume that the distribution function G belongs to a parametric family indexed by the finite-dimensional parameter vector ψ. In particular, we will assume that λ is an independently and identically distributed normal random variable, with mean μ_λ and standard deviation σ_λ. Given observations on compliance behaviour, the income distribution, and the custody and child support orders for a sample of N divorced parents, we can define the conditional (on j) log-likelihood function

$$\mathscr{L}(a_m, a_f, \psi \,|\, j) = \sum_{i=1}^{N} \{d_i \ln p(\mathscr{C}\,|\,S_i) + (1 - d_i) \ln(1 - p(\mathscr{C}\,|\,S_i))\} \tag{14}$$

where $d_i = 1$ if the ith father in the sample complies with the child support order and takes the value 0 otherwise, and where $S_i = \{I_{m,i}, I_{f,i}, \tau_i, T_i, j\}$, with $I_{k,i}$ denoting the income of parent k in sample observation i. Note the dependence of $\mathscr{L}$ on the *assumption* made regarding the explicit coordination rule j adopted.[14] Maximum likelihood estimators for the behavioural parameters corresponding to the arg max of the right-hand side of (14) are well-defined and have standard asymptotic normal distributions for each bargaining model j. The reader is referred to DF for a detailed discussion of the properties of the maximum likelihood estimator for this problem.

Since expenditure data are not available to us, it is not possible to formulate tests between the alternative expenditure coordination mechanisms based on the actual allocations between child specific and adult specific goods. With the estimates of structural parameters obtained under the three assumptions regarding expenditure coordination, we are able to say something about the sensitivity of estimates of parental preference parameters to variations in these assumptions, as well as to address the more interesting question of the implied variability in total parental expenditures on the child under the three mechanisms. Some statistical comparisons between the nonnested models will be conducted using the Akaike Information Criterion (AIC).

Credible threats and cooperative behaviour

In the econometric model of compliance we have performed all estimation conditional on the expenditure allocation mechanism. This is justified if the decisions of whether or not to comply with a given child support order can be treated as independent of the expenditure allocation mechanism adopted. This brief section serves to justify this independence assumption.

The question of independence boils down to whether or not any threat by a parent to choose their expenditures based on the compliance state is credible. Under the noncooperative Nash equilibrium solution, the mother's utility is at least as great under compliance with a child support order than under noncompliance; the father's utility is no greater under compliance than under noncompliance. Can the mother threaten an action which will increase the probability of having the father choose an action which is (weakly) preferred by her? The answer is no, if we require such threats to be credible and if we rule out precommitment possibilities.

Any cooperative solution to the bargaining problem (assuming that it is implementable) yields increases in utility levels over those obtained under noncooperative solutions for *both* parents. Conditional on the compliance state, each party will strictly prefer implementing a cooperative agreement to the bargaining problem. In the absence of precommitment, in this static version of the game played between divorced parents the mother cannot therefore credibly threaten to 'punish' the father for noncompliance by resorting to noncooperative behaviour.

If precommitment is possible, the mother may conceivably opt to punish the father for noncompliance. Assume that the act of precommitment is costless. The mother will precommit to a noncooperative solution to the public good problem if her expected utility under noncooperation exceeds her expected utility under cooperation. By precommitting to noncooperative behaviour in the noncompliance state, the mother reduces her utility yield in that state, but increases the probability of the compliance state which she weakly prefers. For her to precommit she must strongly prefer the compliance state, which means that one parent must specialise in child-good expenditures in Nash equilibrium under one of the two income distributions. If this is the case, then it is possible that precommitment to a noncooperative 'punishment' strategy may be optimal in an expected utility maximisation sense.

The possibility of observing noncooperation in the noncompliance state then rests on the availiability of mechanisms which allow precommitment. In the case of expenditures on child goods, it is difficult to imagine such devices. We conclude that the independence of compliance states and expenditure coordination devices assumed below seems reasonable.

Empirical analysis of compliance data

The data used in this chapter are gathered from court and payment records from divorce, separation, annulment, and paternity cases in 18 counties in Wisconsin. In each of these counties, between 150 and 200 cases over the period 1980–1986 were randomly selected, with approxi-

Table 5.1. *Descriptive statistics for sample of divorced parents with one child*

Variable	Mean	St. dev.
Compliance	0.44	
{*Comply = 1*}		
Joint custody	0.15	
{*Joint Custody = 1*}		
Amount of order	187.43	144.36
Mother's income	646.50	391.01
Father's income	1179.88	695.33
Mother's age	29.10	8.03
Father's age	31.42	8.45
Duration of marriage	8.88	7.71
Age of child	6.22	5.09

mately equal numbers of cases being selected in each year. Only cases from the years 1980–1982 are utilised in this analysis; in none of these cases were mandatory guidelines regarding custody or child support operative. We selected a subsample of divorce cases in which there is only one child under the age of 18 years in the family at the time of the divorce. In addition, only cases of joint custody or mother's custody were included. Over half of all cases in the original sample have missing information on some variable. This is particularly a problem with respect to information regarding income, some of which was merged into this dataset using state income tax returns. Demographic information regarding the parents is also often not recorded. For these reasons, the number of characteristics which can be used as conditioning variables is quite limited.[15] All the cases included in our sample had fixed custody arrangements and child support levels over the period of the sample and have complete information on the focal variables of the analysis. The total sample consists of 390 divorced parents in which the father is under court orders to pay child support to the mother.

As discussed on pp. 125–127, we have modelled compliance as an all-or-nothing decision on the part of the agent under orders to pay child support. Operationally, we have defined compliance to occur whenever the father has paid 90% or more of his child support orders over the entire period of the obligation.[16] Sample means and variances are reported in table 5.1. Only 44% of fathers in this sample complied with child support orders under our definition of compliance. Also note that only 15% of

Table 5.2. *Estimates of preference parameters from the father's compliance decision*

Parameter	(1)	(2)	(3)	(4)
NE solution				
a_m	0.423 (0.172)		0.361 (0.139)	
		0.423 (0.177)		0.375 (0.222)
a_f	0.423 (0.176)		0.328 (0.124)	
μ_λ	− 0.039 (0.020)	− 0.039 (0.021)	0	0
σ_λ	0.163 (0.045)	0.163 (0.044)	0.198 (0.087)	0.232 (0.124)
$\mathscr{L}$	− 257.146	− 257.148	− 259.302	− 259.406
NB solution				
a_m	0.384 (0.114)		0.309 (0.111)	
		0.389 (0.114)		0.309 (0.104)
a_f	0.381 (0.131)		0.309 (0.109)	
μ_λ	− 0.030 (0.023)	− 0.039 (0.021)	0	0
σ_λ	0.146 (0.058)	0.148 (0.054)	0.168 (0.085)	0.168 (0.085)
$\mathscr{L}$	− 256.477	− 257.118	− 258.438	− 258.438
KS solution				
a_m	0.388 (0.112)		0.308 (0.112)	
		0.390 (0.101)		0.309 (0.102)
a_f	0.384 (0.127)		0.309 (0.104)	
μ_λ	0.031 (0.021)	0.031 (0.020)	0	0
σ_λ	0.148 (0.055)	0.148 (0.048)	0.168 (0.084)	0.168 (0.084)
$\mathscr{L}$	− 256.479	− 257.117	− 258.438	− 258.438

fathers have joint custody arrangements. Average child support orders were about 16% of the average income levels of fathers in this sample. The mean income of mothers was approximately 55% of the mean income of fathers. The average age of the child involved in the divorce case was about six years.

Table 5.2 contains m.l. estimates of the behavioural model of compliance under the alternative solutions to the expenditure coordination problem and under various restrictions on the preference parameters. In the top panel of table 5.2 estimates of the preference parameters of the parents under the assumption that all parents make public good expenditure decisions in a noncooperative manner are presented. The estimates of the 'unrestricted' model appear in column (1). Most notable is the fact that the preference weights given to own consumption are identical (0.423) for fathers and mothers. The direct implication of this result is that the only reason mothers spend higher proportions of their own incomes on children than do fathers is custody arrangements which overwhelmingly allot higher proportions of time to the mother than the father. The second thing to note about the estimates in column (1) is the fact that the mean of the random variable representing costs of noncompliance is positive, and that the probability of a father gaining positive utility from the act of noncompliance in and of itself is 0.41.

As is to be expected, the estimates of the model under the restriction that the preference parameters of the parents are equal (column (2)) conform exactly to those in column (1). When the restriction of equality of the αs is relaxed and a zero-mean restriction for λ imposed (column (3)), we do obtain differences in the estimates of the αs. However, we see from the comparison of the log likelihoods associated with the models in columns (3) and (4) that the differences in the α_m and α_f estimates are not statistically significant. Moreover, in comparing the models in columns (3) and (1), the likelihood ratio test statistic value of 4.312 indicates that the null hypothesis of $\mu_\lambda = 0$ should be rejected for a test size of 0.05.

Before discussing the estimates obtained from the compliance probits under the assumption of cooperative behaviour regarding public good expenditures, we wish to point out some numerical problems we experienced in estimating the models. From our previous results we know that there always exists a unique cooperative solution to the parents' expenditure problem in which *both* parents make positive expenditures on the public good. In particular, even when one of the parents spends nothing on the child in Nash equilibrium, he or she will spend a positive amount under a cooperative solution. Such expenditures may be very small, however, thus making exact computation of them infeasible. For cases in which the algorithms for computing the cooperative expenditure levels were not effective, we simply set the cooperative expenditure levels equal to the Nash equilibrium expenditure levels. The justification for this substitution is that since the algorithm only experienced problems for cases in which the solution to the cooperative problem was near zero for one of the parents, the noncooperative solution in which one of the parents treated the child specific good as private is a good approximation. While this approximation always results in an underestimate of the total expenditures on the child, we feel that the size of these approximation errors is negligible.

In the middle panel of table 5.2 we report estimates of the preference parameters using the NB solution. Aside from the fact that the implied weights given to own consumption are noticeably lower in the NB model for both parents, the general pattern of results across columns is similar in the two tables. While there is a small difference between the estimates of a_m and a_f, clearly it is not statistically significant (comparing the log-likelihoods in columns (1) and (2)). The null hypothesis that the mean of the direct cost of noncompliance is zero is rejected at the 0.05 level under either specification of the a parameters (i.e., whether they are assumed identical or are allowed to be different). The variance in the λ is smaller in all columns of the middle panel than in the matching columns of the top panel of table 5.2.

The results presented in the bottom panel of table 5.2 which correspond to the KS solution to the bargaining problem are virtually identical to those contained in the middle panel of the table. In this application, choice between two prominent axiomatic systems for choosing a unique outcome to the cooperative bargaining problem has no effect on the estimates obtained and inferences drawn.

In terms of choosing between competing models of the public good expenditure coordination rule, no classical testing procedure is available because the NE, NB, and KS models are not nested. The models can be compared in terms of overall fit, however, and if we restrict our attention to comparing the same column across the three panels of table 5.2, ranking models in terms of their associated log-likelihoods will be equivalent to ranking them according to an AIC. We note that there exist no detectable differences between the log-likelihoods associated with the NB and KS models, so we will simply compare the results corresponding to the NE and NB solutions to the expenditure problem.

The log-likelihood values corresponding to the NB solution are uniformly greater than those corresponding to the NE solution, indicating that the compliance decision models with cooperative solutions outperform those with noncooperative solutions using the AIC criterion in this application. Admittedly, this indirect 'test' of the form of the expenditure coordination rule is weak, but no obviously superior tests are available in the absence of parent specific expenditure information.

In summary, while the pattern of estimates across columns is similar in all three panels of table 5.2, there are important differences in the implications for public good expenditures between the noncooperative and cooperative models. We know that expenditures on the public good under cooperation exceed those made under noncooperation. In addition, the estimates of the a parameters are greater when cooperation is assumed than when noncooperation is imposed. This will further increase implied expenditures on the public good with respect to the situation which prevails under noncooperation and using the preference parameter estimates from the NE model.[17]

Conclusion

In this chapter we have begun an exploration of the importance of alternative expenditure coordination mechanisms for inferences we draw concerning the preferences of divorced parents using data on divorce arrangements and compliance behaviour. By extending the literature on intra-household bargaining within intact families to the case of divorced parents, we were able to give a more precise definition of cooperative behaviour as it relates to this group of parents. Our contention is that the issues of compliance with legally-stipulated obligations regarding children and cooperation on expenditures are logically distinct, at least in a static context. Empirically, we found that estimates of parental preferences were sensitive to assumptions regarding whether or not behaviour was cooperative, though the specific bargaining rule (Nash or Kalai–Smorodinsky) employed was not relevant.

In this chapter we have explored only the effect of the expenditure coordination device used on expenditures on the child and the welfare of parents. We have not characterised optimal solutions to the problem of an institutional agent who seeks to maximise total expenditures on the child under cooperative or noncooperative behaviour by the parents. A promising area of policy-relevant research would lie in the determination of the manner in which institutional agents can increase the likelihood that parents utilise cooperative rather than noncooperative strategies; to investigate this issue one needs a dynamic version of the model considered in this chapter.

The gain in total child expenditures which can be obtained by getting parents to use cooperative strategies is illustrated in figure 5.1. Using point estimates from the NB model which are contained in the middle panel of table 5.2, we have constructed the total expenditures on the child

Child good ($100\$_{1980}$)

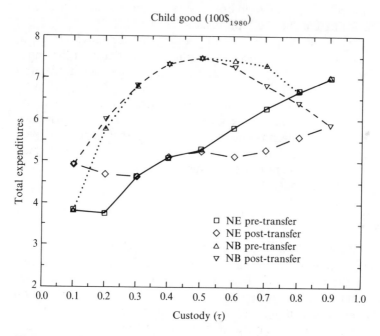

Figure 5.1   Total parental expenditure on child, by custody and compliance status

(in 100 1980 dollars) for a hypothetical household. In this household, the father and mother are assumed to have incomes equal to their respective sample averages and the father is assumed to be under orders to transfer the sample average of child support orders to the mother (figures given in table 5.1). We computed total expenditures on the child for varying levels of father custody [$\tau = 0.1, 0.2, \ldots, 0.9$] under NE and NB assumptions for both pre- and post-transfer income distributions. As we can see from figure 5.1, public good expenditures vary markedly with τ. Given non-compliance with the child support order, NE expenditures are monotone increasing in the amount of time given to the father starting from $\tau = 0.2$. At $\tau = 0.9$, total expenditures on the child are approximately $700, all of which comes from the father. Conversely, NB expenditure levels are concave over the interval [0.1, 0.8], with a maximum around 0.5; at this custody arrangement, total expenditures on the child are approximately $750. Under the income distribution which results from the transfer of the child support order, maximum expenditures on the child also occur at $\tau = 0.9$ in NE; at this value, the father's expenditures on the child are slightly less than $600. In NB, maximum expenditures occur at the same point and assume the same value in the post- and pre-transfer distributions.

We hope that this illustration has served to demonstrate the fact that divorce arrangements (child support *and* custody) can have significant impacts on the expenditures on the children, and that the nature of the effects can be quite sensitive to assumptions regarding the behaviour of parents following a divorce. The estimation of the implied preferences of institutional agents using data on divorce arrangements and parental and child characteristics was begun in DF, and is one of the focuses of our current research.

NOTES

Research support for this chapter has been provided by the National Institute for Child Health and Human Development grant HD28409 and by the C.V. Starr Center for Applied Economics at New York University. We wish to thank our discussant Ian Walker and others for encouraging us to consider cooperative models of expenditure decisions by divorced parents. We are grateful to Francis Gupta and Antonio Merlo for excellent research assistance, and to Ian Walker and two anonymous referees for valuable editorial suggestions. All errors and omissions are our own.

1 According to estimates obtained from Current Population Survey data (Current Population Report, series P–23, no. 167, US Bureau of the Census, 1990), in 1987 the aggregate amount of child support received by women was $10 billion out of $14.6 billion due. The amount received marked an increase of 32% in real terms over the 1985 figure.

2 Manser and Brown also examined other solutions to the bargaining problem, primarily the Kalai–Smorodinsky solution discussed below. The focus of the McElroy and Horney work was the implications for observed household demands of bargaining solutions to the allocation problem instead of allocations resulting from the maximisation of a household utility function with standard concavity properties.

3 Some examples of empirical approaches to the compliance question are Beller and Graham (1985, 1986), Beron (1991), Braver *et al.* (1989), Del Boca (1986), Garfinkel and Oellerich (1989), O'Neill (1985), Hill (1988), Pearson and Thoennes (1988), Peters *et al.* (1991), Selzer (1991), and Weitzman (1985).

4 Other studies include Sonestein and Calhoun (1990), in which measures of friendliness between divorced parents were related to compliance, and Selzer (1990) who looks at the relationship between how the settlement was reached (in terms of the usage of lawyers by the parents) and compliance.

5 Interestingly enough, these authors found that joint custody awards were often a legal response to situations in which the parents could *not* agree on any alternative custody arrangements, which raises doubts concerning the interpretation of joint custody as indicating parental cooperation in parenting.

6 These are really not assumptions so much as products of the characteristics of the compliance model exposited below.

7 Excellent discussions of the problem are contained in the survey by Kalai (1985) and the exhaustive treatment by Roth (1979). Our presentation of the general bargaining problem borrows heavily from Kalai (1985).

8 In the literature, this model of choice is often referred to as the dictatorial model when $\xi \equiv 0$.

9 See Weiss and Willis (1985) for more on this and related points.

10 For a good introduction to such results, see chapter 14 in Kreps (1991).

11 Only cases in which fathers have been ordered to pay child support are included in the data used in the empirical analysis of compliance reported below.

12 Briefly, the reason for such an assumption is as follows. In the NE solution to the expenditure problem for certain values of the behavioural parameters a_m and a_f, income distributions $\{I_m, I_f\}$, and custody arrangements and child support orders $\{\tau, T\}$, optimal expenditure decisions will yield the same value of U_f in the compliance and noncompliance states. If the change in utility attributable directly to the act of noncompliance (λ) is strictly negative, the probability that the father in such a case would not comply with child support orders will be zero. If the father in such a case is observed not to comply with orders, this zero probability event will result in an undefined value of the log-likelihood. Such problems are circumvented when the act of noncompliance *per se* can increase the father's utility.

13 Though in some cases the father's welfare would not decrease as a result of transferring more than the amount ordered. This situation will occur whenever the pre- and post-transfer income distributions are associated with Nash equilibria in which both the father and mother make positive expenditures on the child.

14 The reader should also note the restriction that *all* sample members coordinate expenditures on the public good using the same rule. An interesting extension of the model would be to allow for population heterogeneity in the expenditure coordination rules used.

15 Some descriptive probit models are estimated in DF which include characteristics of the parents and the child other than the parental income distribution and characteristics of the divorce arrangement. In general, we found that these other characteristics did not significantly enhance the predictive power of probits estimated using only the state variables included in the behavioural compliance model.

16 Thus $\theta = 0.9$. Experiments which involved varying θ around 0.9 produced little in the way of qualitative differences in inference from the results reported below.

17 This statement is true conditional on the compliance state, or income distribution. Actual public good expenditures will depend not only the parameters a_m and a_f, but also on ξ. Expected (with respect to compliance behaviour) expenditures on the public good, computed using the point estimates in the top and middle panels of table 5.2, may be larger for some sample cases in the NE case.

REFERENCES

Albiston, C.R., R.H. Mnookin and E. Maccoby (1990) 'Legal conflict and divorcing parents: factors and outcomes in high conflict families', Stanford Center for Conflict and Negotiation, Stanford University, *Working Paper*, 11 (October)

Becker, G.S. (1981) *A Treatise on the Family*, Cambridge MA, Harvard University Press

Beller, A.H. and J.W. Graham (1985) 'Variations in the economic well-being of divorced women and their children: the role of child support income', in M. David and T. Smeeding (eds.), *Horizontal Equity, Uncertainty and Economic Well-Being, NBER Studies in Income and Wealth*, 50, Chicago, University of Chicago Press, 471–509

(1986) 'The determinants of child support income', *Social Science Quarterly*, 67, 353–364

Bergstrom, T.C. (1989) 'A fresh look at the Rotten Kid Theorem and Other household mysteries', *Journal of Political Economy*, 97, 1138–1159

Bergstrom, T.C., L. Blume and H. Varian (1986) 'On the private provision of public goods', *Journal of Public Economics*, 29, 25–49

Beron, K.J. (1991) 'Policy issues and child support payment behavior: empirical findings', *Contemporary Policy Issues*, 8, 124–134

Braver, S., P. Fitzpatrick and C.R. Bay (1989) 'Non-custodial parents' report of child support payments', paper presented at the Population Association of America Annual Meetings

Chambers, D.L. (1979) *Making Fathers Pay*, Chicago, University of Chicago Press

Chiappori, P.-A. (1988a) 'Rational household labour supply', *Econometrica*, 56, 63–89

(1988b) 'Nash-bargained household decisions: a comment', *International Economic Review*, 29, 791–796

Del Boca, D. (1986) 'Children as public goods: an economic approach to child support payments in relation to custody decision', University of Wisconsin-Madison, *IRP Discussion Paper*, 820–886

Del Boca, D. and C. Flinn (1990) 'The effect of child custody and support arrangements on the welfare of children and parents', C.V. Starr Center for Applied Economics, New York University, *Economic Research Report*, 90–16

(1992) 'Expenditure decisions of divorced mothers and income composition', C.V. Starr Center for Applied Economics, New York University, *Economic Research Report*, 92–40, forthcoming in *Journal of Human Resources*

Furstenberg, F., Jr., C. Winquist Nord, J.L. Peterson and N. Zill (1983) 'The life course of children of divorce: marital disruption and parental conflict', *American Sociological Review*, 48, 656–668

Garfinkel, I. and D. Oellerich (1989) 'Non-custodial father's ability to pay child support', *Demography* (May), 219–233

Green, E. and R. Porter (1984) 'Non-cooperative collusion under imperfect price information,' *Econometrica*, 52, 975–994

Hill, M. (1988) 'The role of economic resources and dual-family status in child support payments', paper presented at the Population Association of America Annual Meetings

Kalai, E. (1985) 'Solutions to the bargaining problems', in L. Hurwicz, D. Schmeidler and H. Sonneschein (eds.), *Social Goals and Social Organization*, Cambridge, Cambridge University Press

Kalai, E. and M. Smorodinsky (1975) 'Other solutions to Nash's bargaining problem', *Econometrica*, 43, 513–518

Kemp, M. (1984) 'A note on the theory of international transfers', *Economic Letters* 14, 259–262

Kreps, D. (1991) *A Course in Microeconomic Theory*, Princeton, Princeton University Press

McElroy, M.B. (1990) 'The empirical content of Nash-bargained household behaviour', *Journal of Human Resources*, 25, 559–583

McElroy, M.B. and M.J. Horney (1980) 'Nash-bargained household decisions: towards a generalization of the theory of demand', *International Economic Review*, 22, 333–349

Manser, M. and M. Brown (1980) 'Marriage and household decision-making: a bargaining analysis', *International Economic Review*, 21, 31–44

Mnookin, R. and L. Kornhauser (1979) 'Bargaining in the shadow of the law', *Yale Law Journal*, 88, 950–997

Mnookin, R.H., E. Maccoby, C.R. Albiston and C. Depne (1990) 'Private ordering revisited: which custodial arrangements are parents negotiating?', in S. Sugarman and H. Kaye (eds.), *Divorce Reform at a Crossroad*, New Haven, Yale University Press

Moulin, H. (1988) *Axioms of Cooperative Decisions Making*, Econometric Society Monograph, 15, Cambridge, Cambridge University Press

Nash, J.F. (1950) 'The bargaining problem', *Econometrica*, 28, 155–162

O'Neill, J. (1985) 'Determinants of child support', *Urban Institute Report*, Washington DC

Pearson, J. and N. Thoennes (1988) 'Supporting children after divorce: the influence of custody and support levels and payments', *Family Law Quarterly*, 22, 319–339

Peters, H., L. Argys, E. Maccoby and R. Mnookin (1991) 'Changes in child support payments after divorce: compliance and modifications' (March), mimeo

Radner, R. (1985) 'Repeated partnership games with imperfect monitoring and no discounting', *Review of Economic Studies*, 53, 43–58

Roth, A. (1979) *Axiomatic Models of Bargaining*, Berlin, Springer Verlag

Selzer, J. (1990) 'Legal and physical custody in recent divorces', *Social Science Quarterly*, 71, 250–266

   (1991) 'Legal custody arrangements and the intergenerational transmission of economic welfare', *American Journal of Sociology*, 96, 895–929

Selzer, J., N. Schaeffer and H. Chang (1989) 'Family ties after divorce: the relationship between visiting and paying child support', *Journal of Marriage and the Family*, 51, 1013–1031

Sonestein, F. and C. Calhoun (1990) 'Determinants of child support: a pilot survey of absent parents', *Contemporary Policy Issues*, 8, 75–94

US Bureau of the Census (1990) Current Population Reports, *Poverty in the US*, Series P–23, no. 167

Warr, P. (1983) 'The private provision of a public good is independent of the distribution of income', *Economics Letters*, 13, 207–211

Weiss, Y. and R. Willis (1985) 'Children as collective goods in divorce settlements', *Journal of Labor Economics*, 3, 268–292

(1989) 'An economic analysis of divorce settlements', Economic Research Center/NORC, University of Chicago, *Working Paper*, 89–5 (April)

(1990) 'Transfers among divorced couples: evidence and interpretation', Economic Research Center/NORC, University of Chicago, *Working Paper*, 90–4 (April)

Weitzman, L. (1985) *The Divorce Revolution: The Unexpected Social and Economic Consequences for Women and Children in America*, New York, Free Press

6 Female labour supply, housework and family welfare

PATRICIA APPS

Introduction

The use of observed income and expenditure variables as measures of welfare has a long tradition in studies of taxation and inequality. An objection to the practice is that the variables omit the contribution of nonmarket time. With the increasing availability of household datasets attention has focused on the estimation of labour supply models for the purpose of making welfare comparisons based on a utility function defined on consumption and leisure, with leisure measured as nonmarket time. The approach has been used extensively for analysing reforms to the taxation of married couples. Examples include Arrufat and Zabalza (1986), Blundell *et al.* (1986, 1988), Zabalza and Arrufat (1988) and Symons and Walker (1990). An obvious criticism of the approach is that the nonmarket activities of married women do not easily fit the conventional notion of 'leisure'. Much of their time is spent on housework, producing goods and services for which there are substitutes in the market place, and so it may be more appropriate to treat domestic activity in the same way as market activity, as suggested by Becker (1965).

A long-standing and central concern in the taxation of families is that of horizontal equity in the treatment of those with different time allocations to household production and market work. Conflicting interpretations of what the criterion implies for policy typically reflect different weightings on household production in the calculation of the welfare indicator used to assess the distributional merits of a particular reform. The traditional objection to household income as a welfare indicator in this context is that it implies a zero weighting of the benefits of nonmarket work, and therefore understates the relative welfare position of families in which a spouse, typically the wife, specialises in home work. An evaluation of the distributional effects of tax changes with reference to the pre-reform ordering of families by household income can therefore be expected to generate results which overstate the equity merits of reforms disadvantaging employed married women.[1] As Pechman (1977) explains, the equity argument for selectively taxing the earnings of married women at higher rates, by basing taxes on household income rather than on individual incomes, depends on the view that the work of married women at home does not contribute to family welfare.[2] The question this study seeks to answer is whether an analysis based on a labour supply model which treats the nonmarket work of married women as leisure represents a significant departure from this view.

The tax reform studies cited above employ models estimated on the market hours of wives, with husbands' hours treated as fixed. Because of wide variation in the market hours of married women with similar economic and demographic characteristics, models estimated on data for market work inevitably yield large discrepancies between observed and predicted hours which cannot be attributed plausibly to optimisation errors or to errors in the observation of hours. Moreover, because the discrepancies are so large, the use of predictions can lead to entirely fictitious results when the analysis is concerned with reforms to the selective taxation of married women as second earners. In the face of these difficulties, the approach widely adopted is to allow diversity in preferences with demographic characteristics and to attribute the residual variance to random preferences, by introducing an error term in the utility function which ensures that pre-reform predicted hours correspond to observed hours.

While the identification problem which arises when tastes vary is well recognised (Pollak and Wales, 1979; Deaton and Muellbauer, 1980b), it is nevertheless an accepted practice to report results for a pre-reform ordering of families by a welfare measure derived from the conditional cost function of a heterogeneous preference model. It is therefore of interest to investigate the sensitivity of such orderings to the treatment of nonmarket time. Of particular concern is the role of the error term and of demographics entering the specified utility function. The data indicate that married women who work fewer market hours typically allocate more time to work at home, and so much of the preference heterogeneity captured by the error term may be generated by the omission of housework. If measures of family welfare are sensitive to the error term, orderings defined on the measures may be no more than an artefact of the treatment of housework as leisure. A second concern is that the leisure assumption of the model can have perverse effects on demographic coefficients. Models estimated on market hours typically yield negative coefficients on variables indicating the presence of young children. However this result may reflect a greater overall burden of work on families with young children. Wives may work fewer hours in the market place because, under existing institutional arrangements and social custom,[3] they must work longer hours at home. Estimation of the models on hours data which include work at home may therefore yield positive coefficients on the same variables.

The strategy adopted to investigate these issues is to estimate two labour supply models for married women, the first with the dependent hours variable measured as market hours and the second with the dependent hours variable calculated as the sum of market and housework hours. The models are estimated on data for a sample of relatively homogeneous families with an employed husband. The functional form selected for estimation is that of the 'Almost Ideal Demand System' (Deaton and Muellbauer, 1980a). The present chapter compares the orderings of families generated by the equivalent incomes of the estimated systems with a ranking by net household income. The results show that a model which treats time at home as leisure can, under certain conditions, generate an equivalent income ordering which approximates one defined on household income. When housework is introduced, the ordering approaches rankings defined on measures of income adjusted for an imputed value of housework or calculated on the basis of a given number of market hours of work by the wife. The findings suggest that the concept of leisure underlying a conventional labour supply model is too specialised for analysing welfare and policy issues concerning the family.

The second section of the chapter sets out the specification of the models. The third section describes the unit record files and criteria used for selecting the data sample for the study. The fourth section reports the parameter estimates for each demand system. The comparative analysis of family orderings defined on equivalent incomes generated by the systems and on selected household income variables is presented in the fifth section. The sixth section draws concluding comments.

Specification of the estimated labour supply models

The two labour supply systems estimated for married women are reported as Model 1 and Model 2. Model 1 is a conventional system with the dependent hours variable measured as wife's market hours of work. In Model 2, the dependent hours variable is calculated as the sum of wife's hours of market work and housework. The two systems can be seen as special cases of the more general household model in which husband's behaviour is assumed to be exogenous. The family maximises a utility function, assumed to be twice-differentiable and strictly quasi-concave, of the form

$$U = U(x^m, x^d, l) \tag{1}$$

where x^m represents market consumption, x^d is domestic consumption and l is wife's leisure. Constraints on the family's utility-maximisation problem are

$$x^m = wh_m + M \tag{2}$$

$$x^d = f(h_d) \tag{3}$$

where w is the wife's net wage, h_m is her hours of market work and h_d her hours of domestic work and $f(.)$ is a household production function, assumed to be strictly increasing, twice-differentiable and concave. M is virtual income calculated as the level of net household income, including husbands' income, corresponding to the intercept of the linearised budget constraint. The time constraint is

$$T = l + h_m + h_d \tag{4}$$

where T is total time available.

Model 1 sets $h_d = x^d = 0$. In Model 2 market and domestic output are treated as perfect substitutes as in Gronau (1977). The utility function takes the form

$$U = U(x^m + x^d, l) \tag{5}$$

where $x^d = wh_d$.

The essential difference between the two systems is that Model 1 assumes that all nonmarket time is leisure, an identical 'commodity' across households with a price varying with the net wage, whereas Model 2 allows the marginal product of time allocated to housework to vary with the net wage, holding the price of domestic output constant. By treating housework in the same way as market work, Model 2 implies that the productivity of time is perfectly correlated with the wage rate in domestic production as well as in market production, an equilibrium which can be attributed to the mechanism of a perfectly competitive labour market across both spheres of production. While Model 2 obviously employs strong assumptions on domestic production, those of Model 1 are no less specialised. For example, objections to the specification of a model yielding a constant price for output could be made in the context of both models (there are cases where market goods prices can be observed to differ across households and we would expect the price of domestic goods to vary, although not necessarily with the net wage). Ideally, as in Becker (1965), we require a model which discards the concepts of leisure by specifying production functions for all household activities with inputs of

goods and labour of varying productivities.[4] The informational requirement of such a model would, however, be prohibitive. In particular, the
estimation of the system would require data on domestic output levels, as
well as information on time and goods inputs.

If we let $x = x^m + x^d$ and $h = h_m + h_d$, the direct utility function for
both models can be written as

$$U = U(x, l) \tag{6}$$

and the pooled household budget as

$$x + wl = Y = wT + M \tag{7}$$

where Y is household full income and the price of x as numeraire is set to
one.

Selecting the 'Almost Ideal Demand System' for estimation, the cost
function can be specified as

$$\ln C(w, Y; z, e) = \ln A(w; z, e) + V(w, Y; z, e) B(w) \tag{8}$$

where z is a vector of demographic characteristics and e is the error term
capturing preference heterogeneity. $V(.)$ is the indirect utility function
given by

$$V(w, Y; z, e) = \ln(Y/A(w; z, e))/B(w). \tag{9}$$

The price indices $A(.)$ and $B(.)$ take the form

$$\ln A(w; z, e) = a_0 + a_l(z, e)\ln w + 0.5\gamma_{ll}\ln^2 w \tag{10a}$$

$$B(w) = w^{\beta_l} \tag{10b}$$

where a_0, a_l, γ_{ll}, β_l are parameters of the system.

The demands for leisure and consumption in share form are given by

$$S_i = a_i(z, e) + \gamma_{ii}\ln w + \beta_i\ln(Y/A(w; z, e)) \tag{11}$$

for $i = l$, x. The leisure share is calculated as $S_l = wl/Y$ and the consumption share as $S_x = x/Y$. Adding up requires $\Sigma_i a_i = 1$, $\Sigma_i \gamma_{ij} = 0$ and
$\Sigma_i \beta_i = 0$. In addition we require: homogeneity, $\Sigma_j \gamma_{ij} = 0$; symmetry,
$\gamma_{ij} = \gamma_{ji}$; and concavity of the expenditure function which is satisfied if the
Slutsky matrix is negative semi-definite.

The specification of demographic variables in the system is deliberately
kept simple. Household size and three dummy variables for age of
youngest child are entered with the error term in the leisure share intercept as

$$a_i(z, e) = a_i^0 + a_i^1 D^1 + a_i^2 D^2 + a_i^3 D^3 + a_i^4 \ln N + e_i \tag{12}$$

for $i = l$, x. D^1, D^2 and D^3 are dummy variables which take the value of one if the age of the youngest child is 0–2, 3–4, and 5–9 years, respectively. N is the number of dependent children in the family.[5]

Equivalent income, Ye, is calculated as

$$Ye = \exp((B^r(w^r)/B(w))(\ln(Y/A(w;z,e)) + \ln A^r(w^r;z^r,e^r)) \tag{13}$$

where $B^r(.)$ and $A^r(.)$ are reference price indices defined on a reference wage rate and reference demographics and error term. Orderings of families by equivalent income derived from each model are compared with rankings defined on net household income, on an income variable adjusted for an imputed value of housework and on potential net income, calculated as the income the family would earn if all wives worked the same number of hours.

The problem of identifying unconditional preferences when demographic profiles differ has been given considerable attention in the literature on family welfare measurement and equivalence scales. As Pollak and Wales (1979) explain, welfare comparisons based on a demand system employing a utility function of the form $v(.;z)$ for example are conditional upon z. Comparisons across families that vary with respect to z imply specialised assumptions because family welfare depends not only on consumption and leisure, but also on how parents feel about children.[6] In addition to demographic differences, the utility function $V(.)$ in (9) includes stochastic variation. While recognising the difficulties associated with interfamily welfare comparisons when tastes vary, it is worth investigating family orderings defined on measures derived from the utility function $V(.)$ in order to assess the extent to which preference heterogeneity, and its impact on the ordering, is an artefact of the work–leisure assumptions of the model.

Of central concern is the role of z and e in a utility function of the form $V(.;z,e)$. In the model above these terms enter the index $A(.)$, weighting full income for preference diversity for leisure as well as for variation in the price of leisure. The model implies that if the ratio of the wage to the price of the market good is greater than one, equivalent income is lower for those with a stronger preference for leisure because they are effectively constrained to purchasing more of the higher priced good. The estimation of Model 1 on data for households facing a wage/price ratio greater than one can therefore be expected to generate an equivalent income ordering in which families with a greater commitment to market work are ranked, *ceteris paribus*, systematically above those who work fewer market hours. The empirical analysis illustrates this result and its sensitivity to the treatment of housework.

Sample selection and the construction of the housework variable

The data for the study are drawn from two unit record files, the ABS 1985/6 Income Distribution Survey Sample file and the 1987 ABS Time Use Pilot Survey file (see ABS, 1988). The two surveys provide detailed information on the same demographic and personal characteristics of family members and on market hours of work. The 1987 ABS file includes data on hours of housework but does not separate earnings from nonlabour income and so does not permit the calculation of hourly earnings as a measure of the gross wage. The ABS 1985/6 file reports earnings separately from nonlabour income but does not record hours of housework. The latter file also provides information for a much larger sample of families. For these reasons the study employs data for a sample of families selected from the ABS 1985/6 file, with information on hours of housework for each record generated by a regression model estimated on a sample of married women from similar families drawn from the 1987 ABS file.

The ABS 1985/6 file contains records for persons and income units. An income unit is defined to contain either one nondependent 'head' or two nondependent persons forming a couple with the male partner classified as 'head' and the female partner as 'spouse'. Dependents are defined as unmarried persons living with their parent(s) and either under 15 years of age or full-time students aged 15 to 20 years. The sample comprises 10,815 income unit records in complete households. Of these, 4,522 represent 'couple' income units. The sample of families for the study is selected from the couple income unit records on the following criteria:

1 Head and spouse (if employed) earning labour income only (excludes couples with earnings from partnerships, own business or farms); no. of records: 3,795.
2 Head aged 20 to 64 years; no. of records: 3,240.
3 Presence of dependents under 15 years; no. of records: 1,647.
4 Head working 500 hours or more p.a., with a gross wage exceeding $3.00; no. of records: 1,483.
5 Head and spouse with consistent hours and earnings data; no. of records: 1,447.

The measure of the gross wage used for participants is gross hourly earnings, calculated from market hours and earnings. Wage rates for nonparticipants are constructed from a female wage equation estimated on data for a sample of 586 participants employed for 500 hours or more p.a. The lower bound of 500 hours is chosen in order to reduce measurement error in gross hourly earnings arising from limitations of the data

for those working fewer hours.[7] In the estimation of the wage equation
the Heckman procedure is applied to correct for sample selection bias,
explaining whether a wife works 500 hours or more in terms of specified
market and reservation wage variables.

The 1987 ABS file contains records for 1,611 persons (respondents) and
activity episodes (up to 72 records per diary day, depending on the
number of activities reported). The activity records report time allocations to labour force activities and to household activities including
housework, education and active and passive leisure activities. Hours of
housework are calculated as the sum of hours allocated to the housework
activities in the categories: 'domestic', 'child care/minding' and 'purchasing goods and services'.[8]

An hours of housework equation is estimated on data for a sample of
222 married women with dependants under 15 years. The equation is
specified as the following linear function of variables for which information is available in both data files:

$$h_d = a_0 + a_1 D^1 + a_2 D^2 + a_3 \ln N + a_4 \ln A$$
$$+ a_5 E^1 + a_6 E^2 + a_7 E^3 + a_8 E^4 + a_9 h_m + a_{10} P + v \qquad (14)$$

where h_d is hours of housework per week, D^1 and D^2 are dummy variables
for the presence of the youngest child aged 0–4 and 5–9 years, N is
number of dependent children, A is age, and E^1 to E^4 represent dummies
for highest educational qualifications in the categories: completed highest
level of secondary school available, no qualifications since school; post-
school trade or apprenticeship; post-school certificate or diploma; Bach-
elor degree or higher. The number of hours of market work per week, h_m,
is included as an independent variable because it is fundamental in
explaining domestic hours of work: women who work longer hours in the
market place typically work fewer hours at home. Demographic characteristics explain relatively little of the observed variation in market
hours.[9] If actual market hours are assumed to be endogenous and
replaced by an instrument estimated on demographic and personal characteristics, the system will generate the discrepancies between observed
and predicted hours characteristic of a conventional model of the labour
supply of married women. To avoid this problem market hours must be
treated as exogenous. An employment status dummy, P, which takes the
value of one for participation in market employment and zero for non-
participation, is also included as a regressor. The random error is denoted
by v.

The estimated parameters are presented in table 6.1. As expected, the
most significant variable is hours of market work. Time allocated to
housework falls by 0.58 of an hour for every extra hour a wife works in

Table 6.1. *Hours of housework*

Parameter	Estimate (St. error)
a_0	43.819
	(25.154)
a_1 (D^1)	4.3234
	(3.6085)
a_2 (D^2)	-2.1062
	(3.4780)
a_3 ($\ln N$)	6.7711
	(2.5722)
a_4 ($\ln A$)	1.9974
	(7.1045)
a_5 (E^1)	-1.1413
	(4.5246)
a_6 (E^2)	2.7570
	(6.4052)
a_7 (E^3)	5.6518
	(2.4307)
a_8 (E^4)	4.0390
	(3.8097)
a_9 (h_m)	-0.5863
	(0.1232)
a_{10} (P)	-3.5607
	(3.3720)
R^2	0.3712
no. of records:	222

the market place. Hours of housework rise significantly with the number of dependants. The dummy variables for the age categories of youngest child, 0–4 and 5–9 years, are not significant. Of post-school qualifications only the dummy variable for those in the category 'certificate or diploma' (E^3) has a positive and significant effect on hours of housework.

The labour supply systems are estimated on data for a subsample of 551 participants employed for 500 hours or more, selected on the additional criterion that the wife has net hourly earnings greater than \$3.00 and less than \$20.00. Net wage rates and virtual incomes are calculated by applying the 1985/6 marginal tax rate schedule and rebates to reported incomes. In the estimation of Model 2 the predicted hours of housework variable is treated as a generated regressor. The standard errors of the parameters are corrected for heteroskedasticity and the inclusion of a generated regressor using the methodology described in Arellano and Meghir (1992) adapted for a nonlinear system.

The means of the data for the full sample of 1,447 families are listed in table 6A.1 (Data Appendix, p. 159). Table 6A.1 also reports data means for the 586 families with a wife employed 500 hours or more p.a., and for the 861 families with a wife employed for less than 500 hours p.a. Family orderings defined on alternative measures of welfare and income are reported for these subsamples.

Parameter estimates

The results for the maximum likelihood estimation of the parameters of Models 1 and 2 are reported in table 6.2. Since each system has two equations and is constrained to satisfy the adding up restrictions, the composite good share equation can be omitted for estimation. Annual leisure hours are obtained by subtracting annual hours of work from time available, T, which is set to 5,840 hours (16 hours per day for 365 days). The intercept term, a_0, is set to 9.5 in each model.

In both models there will be bias in the parameter estimates due to the fact that with varying marginal tax rates the net wage and virtual income will depend on hours of market work. To help deal with this problem, a two-stage estimation procedure is employed in which the net wage is not used as its own instrument. In Models 1 and 2 the net wage is replaced by the predicted value from a regression equation of the log of the wage, estimated on logged and dummy variables for demographic character- istics, age left school, and for highest educational qualifications in the categories listed previously.[10]

The parameter estimates for the demand systems illustrate the effect of treating housework as leisure. The leisure share intercept, evaluated at demographic means, is 0.5102 for Model 1 and 0.3869 for Model 2. As expected, the presence of children in the youngest category, 0–2 years, is positive in Model 1 but negative in Model 2, and significant in both cases. The coefficients on the dummy for youngest child in the 3–4 age group is not significant in Model 1 but significant and negative in Model 2. These results are consistent with the observation that mothers of very young children tend to work fewer market hours but longer hours at home. Unfortunately Model 1 attributes their reduced commitment to market work to a greater preference for leisure, when in fact they are working longer hours overall, as indicated by Model 2. The coefficient on household size is not significant in Model 1 but negative and significant in Model 2, indicating that married women work longer total hours as

Table 6.2. *Parameter estimates*

Parameter	Model 1 estimate (St. error)	Model 2 estimate (St. error)
α_l^0	0.5020 (0.0440)	0.4107 (0.0432)
$\alpha_l^1(D^1)$	0.0131 (0.0042)	− 0.0291 (0.0083)
$\alpha_l^2(D^2)$	0.0035 (0.0054)	− 0.0218 (0.0101)
$\alpha_l^3(D^3)$	0.0036 (0.0042)	0.0053 (0.0042)
$\alpha_l^4(\ln N)$	0.0057 (0.0037)	− 0.0289 (0.0074)
β_l	− 0.3845 (0.0195)	− 0.2197 (0.0165)
γ_{ll}	0.0673 (0.0315)	0.0168 (0.0293)
σ^2	0.0034	0.0025
Log L	782.20	871.87
	no. of records: 551	

household size increases, again a result we would expect and missed by Model 1. These findings suggest that, in addition to the objections raised by Pollak and Wales (1979) to welfare comparisons between families with different demographic profiles, a conventional demand system may yield results which are no more than a reflection of the influence of institutional and social constraints on the work location of married women.

The coefficient on income is significant in both models and yields a mean income elasticity of demand for leisure of 0.1743 for Model 1 and of 0.1519 for Model 2, indicating that leisure is a strong necessity in both cases. The wage coefficient is significant and positive in Model 1, but not significant in Model 2. Evaluated at variable means, the parameters of the systems yield uncompensated and compensated wage elasticities of 0.7332 and 0.8149 for Model 1 and 0.3597 and 0.3992 for Model 2, respectively. The results for Model 1 are not inconsistent with previous estimates in the literature (see, Killingsworth, 1983).

Comparative analysis of family rankings

This section compares the ranking of families by annual net household income with orderings defined on equivalent incomes generated by the preceding models. Comparisons are also made with rankings by an income variable adjusted for an estimated value of housework and by potential net income, defined as the income the household would earn if the wife worked 30 hours per week in the market place.[11] Tables 6.3, 6.4 and 6.5 present quintile rankings of families, in ascending order, by annual net household income and by equivalent incomes derived from Models 1 and 2, respectively. Tables 6.6 and 6.7 report rankings by income adjusted for an imputed value of housework and by potential net income. The first row of the tables gives the mean net income of households in each quintile. The second and third rows report the percentage of households with a wife employed for 500 hours or more annually and full-time. The fourth and fifth rows show mean annual hours of market work and housework and the sixth records mean total annual hours of work. The seventh row gives the percentage of households in which the youngest child is aged 0–4 years and the eighth, the percentage of families with more than two dependent children. The two subsequent rows report the mean net wage rate for wives and mean full income per annum. Overall means and total percentages are shown in the final column of each table. Concavity violations are ignored because almost all records satisfy the required conditions for both models (over 99%).

As we would expect, the ranking by net household income in table 6.3 concentrates families with a wife employed in the market place in the upper quintiles. For example, 79.8% of families in quintile 5 represent couples with a wife employed for 500 or more hours annually, almost twice the overall figure of 40.5%, and 43.9% represent those with a wife employed full-time, over three times the overall figure of 13.9%. In contrast, quintile 1 contains only 6.2% of couples with a wife employed for 500 or more hours annually, and 1.0% of those with a wife employed full-time. Consistent with these figures, mean annual hours of market work rise from 87 in quintile 1 to 1,366 in quintile 5 while mean annual hours of housework fall from 2,761 in quintile 1 to 1,788 in quintile 5. Because of the inverse relationship between market hours and housework hours, the profile of total hours of work across quintiles is relatively flat, increasing from 2,848 in quintile 1 to 3,154 in quintile 5. Couples with young children and those with larger families (over two children) tend to predominate in the lower quintiles because, as suggested by the demographic coefficients of Model 1, wives in these families tend to spend more time at

Table 6.3. *Quintile ranking by annual net household income, $ p.a.*

Quintile	1	2	3	4	5	Overall
Mean h/income, $ p.a.	15,733	20,182	23,570	27,993	38,302	25,129
% wife emp ≥ 500 hours	6.2	17.2	35.5	64.1	79.8	40.5
% wife emp F/T	1.0	2.4	4.1	18.3	43.9	13.9
Mean market hours	87	214	440	868	1,366	593
Mean housework hours	2,761	2,651	2,530	2,077	1,788	2,362
Mean total hours	2,848	2,865	2,970	2,945	3,154	2,955
% youngest child 0–4	67.6	59.3	56.2	50.0	41.8	55.0
% 2 + child families	27.6	24.1	23.8	17.7	20.6	23.2
Mean net wage, $	7.79	7.30	7.07	6.79	6.71	7.13
Mean full income, $ p.a.	60,769	61,586	62,422	62,435	68,889	63,209

Table 6.4. *Model 1: Quintile ranking by equivalent income, $ p.a.*

Quintile	1	2	3	4	5	Overall
Mean h/income, $ p.a.	15,859	20,332	23,601	27,870	38,115	25,129
% wife emp ≥ 500 hours	5.9	10.7	38.3	65.9	82.2	40.5
% wife emp F/T	1.4	1.7	3.1	17.6	46.0	13.9
Mean market hours	84	146	434	894	1,416	593
Mean housework hours	2,749	2,740	2,517	2,028	1,769	2,362
Mean total hours	2,833	2,886	2,951	2,912	3,175	2,955
% youngest child 0–4	68.6	59.3	59.0	46.9	41.1	55.0
% 2 + child families	27.6	25.5	22.4	21.7	18.5	23.2
Mean net wage, $	7.90	7.47	7.05	6.68	6.54	7.13
Mean full income, $ p.a.	62,441	64,217	62,156	60,877	66,384	63,209

home. The mean net wage rate falls from $7.79 to $6.71 across quintiles, while mean full income increases only slightly, from $60,769 in quintile 1 to $68,889 in quintile 5. The profiles of these two variables reflect the effect of a progressive tax rate schedule. While estimates yield mean gross wage rates for nonparticipants which are close to those for participants, net wage rates for nonparticipants are typically higher because their taxable incomes place them in income bands attracting lower marginal tax rates.

The ranking by equivalent income in table 6.4, derived from Model 1, yields similar results. The percentage of families with a wife employed for 500 hours or more annually rises from 5.9% in quintile 1 to 82.2% in quintile 5, and for those with a wife employed full-time, from 1.4% to 46.0%. The quintile distributions of annual market hours and housework hours are also similar. Mean annual hours of market work increase from 84 in quintile 1 to 1,416 in quintile 5. Mean housework hours decline from 2,749 in quintile 1 to 1,769 in quintile 5. Again total hours of work form a relatively flat profile across quintiles. The distributions of demographic characteristics, of the mean net wage and mean full income also closely approximate those of the net household income ranking.

The concentration of families with a wife working fewer market hours in the lower quintiles of the net household income ranking reflects the effect of ordering families by a measure of income which omits the value of housework. The ranking by equivalent income calculated from Model 1 generates a similar result because the system treats the nonmarket time of married women as leisure, a homogeneous 'commodity' priced at the net wage, and attributes discrepancies between predicted and actual market hours to preference heterogeneity. Those who choose to work at home have, according to the model, an extreme preference for leisure, the higher price good. Consequently, their equivalent income, measured as the income required to obtain the level of utility at the reference wage rate and reference demographics and error term, is lower than that required by families in which the wife has a less extreme preference for leisure. Because household income depends on female earnings, it tends to be directly related to female hours of market work as indicated in table 6.3. As a result, equivalent incomes generated by Model 1 are directly related to household incomes. Demographic variables, while significant at the 95% level in the case of the dummy for a youngest child in the 0–2 year age category, have relatively little explanatory power, leaving a large role for the stochastic term in the model. The ranking is therefore driven largely by the error term in the utility function.

The ordering of households by equivalent income calculated for Model 2, shown in table 6.5, yields results which differ dramatically from those for the ranking by the equivalent income of Model 1 in table 6.4. Families in which the wife works 500 hours or more in the market place are distributed more uniformly across quintiles. The reordering of families caused by introducing housework in Model 2 reflects the effect of treating nonmarket work in the same way as market work. Because the dependent hours variable is defined on total hours of work, the error term is now inversely related to total hours: those with fewer total hours have a greater preference for leisure. While women who work fewer market

Table 6.5. *Model 2: Quintile ranking by equivalent income, $ p.a.*

Quintile	1	2	3	4	5	Overall
Mean h/income, $ p.a.	19,347	22,355	24,801	29,196	33,026	25,129
% wife emp ⩾ 500 hours	40.7	40.3	42.8	39.3	39.4	40.5
% wife emp F/T	8.3	10.7	17.6	15.2	17.8	13.9
Mean market hours	531	538	654	601	641	593
Mean housework hours	1,680	2,097	2,320	2,675	3,045	2,362
Mean total hours	2,211	2,645	2,947	3,276	3,686	2,957
% youngest child 0–4	40.7	55.5	53.8	58.3	66.9	55.0
% 2 + child families	21.4	22.1	19.3	23.4	29.6	23.2
Mean net wage, $	6.86	7.02	6.93	7.20	7.65	7.13
Mean full income, $ p.a.	56,469	60,237	61,521	64,557	73,365	63,209

hours typically work longer hours at home as indicated in tables 6.3 and 6.4, overall they work slightly fewer total hours (mean annual total hours of work are 2,852 for wives employed for less than 500 market hours, and 3,107 for those with 500 market hours or more). Comparing table 6.5 with table 6.4 we find that mean market hours rise much less steeply across quintiles, from 531 in quintile 1 to 641 in quintile 5, and total hours increase more steeply, from 2,211 to 3,686 across the same quintiles. Because, in contrast to market hours, there is relatively little variation in total hours worked by wives with similar wage rates and full incomes, preference heterogeneity is relatively unimportant in Model 2 and so the error term has a reduced role in the utility function. Consequently equivalent income is more directly related to full income, as indicated by the steeper increase in mean full income, from $56,469 in quintile 1 to $73,365 in quintile 5.

The distribution of households by demographic characteristics in table 6.5 is also worth noting. Wives in larger families and those with young children, while working fewer market hours, work longer total hours and so they are more concentrated in the upper quintiles of table 6.5, in contrast to their stronger representation in the lower quintiles of table 6.4. This feature of the ranking is consistent with the change in the coefficients on these demographic characteristics across the demand systems.

Table 6.6 illustrates the effect of defining a ranking on a measure of household income adjusted for an imputed value of housework. In contrast to table 6.3, families with a wife employed for 500 hours or more annually are more strongly represented in the lower and middle quintiles.

Table 6.6. *Quintile ranking by household income plus an imputed value for housework, $ p.a.*

Quintile	1	2	3	4	5	Overall
Mean h/income, $ p.a.	19,884	22,910	24,670	26,941	31,303	25,129
% wife emp ⩾ 500 hours	45.2	43.4	44.1	39.0	30.7	40.5
% wife emp F/T	11.7	15.5	16.9	14.5	10.8	13.9
Mean market hours	624	645	634	602	460	593
Mean housework hours	1,838	2,149	2,327	2,498	3,005	2,362
Mean total hours	2,462	2,794	2,961	3,100	3,465	2,955
% youngest child 0–4	45.2	48.6	58.3	53.1	70.0	55.0
% 2 + child families	19.7	20.7	20.7	25.5	29.3	23.2
Mean net wage, $	5.06	6.06	6.96	7.70	9.11	7.13
Mean full income, $ p.a.	46,399	54,832	61,445	67,981	80,970	63,209

Comparing the change in the ranking of families which occurs from tables 6.4 to 6.5 with the change from tables 6.4 to 6.6, we find the reordering follows the same direction in both cases but is stronger in the latter case. In table 6.6 families in which the wife works longer market hours are distributed more strongly towards the lower and middle quintiles. The proportion of families in which the wife is employed for 500 hours or more annually, while relatively flat across quintiles in table 6.5, actually falls in table 6.6, from 45.2% to 30.7%. The mean net wage rises from $5.06 to $9.11 in table 6.6, while varying by less than a dollar in table 6.5. Mean full income increases more steeply, from $46,399 in quintile 1 to $80,970 in quintile 5. However, mean hours of total work rise less steeply in table 6.6. The explanation for these differences across the tables is that the income variable adjusted for housework is more strongly correlated with the net wage and full income, while the equivalent income of Model 2 is more highly correlated with total hours of work.

The stronger reordering of families with a wife working longer market hours towards the lower quintiles in table 6.6 is due to the endogeneity of the net wage under a progressive tax rate schedule. As already noted, while nonparticipants and participants have similar gross wage rates, the former tend to have higher net wage rates due to the tax system, and so an hour of their housework is valued at a higher price. The impact of the higher valuation of time for nonparticipants is partly offset by the fact that they work fewer total hours. However, the marginal tax rate effect tends to dominate. Tax rates have a similar impact on full incomes: those working fewer hours tend to have higher full incomes due to higher net wage rates. However, in the derivation of equivalent incomes from Model 2, the error term has the effect of reversing the impact of tax rates for nonparticipants: they work fewer total hours and their greater preference for leisure as the higher priced good is just sufficient to offset, on average, gains from higher net wages. This explains the relatively flat quintile distribution of families with a wife employed for less than 500 hours annually reported in table 6.5.

The equivalent income rankings in tables 6.4 and 6.5 illustrate the arbitrariness of family welfare measures which are sensitive to specialised assumptions on leisure, particularly in the context of policy issues concerning horizontal equity in the treatment of families with different hours of market work but identical earning capacities, nonlabour incomes and demographic characteristics. Table 6.6 illustrates the limitations of using a measure of household income adjusted for housework valued at the net wage when marginal tax rates vary.

The ranking of families by potential net income shown in table 6.7 is of interest in the context of the preceding results because it illustrates the implications of defining an ordering on an income variable calculated on the basis of a fixed number of market hours of work by married women. Not surprisingly, we find the ranking generates relatively flat profiles of mean actual market hours and housework hours, and of mean total hours. The proportion of wives in each quintile working full time varies by less than two percentage points, the minimum being 13.1 in quintile 2 and the maximum 14.5 in quintile 3. In contrast to hours of work, the mean net wage rises relatively sharply across quintiles, from $5.44 in quintile 1 to $8.23 in quintile 5. Mean full income also rises quite steeply, from $47,173 in quintile 1 to $78,761 in quintile 5. These figures suggest that the use of potential net income as a welfare indicator for the purpose of assessing the equity merits of family tax policies may yield results which are less dominated by the employment status of the wife and more sensitive to potential earning capacities and nonlabour incomes.[12]

Ideally, we require welfare indicators which take account of employment opportunities for married women and the impact of institutional constraints and of the long-standing social pressures which account for asymmetries in the employment behaviour of husbands and wives, and for gender wage differentials. In the absence of this kind of information, however, it would seem to be important to avoid the use of measures which can generate results overstating the case for policies likely to reinforce traditional constraints on the employment choices of married women.[13]

Table 6.7. *Quintile ranking by potential net income, $ p.a.*

Quintile	1	2	3	4	5	Overall
Mean h/income, $ p.a.	18,218	21,452	24,246	26,897	34,933	25,129
% wife emp ≥ 500 hours	38.6	39.7	41.4	43.4	39.4	40.5
% wife emp F/T	14.5	13.1	14.5	13.1	14.3	13.9
Mean market hours	590	557	613	607	600	593
Mean housework hours	2,381	2,364	2,402	2,307	3,357	2,362
Mean total hours	2,971	2,921	3,015	2,914	2,957	2,955
% youngest child 0–4	60.7	49.7	56.6	52.8	55.4	55.0
% 2 + child families	22.8	20.3	21.7	21.0	30.0	23.2
Mean net wage, $	5.44	6.47	7.14	7.60	8.23	7.13
Mean full income, $ p.a.	47,173	56,093	62,252	67,324	78,761	63,209

Conclusions

Models of female labour supply specifying heterogeneous preferences have been used extensively in the analysis of reforms to the taxation of families. The models treat the nonmarket time of married women as leisure, yet the available data indicate that those who spend more time at home typically spend much of that time on housework. This study has investigated the sensitivity of measures of family welfare to the assumption that housework by married women is leisure by contrasting family orderings by equivalent income derived from a conventional model of female labour supply and from a system which treats housework in the same way as market work. The orderings are matched with family rankings defined on net household income, net income adjusted for an imputed value of housework and potential net income.

   The analysis illustrates the specialised nature of 'leisure' in a conventional labour supply model, and suggests that the underlying assumptions of the model are not appropriate for analysing family welfare and policy issues which have long been recognised as central concerns in public finance. In particular, the study has shown that a labour supply model which treats the nonmarket time of married women as leisure does not provide an appropriate basis for analysing equity issues which arise in the tax treatment of families with varying degrees of specialisation in market versus nonmarket work. The analysis identifies the way in which a conventional system can lead to results which, in common with studies using household income as a family welfare indicator, overstate the distributional merits of policies disadvantaging employed married women. The models are also shown to be of questionable relevance to issues concerning the appropriate treatment of families with different demographic characteristics. The data indicate that larger families and those with young children typically spend longer total hours working in the market place and at home, but because they work fewer hours in the former location, the parameter estimates of a model which ignores work at home imply that they have a greater preference for leisure.

A significant implication of the analysis is that much of the preference heterogeneity captured by labour supply models employed in recent tax reform studies, and the consequent problems for interfamily welfare comparisons, may be generated largely by the concept of leisure on which the models are based. In addition the studies ignore the role of social conditions in generating behavioural differences by gender. Ideally we require an analysis of family welfare which treats each family member as an individual, including children,[14] and takes account of the effects of institutional constraints on their present and future incomes.

Data appendix

Table 6A.1. *Means of data (st. dev. in parentheses)*

Variable name	Full sample	Wife employed ≥ 500 hours	Wife employed < 500 hours
Wife:			
Gross wage, $	–	8.97	–
(gross hourly earnings)		(3.07)	
Non-labour income, $ p.a.	1,344	1,328	1,355
	(2,456)	(2,697)	(2,279)
Hours of market work p.a.	593	1,402	43
	(763)	(569)	(107)
Hours of housework p.a.	2,362	1,705	2,809
	(932)	(843)	(695)
Age	33.2	34.3	32.5
	(6.3)	(6.2)	(6.3)
E^1: completed highest level	0.12	0.11	0.12
of secondary school available	(0.32)	(0.31)	(0.33)
E^2: post-school trade	0.04	0.05	0.04
or apprenticeship	(0.20)	(0.21)	(0.20)
E^3: post-school certificate	0.27	0.32	0.25
or diploma	(0.45)	(0.47)	(0.43)
E^4: Bachelor degree or higher	0.07	0.10	0.04
	(0.25)	(0.30)	(0.20)
Husband:			
Gross wage, $	11.48	11.33	11.55
(Average hourly earnings)	(4.09)	(4.99)	(4.00)
Nonlabour income, $ p.a.	1,123	1,624	781
	(6,099)	(8,785)	(3,124)
Hours of market work p.a.	2,179	2,200	2,165
	(360)	(330)	(378)
Income unit:			
Household size	4.01	3.82	4.14
	(0.91)	(0.80)	(0.95)
Children aged 0–4 years	0.75	0.49	0.92
	(0.79)	(0.65)	(0.82)
Children aged 5–9 years	0.68	0.61	0.73
	(0.80)	(0.75)	(0.83)
Children aged 10–14 years	0.36	0.42	0.31
	(0.56)	(0.59)	(0.54)
No. of records	1,477	586	861

NOTES

The research for this chapter was supported by a grant from the Australian Research Council.

The chapter is a revised section of a longer paper which was first presented at the session on 'Tax Induced Distortions in Consumption and Labor Supply' of the American Economic Association Meetings, New York City (28–30 December 1988). I would like to thank Mark Killingsworth for his constructive comments as discussant of the paper at that conference. I am also indebted to Martin Ravallion for his detailed suggestions on all aspects of the study which have been most useful in revising the chapter. Thanks are also due to Ian Walker for extensive comments on revised versions of the chapter, and to Lorraine Dearden, Tony Hall, Glenn Jones, Ray Rees, and Elizabeth Savage for helpful comments.

1 For a study illustrating the distributional implications of basing taxes on household income, see Apps (1990).

2 Pechman (1977) suggest that the traditional horizontal equity argument in favour of basing taxes on household income, or the combined income of husband and wife, depends on two assumptions: first that husband and wife share their incomes equally and, second, that household income is directly related to family welfare or ability to pay. In discussing the debate he observes that the first, the premise of income sharing or pooling, is almost universally accepted; that differences of opinion centre on the second and arise primarily from opposing views on the contribution of domestic work to family welfare in households with a traditional division of labour. More recent studies recognise objections to the first assumption and take an individual decision making approach which does not necessarily imply intra-family equality. Examples include Manser and Brown (1980), McElroy and Horney (1981), Apps (1982), Apps and Jones (1988), Apps and Rees (1988), Chiappori (1988) and Apps and Savage (1989). The estimation of an individual decision model incorporating housework can be found in Apps (1991b).

The Pechman analysis ignores incentive effects. In contrast, Boskin and Sheshinski (1983) focus on incentive effects and find that individual taxation is superior to combined income taxation for reasons of efficiency. Interestingly, Boskin and Sheshinski ignore both of the intra-family and inter-family equity issues recognised by Pechman, by specifying a household decision model and assuming identical preferences.

3 For example, inadequate provision of pre-school child care, combined with social custom, may constrain women with very young children to longer hours of work at home and, in turn, to longer total hours.

4 A number of studies specify demand systems incorporating a household production function. Examples include Gronau (1977) and Blundell and Walker (1984). The studies are not directly concerned with the issues raised in the present analysis, the welfare implications of treating nonmarket time as a homogeneous commodity (or input to production) with a price varying with the net wage. Gronau does not comment on this problem. The Blundell and Walker analysis is conerned primarily with specifying children as an argument of the household utility function.

5 The ordering of families by equivalent income derived from the utility function in (9) was found to be robust to alternative and more complex specifications of demographic characteristics. For expositions of the different approaches to entering demographic effects, see Pollak and Wales (1981) and Lewbel (1985).

6 For further discussion, see Deaton and Muellbauer (1980b).

7 Earnings for Australian workers with a casual labour force attachment may include 'loadings' to compensate for the benefit of full-time employment, and so gross hourly earnings are likely to overstate the wage rates of those working very few hours.

8 The data file provides information on time allocations to the following:

(1) Domestic activities:
    Housework – Food and drink preparation, clean-up; Laundry, ironing and clothes care; Other housework.
    Other domestic activities – Gardening, lawn care and pool care; Pet/ animal care; Home maintenance, improvement and care; Household paperwork, bills, etc.; Providing transport for other household members.

(2) Child care/minding:
    Own children – Physical care and minding; Care for sick or disabled; Teaching, helping, reprimanding; Playing, reading to, talking to.
    Other children – Physical care and minding; Care for sick or disabled; Teaching, helping, reprimanding; Playing, reading to, talking to; Associated travel.

(3) Purchasing goods and services: Goods; Services; Associated travel.

9 Demographic variables are also weak in explaining the participation decision. The results for the participation equation estimated to correct for selection bias in the female wage equation indicate that while household size and the presence of young children are significant at the 95% level, they have relatively poor explanatory power. This is consistent with the data means reported in Table 6A.1 (p. 159) which suggest that there is little difference in the mean size of families in subsamples defined on whether the wife works 500 hours or more annually, and that while the majority of wives with young children work less than 500 hours annually, there is a large proportion working longer hours.

10 Detailed results are available from the author. For an analysis of the sensitivity of parameters to controlling for taxes by instrumenting the net wage, see Mroz (1987). Because the system is estimated on data for families in which the wife works 500 hours or more annually, the parameters may be subject to self-selection bias. The leisure share equations have been estimated without controlling for self-selection because the complexity of the system precludes the estimation of the inverse of Mill's ratio from the reduced form of a complete model, so that only an approximate, nonutility consistent correction is feasible (see Kooreman and Kapteyn, 1986).

11 The wage rate for a nonparticipant used to impute a value for housework and to calculate potential net income is the wife's predicted wage plus an error term drawn randomly from the vector of terms generated by the female wage equation.

12 Primary earner income is an alternative measure with similar properties. Rankings by primary earner income are investigated in Apps and Savage (1989).

13 The analysis of tax reforms of this kind in Apps (1991a) presents results for households ranked by potential net income for this reason.

14 The importance of developing an analysis of welfare which treats children as individuals in their own right has been emphasised by Pollak and Wales (1979). In the case of children, taking an approach which recognises the role of the family as a lending institution, and the implications of capital market constrains facing those in low income families, may lead to results supporting family allowances and income maintenance schemes for reasons of both efficiency and equity (see Apps, 1989).

REFERENCES

ABS (1988) *Information Paper: Time Use Pilot Survey*, Sydney (May–June 1987), Cat. no. 4113.1
Apps, P.F. (1982) 'Institutional inequality and tax incidence', *Journal of Public Economics*, 18, 217–242
   (1989) 'Welfare options under less progressive tax rates: an analysis of distributional effects for working families', *Australian Economic Review*, 4th Quarter, 52–65
   (1990) 'Tax transfer options: a critique of joint income and flat rate Proposals', in J.G. Head and R.E. Krever (eds.), *Flattening the Tax Rate Scale: Alternative Scenarios and Methodologies*, Melbourne, Longman, 211–235
   (1991a) 'Tax reform, population ageing and the changing labour supply of married women', *Journal of Population Economics*, 4, 201–216
   (1991b) 'Labour supply and welfare: some effects of neglecting housework and intra-family inequality', Working Papers in Economics and Econometrics, Research School of Social Sciences, Australian National University, Canberra, *Working Paper*, 240
, *Working Paper*Apps, P.F. and G.S. Jones (1988) 'Selective taxation of couples', *Zeitschrift für Nationalökonomie, Suppl.*, 5, 63–74
Apps, P.F. and R. Rees (1988) 'Taxation and the household', *Journal of Public Economics*, 39, 335–364
Apps, P.F. and E.J. Savage (1989) 'Labour supply, welfare rankings and the measurement of inequality', *Journal of Public Economics*, 29, 335–364
Arellano, M. and C. Meghir (1992) 'Female labour supply and on-the-job search: an empirical model estimated using complementary data sets,' *Review of Economic Studies*, 59, 537–557
Arrufat, J.L. and Z. Zabalza (1986) 'Female labor supply with taxation, random preferences, and optimization errors', *Econometrica*, 54, 47–63
Becker, G.S. (1965) 'A theory of the allocation of time', *Economic Journal*, 75, 493–517

Blundell, R.W. and I. Walker (1984) 'A household production specification of demographic variables in demand analysis', *Economic Journal*, 94, Suppl., 59–68

Blundell, R.W., C. Meghir, E. Symons and I. Walker (1986) 'A labour supply model for the simulation of tax and benefit reforms', in R.W. Blundell and I. Walker (eds.), *Unemployment, Search and Labour Supply*, Cambridge, Cambridge University Press

  (1988) 'Labour supply specification and the evaluation of tax reforms', *Journal of Public Economics*, 36, 23–52

Boskin, M.J. and E. Sheshinski (1983) 'Optimal tax treatment of the family: married couples', *Journal of Public Economics*, 20, 281–297

Chiappori, P.-A. (1988) 'Rational household labour supply', *Econometrica*, 56, 63–89

Deaton, A.S. and J. Muellbauer (1980a) 'An almost ideal demand system', *American Economic Review*, 70, 312–326

  (1980b) *Economics and Consumer Behaviour*, Cambridge, Cambridge University Press

Gronau, R. (1977) 'Leisure, home production, and work – the theory of the allocation of time revisited', *Journal of Political Economy*, 85, 1099–1123

Killingsworth, M. (1983) *Labour Supply*, Cambridge, Cambridge University Press

Kooreman, P. and A. Kapteyn (1986) 'Estimation of rationed and unrationed household labour supply functions using flexible functional forms', *Economic Journal*, 96, 398–412

Lewbel, A. (1985) 'A unified approach to incorporating demographic or other effects into demand systems', *Review of Economic Studies*, 52, 1–18

McElroy, M.B. and M.J. Horney (1981) 'Nash-bargained household decisions: towards a generalization of the theory of demand', *International Economic Review*, 22, 333–349

Manser, M. and M. Brown (1980) 'Marriage and household decision-making: a bargaining analysis', *International Economic Review*, 21, 31–44

Mroz, T.A. (1987) 'The sensitivity of an empirical model of married women's hours of work to economic and statistical assumptions', *Econometrica*, 55, 765–799

Pechman, J.A. (1977) *Federal Tax Policy*, Washington, DC, The Brookings Institution

Pollak, R.A. and T.J. Wales (1979) 'Welfare comparisons and equivalence scales', *American Economic Review*, 69, 216–221

  (1981) 'Demographic variables in demand analysis', *Econometrica*, 49, 1533–1551

Symons, E. and I. Walker (1990) 'Tax reform analysis; the effects of proportional tax system', in J.G. Head and R.E. Krever (eds), *Flattening the Tax Rate Scale: Alternative Scenarios and Methodologies*, Melbourne, Longman, 251–265

Zabalza, Z. and J.L. Arrufat (1988) 'Efficiency and equity effects of reforming the british system of direct taxation: a utility-based simulation methodology', *Economica*, 55, 21–45

7 Engel equivalence scales in Sri Lanka: exactness, specification, measurement error

MAMTA MURTHI

Introduction

Equivalence scales – index numbers that attempt to measure the cost to a household of a change in its composition – are of considerable importance in the study of poverty and distribution and in the formulation of government policy. Yet there appears to be no consensus on what model of equivalence scales is the most appropriate, or whether, if at all, comparisons of household welfare can be based on household expenditure data. The reader is referred to Coulter, Cowell and Jenkins (1991) and Browning (1991) for recent surveys of the literature.

The model of equivalence scales usually attributed to Engel (1857) is perhaps the simplest and most easy to compute. It relies on the use of the share of food, sometimes broadly interpreted to include other necessities, as an indicator of household welfare. The equivalence scale is simply the ratio of expenditures that imply equal levels of the budget share of food for households of different demographic compositions. In general, it is impossible *to test* the assumption used to identify household welfare from household behaviour; it is only possible to test the implications for household demand of an identifying assumption. This makes rejections conclusive, but not acceptances.

The restriction on household demand implied by the Engel model have been explicitly spelled out by Deaton (1981) and, more recently, Browning (1988) and Blackorby and Donaldson (1988). In the absence of information on price variation it is not possible in this chapter to test these restrictions explicitly. Instead, the chapter addresses some practical issues which are of relevance because of the wide use of the method.

The size of the estimated equivalence scales will, in general, depend on the level of food share at which the comparison of household expenditures is made or, equivalently, the level of expenditure of the reference household. If the equivalence scale is independent of expendi-

164

ture then the same scale can be used for *all* comparisons with the reference household irrespective of the level of expenditure or welfare the comparison pertains to. For this reason expenditure independence or *equivalence scale exactness* (Blackorby and Donaldson, 1988; Lewbel, 1989) is an attractive property. In general, exactness implies testable restrictions on the pattern of demand across household types. The second section tests the restrictions implied by the exactness of Engel scales in the context of different parametric forms of the Engel curve. The chapter then proceeds to examine various propositions about the nature of the estimated exact equivalence scales. The third section considers whether the estimates are sensitive to the parametric form of the Engel curve, while the fourth section examines their robustness to the generalisation of the equation for food share. The effect of measurement error on the findings of the earlier sections is assessed in the fifth section while the sixth section draws some conclusions.

Exactness of Engel equivalence scales

Proposed tests

Engel equivalence scales can be determined from estimates of the Engel curve for food. The equivalence scale, M, is given by the ratio of expenditures that implies equal levels of the budget share of food for households of different types. If the scales are independent of household expenditure, the model can be expressed as:

$$w_f = f(X/M) \qquad (1)$$

where w_f is the expected budget share of food, X is total expenditure and $M = g(z)$, the household equivalence scale, is a function only of the demographic characteristics of the household.[1] The exactness of M implies restrictions on Engel curves across household types.

If expenditure shares are of the Working–Leser form (see Working, 1943; Leser, 1963) then equation (1) implies that for each household type i,

$$w_{fi} = a_1 + \beta_1 \ln(X_i/M_i)$$

$$= a_1 + a_{1i} + \beta_1 \ln(X_i) \qquad (2)$$

where $a_{1i} = -\beta_1 \ln(M_i)$. Exactness, in the context of the Working–Leser parametric form, thus implies that the coefficient on the logarithm of expenditure, β_1, is the same for all household types. This can be tested for the data on hand (described below) by estimating the unpooled regression:

$$w_{fi} = a_1 + \sum_{i=1}^{8} a_{1i} D_i + \left(\beta_1 + \sum_{i=1}^{8} \beta_{1i} D_i\right) \ln(X_i) \tag{3}$$

where the D_is are dummies for the eight houshold types other than the reference household, and examining the hypothesis that $\beta_{1i} = 0$ for all i (R0). A rejection of (R0) implies that exactness is not borne out in the context of this parametric form of the Engel curve.

Consider now the augmented Working–Leser form which includes the square of the log of expenditure as an explanatory variable (Deaton, 1981; Gorman, 1981). Exactness of M implies that for each family type i:

$$w_{fi} = a_2 + \beta_2 \ln(X_i/M_i) + \gamma_2 [\ln(X_i/M_i)]^2$$

which on rewriting becomes,

$$w_{fi} = a_2 + a_{2i} + (\beta_2 + \beta_{2i}) \ln(X_i) + \gamma_2 [\ln(X_i)]^2 \tag{4}$$

where $a_{2i} = -\beta_2 \ln(M_i) + \gamma_2 [\ln(M_i)]^2$, and $\beta_{2i} = -2\gamma_2 \ln(M_i)$.

One implication is that the coefficient on the square of the logarithm of expenditure is the same for all family types. If γ_{2i} measures the deviation of the coefficient on the square of the log of expenditure in household type i from the coefficient for the reference household type, then exactness implies the restriction that $\gamma_{2i} = 0$ for all i (R1). Also,

$$\beta_{2i} = -2\gamma_2 \ln(M_i) \Rightarrow \ln(M_i) = -\beta_{2i}/2\gamma_2,$$

which on substitution into a_{2i}, yields the restriction (R2):

$$a_{2i} = \frac{\beta_{2i}(\beta_{2i} + 2\beta_2)}{4\gamma_2}$$

for all i (R2). (R2) is a set of nonlinear restrictions which may be imposed as they stand. However, a simpler way of testing (R1) and (R2) is by comparing twice the log-likelihood of the unpooled regression:

$$w_{fi} = a_2 + \sum_{i=1}^{8} a_{2i} D_i + \left(\beta_2 + \sum_{i=1}^{8} \beta_{2i} D_i\right) \ln(X_i) + \left(\gamma_2 + \sum_{i=1}^{8} \gamma_{2i} D_i\right) \ln(X_i)^2, \tag{5}$$

with the regression:

$$w_{fi} = a_2 + \beta_2 [\ln(X_i) - \ln(M_i)] + \gamma_2 [\ln(X_i) - \ln(M_i)]^2 \tag{6}$$

where $M_i = 1 + \sum_{i=1}^{8} \mu_i D_i$.

The D_is are the usual dummies for family types. It should be clear that (6) is obtained by imposing the restrictions (R1) and (R2) on (5). The difference in twice the log-likelihoods, the likelihood ratio test statistic, is distributed as a chi-squared with 16 degrees of freedom. (The degrees of freedom equals the number of restrictions imposed. There are 16 restrictions, eight from (R1) and an equal number from (R2).)

A third parametric form of the Engel curve is a logistic function of log expenditure. For each household type i:

$$w_{fi} = a_3 \left(1 - \frac{1}{1 + \delta_3 e^{-\gamma_3 \ln(X_i)}}\right), \quad a_3, \gamma_3, \delta_3 > 0. \tag{7}$$

From dw_{fi}/dX, which is less than zero for all X, it follows that food share varies monotonically with expenditure. It approaches an upper limt of a_3 as expenditure falls to zero and falls asymptotically to zero as expenditure tends to infinity. In this sense the function is a natural choice for a share Engel curve. If $w_{fi} = f(X_i/M_i)$, then

$$w_{fi} = a_3 \left(1 - \frac{1}{1 + \delta_3 e^{-\gamma_3 \ln(X_i) - \ln(M_i)}}\right)$$

$$\Rightarrow w_{fi} = a_3 \left(1 - \frac{1}{1 + \delta_3 e^{\gamma_3 \ln(M_i)} e^{-\gamma_3 \ln(X_i)}}\right). \tag{8}$$

The restrictions implied by exactness are that a_3 and γ_3 are the same for all i, a total of 16 restrictions on the unpooled regression:

$$w_{fi} = \left(a_3 + \sum_{i=1}^{8} a_{3i} D_i\right)\left(1 - \frac{1}{1 + \left(\delta_3 + \sum_{i=1}^{8} \delta_{3i} D_i\right) e^{\left(-\gamma_3 - \sum_{i=1}^{8} \gamma_{3i} D_i\right)(\ln(X_i))}}\right). \tag{9}$$

These may be tested by comparing twice the log-likelihood of (9) with that of:

$$w_{fi} = a_3 \left(1 - \frac{1}{1 + \left(\delta_3 + \sum_{i=1}^{8} \delta_{3i} D_i\right) e^{-\gamma_3 \ln(X_i)}}\right). \tag{10}$$

The test statistic is distributed as a chi-squared with 16 degrees of freedom.

The logistic parametric form can be augmented so that:

$$w_{fi} = a_4 \left(1 - \frac{1}{1 + \delta_4 e^{-\gamma_4 \ln(X_i)}}\right) - \frac{\theta_4}{X_i}.$$

The additional term $(-\theta_4/X_i)$ tends to zero as X_i becomes very large and tends to minus infinity as X_i tends to zero. Its inclusion allows the relation between food share and expenditure, which is otherwise inverse, to be nonnegative at the lower end of the distribution of expenditure.[2] The exactness of Engel equivalence scales in the context of this functional form implies that:

$$w_{fi} = a_4 \left(1 - \frac{1}{1 + \delta_4\, e^{-\gamma_4(\ln(X_i) - \ln(M_i))}}\right) - \frac{\theta_4 M_i}{X_i}.$$

$$\Rightarrow w_{fi} = a_4 \left(1 - \frac{1}{1 + \delta_4\, e^{-\gamma_4 \ln(X_i)}\, e^{\gamma_4 \ln(M_i)}}\right) - \frac{\theta_4 M_i}{X_i}.$$

for all i. The implied restrictions are more complex than in the cases considered previously, but the reader may verify that these restrictions can be tested by comparing twice the log-likelihood of:

$$w_{fi} = \left(a_4 + \sum_{i=1}^{8} a_{4i} D_i\right)\left(1 - \frac{1}{1 + \left(\delta_4 + \sum_{i=1}^{8} \delta_{4i} D_i\right) e^{\left(-\gamma_4 - \sum_{i=1}^{8} \gamma_{4i} D_i\right)(\ln(X_i))}}\right)$$

$$- \frac{\theta_4 + \sum_{i=1}^{8} \theta_{4i} D_i}{X_i} \tag{11}$$

with:

$$w_{fi} = a_4 \left(1 - \frac{1}{1 + \delta_4\, e^{-\gamma_4(\ln(X_i) - \ln(M_i))}}\right) - \frac{\theta_4 M_i}{X_i} \tag{12}$$

where $M_i = 1 + \sum_{i=1}^{8} \mu_i D_i$.

The likelihood-ratio test statistic is distributed as a chi-squared with 24 degrees of freedom. (The degrees of freedom can be determined from the reduction in the number of dimensions in the parameter space that results from imposing the restrictions. This is $36 - 12 = 24$.)

Results

The exactness of M was tested in the context of different forms of the Engel curve for food using data from a Sri Lankan household expenditure survey. The data are described in greater detail in the Appendix (pp. 183–187).

Each equation was estimated using the principle of least squares making standard assumptions about the distribution of the error terms. A two-adult household was used as the reference. The restrictions implied by the exactness of M are tested in table 7.1.

In the case of the Working–Leser model (WL), equation (3), a hetero-skedasticity-consistent Wald test of the restrictions was performed.[3] The test statistic, distributed as a chi-squared with eight degrees of freedom, is less than the 99% critical value. Exactness is thus not rejected in the context of this parametric form.

Table 7.1. *Tests of Exactness*

Equation	DF	Test statistic	Critical T_1 value at 1%
(1.1) Working–Leser (WL)	8	9.86*	20.09
(2.1) Augmented Working–Leser (AWL)	16	58.63$	32.00
(3.1) Logistic (L)	16	24.04$	32.00
(4.1) Augmented Logistic (AL)	24	26.22$	42.98

$ Likelihood-ratio test.
* Heteroskedasticity-consistent Wald test.

In the case of the augmented Working–Leser model (AWL), however, exactness *is* rejected at the 1% level of significance. When the origin of the rejection was investigated, it was found to be related to the existence of one household of the (3,1) type with a high value of total expenditure. If this observation is dropped, the restrictions implied by exactness are not rejected by the data. The AWL form is very sensitive to observations in the tails of the distribution of (log) expenditure. It does not come as a surprise, therefore, that one sampled household with a high level of total expenditure should so affect the Engel curve for its household type that the estimated coefficients are significantly different from those implied by the exact Engel model.

In the case of the other two parametric forms, the logistic (L), equation (9), and the augmented logistic (AL), equation (11), the restrictions implied by exactness are not rejected at 1%.

A question that arises is whether the errors in equations (5), (9) and (11) have been correctly specified, i.e., can they be taken to be homoskedastic? When the AWL, L, and AL models were estimated separately for each family type (details available from the author), homoskedasticity was not rejected in any equation. This establishes that the errors are homoskedastic within family types. However, they may be heteroskedastic *across* family types. One way of testing for heteroskedasticity across sub-equations in an unpooled regression is to regress the squared errors from the n sub-equations on a constant and $(n - 1)$ subequation dummies, and perform an F-test of the joint significance of the dummies. These F-statistics for the joint significance of eight family-type dummies are 1.52 (AWL, full sample), 1.55 (AWL, 2,926 observations), 1.62 (L) and 1.66 (AL), all less than the critical value (at 1%) of 2.51. The error variances in equations (5), (9), and (11) may, therefore, be taken to be homoskedastic.

Table 7.2A. *Sensitivity of Engel scales to shape of Engel curve*
Two-adult household = 1.00   Equivalence scale = $1 + \mu_i$

	(WL)	(AWL)	(L)	(AL)
	$a_1 = 1.8697$	$a_2 = -0.7920$	$a_3 = 0.7896$	$a_4 = 0.8893$
	$(0.028)^*$	$(0.182)^*$	$(0.008)^*$	$(0.045)^*$
	$\beta_1 = -0.1892$	$\beta_2 = 0.6250$	–	–
	$(0.004)^*$	$(0.055)^*$		
	–	$\gamma_2 = -0.0619$	$\gamma_3 = 0.8462$	$\gamma_4 = 0.7318$
		$(0.004)^*$	$(0.035)^*$	$(0.050)^*$
	–	–	$\delta_3 = 2.2789$	$\delta_4 = 1.7407$
			$(0.132)^*$	$(0.205)^*$
	–	–	–	$\theta_4 = 20.7030$
				(8.305)
$\mu_1(2,1)$	0.3242	0.3311	0.3368	0.3353
	$(0.052)^*$	$(0.048)^*$	$(0.045)^*$	$(0.045)^*$
$\mu_2(2,2)$	0.6418	0.6138	0.6000	0.5920
	$(0.060)^*$	$(0.058)^*$	$(0.054)^*$	$(0.053)^*$
$\mu_3(2,3)$	0.9322	0.9146	0.8887	0.8784
	$(0.074)^*$	$(0.073)^*$	$(0.069)^*$	$(0.067)^*$
$\mu_4(3,0)$	0.3604	0.3705	0.3700	0.3686
	$(0.060)^*$	$(0.052)^*$	$(0.050)^*$	$(0.049)^*$
$\mu_5(3,1)$	0.7992	0.8208	0.7239	0.7269
	$(0.082)^*$	$(0.077)^*$	$(0.068)^*$	$(0.067)^*$
$\mu_6(3,2)$	1.0512	1.0182	0.9950	0.9914
	$(0.088)^*$	$(0.089)^*$	$(0.083)^*$	$(0.082)^*$
$\mu_7(4,0)$	0.8254	0.8164	0.8299	0.8202
	$(0.081)^*$	$(0.074)^*$	$(0.080)^*$	$(0.070)^*$
$\mu_8(4,1)$	1.0502	1.0293	1.0287	1.0209
	$(0.092)^*$	$(0.087)^*$	$(0.080)^*$	$(0.082)^*$
RMSE	0.0971	0.0936	0.0924	0.0923
R^2	0.4813	0.5175	0.5306	0.5316
n	2926	2926	2926	2926
L	2676.86	2783.22	2823.36	2827.19

Asymptotic standard errors in brackets. Standard errors for WL are robust.

Sensitivity to the functional form of the Engel curve

Having established that it is not a distortion to think of the Engel
equivalence scales in this sample as exact, at least in the context of three of
the four parametric forms used here, we may now turn to the question of
whether the estimates are sensitive to the parametric form of the Engel

Table 7.2B. *Ordinary least squares estimates*
Two-adult household = 1.00   *Equivalence scale* = $1 + p_4[N_{15+} - 2] + p_{23}N_{0-14}$

	(WL)	(AWL)	(L)	(AL)
	$a_1 = 1.8697$	$a_2 = -0.7623$	$a_3 = 0.7898$	$a_4 = 0.8875$
	(0.028)*	(0.180)*	(0.008)*	(0.045)*
	$\beta_1 = -0.1889$	$\beta_2 = 0.6152$		
	(0.004)*	(0.055)*		
		$\gamma_2 = -0.0610$	$\gamma_3 = 0.8439$	$\gamma_4 = 0.7314$
		(0.004)*	(0.035)*	(0.050)*
			$\delta_3 = 2.3169$	$\delta_4 = 1.7748$
			(0.124)*	(0.208)*
				$\theta_4 = 20.4600$
				(8.319)
p_4	0.3973	0.3915	0.3834	0.3808
	(0.029)*	(0.027)*	(0.025)*	(0.025)*
p_{23}	0.3186	0.3076	0.2958	0.2925
	(0.021)*	(0.021)*	(0.019)*	(0.019)*
RMSE	0.0971	0.0936	0.0923	0.0922
R^2	0.4816	0.5174	0.5310	0.5320
n	2926	2926	2926	2926
L	2674.74	2780.09	2821.62	2825.33

Asymptotic standard errors in brackets. Standard errors for WL are robust.

curve. If they are not, then any parametric form (for which exactness is not rejected) would do equally well for the purposes of estimation. Exact equivalence scales based on the four parametric forms considered previously are estimated in table 7.2A. For AWL and AL, the equations used are (6) and (1) respectively. In the case of WL and L the estimates are based on:

$$w_f = a_1 + \beta_1 \ln(X) - \ln(M) \tag{13}$$

for WL, and

$$w_f = a_3 \left(1 - \frac{1}{1 + \delta_3\, e^{-\gamma_3 \ln((X_i) - \ln(M))}}\right) \tag{14}$$

for L where

$$M = 1 + \sum_{i=1}^{8} \mu_i D_i.$$

A childless two-adult household is used as reference.

The first point to note about table 7.2A is that all the equivalence scales, $1 + \mu_i$, are significantly different from the headcount, or equivalently, the number of individuals in the household relative to the reference. For example, in the first column, $1 + \mu_i = 1.3242$, which has a standard error of 0.052. This implies that households with two adults and one child are equivalent, in effective size, to 1.32 reference households. This is significantly different (at 1%) from $3/2 = 1.5$.

A close look at table 7.2A reveals that the estimated scales vary with the parametric form of the Engel curve, tending to be higher in the case of the WL form which is estimated with a high equation standard error compared to the other forms, and lower in the case of the L and AL forms which are estimated with relatively low equation standard errors. While the differences between the estimates are not statistically significant, and the suggested ranking does not always hold – compare the estimate of μ_4 in the four equations, for example – there is sufficient conformity to warrant comment.

It would be interesting to see if a parametric form which is likely to have a worse fit, e.g., one that is linear in expenditure, yields higher estimates of the equivalence scales than the WL model. A suitable candidate for this exercise is a share equation from the Linear Expenditure System (LES):

$$w_f = a_5 + \beta_5/(X/M). \tag{15}$$

The LES is commonly used in time-series analysis but is, in general, quite restrictive because of the presumed linearity between the expenditure on a good and total household expenditure. (15) is estimated below subject to the hypothesis that the equivalence scale is a simple linear function of the (normalised) number of adults ($N_{15+} - 2$) and the number of children (N_{0-14}) in the household:

$$M = 1 + \rho_{23} \text{ (no. of children)} + \rho_4 \text{ [no. of adults} - 2].$$

The estimate of (15) may be compared with the estimates of (6), (12), (13), (14), all subject to the hypothesis, in table 7.2B.

$$\hat{w}_f = 0.4902 + (86.040/X)(1 + 0.3554 N_{0-14}$$
$$(0.005)^* \quad (3.549)^* \quad (0.027)^*$$
$$+ \quad 0.4539(N_{15+} - 2))$$
$$(0.040)^*$$

$$\text{RMSE} = 0.1107 \quad R^2 = 0.3257 \quad n = 2,926 \quad L = 2290.00$$

As anticipated, (15) is estimated with a higher equation standard error than the WL form or any of the equations in table 7.2B. The estimates of ρ_{23} and ρ_4 are also higher in this equation than in the others. The estimates of ρ_{23} and ρ_4 fall uniformly with equation standard error, so much so that if the logistic or the augmented logistic model is our maintained hypothesis, the estimates of ρ_{23} and ρ_4 in (15) are significantly greater. In this result, we are helped no doubt by the lower standard errors of the demographic coefficients in table 7.2B that arise out of the economy of (M2) relative to (M1). This has not been at the cost of goodness of fit, however, as the equations in table 7.2B fit as well, and in some cases better, than the equations in table 7.2A.

What all this seems to suggest is that the parameterisation of the Engel curve, far from being innocuous, is potentially of considerable significance for the sizes of the estimated equivalence scales.

The estimates in table 7.2B also allow us to comment on another issue. In terms of the logistic model, a child is seen to be equivalent to 0.2958 (0.019) reference households while an additional adult is equivalent to 0.3834 (0.025) reference households. The sizes of the coefficients do not contradict notions of relative needs, but the equivalence scale for a child does appear on the high side relative to the estimate for an additional adult. The estimates thus give some support to the argument that Engel scales are likely to overcompensate households for the presence of children (Deaton and Muellbauer, 1986). Notice, however, that while ρ_{23} may be high relative to ρ_4, the coefficients are significantly different from each other, and from 0.5, the *per capita* deflator. This is true of the estimates in all equations.

Alternative specifications of demographic and other effects

The aims of this section are twofold. First, to decompose the estimated scales into the 'effects' of particular demographic groups within the household and second, to examine the robustness of the estimates to the inclusion of other demographic information about the household, and the generalisation of the Engel curve to take account of regional and seasonal influences. Adults (N_{15+}) will not be classified by age; children (N_{0-14}) will be divided into two groups: 0–4 years (N_{0-4}), and 5–14 years (N_{5-14}), and will be described as 'young' and 'old' respectively. A dummy variable (*FXDCOST*) will be introduced that assumes a value of one for households with children but is zero otherwise. It should help to capture any economies of scale associated with children. An interaction term (*CARECOST*), the product of (N_{0-4}) and the number of other members in the household less two ($N_{15+} - 2$) will also be used. If there are costs of minding young children that increase the budget share of food then, given the number of such children, the greater the number of other members (all potential child minders), the smaller the expected value of food share.

CARECOST may thus be expected to be negative. It may also be negative on account of scale economies in food consumption.

Only one function was selected for the decomposition exercise: the logistic (14). The reasons for selecting this equation are the following: of the equations estimated in table 7.2B, the logistic appears to combine parsimony in parameterisation with goodness of fit; it was accepted in preference to the AWL form in a *J*-test of nonnested hypotheses;[4] the restrictions implied by exactness are not rejected in its context; and nonparametric estimation of the regression of food share on log expenditure suggests that it is consistent with the logistic form (details available from the author). The estimated equation is:

$$w_f = a_3 \left(1 - \frac{1}{1 + \delta_3(X/M)^{-\gamma_3}} \right)$$

where we adopt the hypothesis that

$$M = 1 + \rho_1(FXDCOST) + \rho_2(N_{0-4}) + \rho_3(N_{5-14})$$
$$+ \rho_4(N_{15+} - 2) + \rho_5(CARECOST)$$

and is reported in table 7.3.

In column (1), we see that a young child and older child are equivalent to 0.2190 (0.092) and 0.2679 (0.031) reference households respectively, which presumably reflects the difference in their relative food requirements. The coefficients are not significantly different from each other. An additional adult is observed to be equivalent to 0.3801 (0.026) reference households. The *FXDCOST* term is not significant; the *CARECOST* term is of the wrong sign, but is insignificant. Dropping both *FXDCOST* and *CARECOST* (column (4)) we see that the coefficient on N_{0-4} rises to 0.3007 (0.026), which is larger than that on N_{5-14} but not by a significant margin. All three demographic coefficients are significantly different from 0.5, and N_{15+} is significantly bigger than either N_{0-4} or N_{5-14}.

In including the number of children in two age bands, the scales in table 7.3 introduce a discontinuity with respect to age in the estimated equivalence scales. This may be responsible for the insignificant differences between the coefficients on N_{0-4} and N_{5-14}. One way of getting round this problem would be to estimate the following:

$$M = 1 + \rho_2(N_{0-4}) + \rho_4[(N_{15+}) - 2] + \sum_{j=1}^{3} (k_0 + k_1(\text{age}_j)^{k_2})$$

where the age_j is the age of the *j*th older child. *M* is sensitive to the ages of the older children in the household but not to the ages of young children or adults. The index, *j*, runs from 1 to 3 because the number of

Table 7.3. *Alternative demographic specifications*
Two-adult household = 1.00

$$w_f = a_3 \left(1 - \frac{1}{1 + \delta_3 e^{-\gamma_3[\ln(X) - \ln(M)]}} \right)$$

$M = 1 +$ combinations of demographic variables

	(1)	(2)	(3)	(4)	(5)
a_3	0.7902	0.7899	0.7899	0.7897	0.7898
	(0.008)*	(0.008)*	(0.008)*	(0.008)*	(0.008)*
γ_3	0.8427	0.8425	0.8447	0.8430	0.8439
	(0.035)*	(0.035)*	(0.035)*	(0.035)*	(0.035)*
δ_3	2.2940	2.3210	2.2900	2.3151	2.3169
	(0.126)*	(0.126)*	(0.125)*	(0.124)*	(0.124)*
$FXDCOST$	0.0519	–	0.0409	–	–
	(0.050)		(0.048)		
N_{0-4}	0.2190	0.2696	0.2820	0.3007	–
	(0.092)*	(0.081)*	(0.033)*	(0.026)*	
N_{5-14}	0.2679	0.2899	0.2782	0.2933	–
	(0.031)*	(0.023)*	(0.028)*	(0.021)*	
$N_{15+} - 2$	0.3801	0.3813	0.3854	0.3842	0.3834*
	(0.026)*	(0.026)*	(0.026)*	(0.025)*	(0.025)*
$CARECOST$	0.0221	0.0199	–	–	–
	(0.031)	(0.030)			
N_{0-4}	–	–	–	–	0.2958
					(0.019)*
RMSE	0.0923	0.0923	0.0923	0.0923	0.0923
R^2	0.5307	0.5307	0.5308	0.5308	0.5310
n	2926	2926	2926	2926	2926
L	2822.26	2821.73	2822.02	2821.66	2821.62

Asymptotic standard errors in brackets.

older children in any household in the sample is at most three. If $k_2 = 0$, M reduces to a function of the number of children in the age groups 0–4 years and 5–14 years, and the number of adults, as in column (4) of table 7.3. If $k_2 = 1$, M is a piecewise linear function of age; if $k_2 = 2$, the equivalence scale is a quadratic in the age of older children. Continuity in age may be ensured by restricting p_2 and p_4 in the following way:

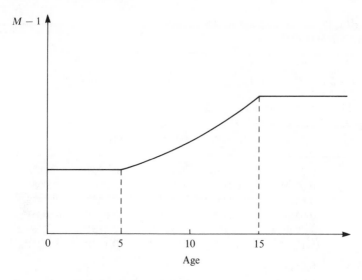

Figure 7.1   Relation between $M - 1$ and age

$$M = 1 + (N_{0-4})(k_0 + k_1(5)^{k_2}) + (N_{15+})(k_0 + k_1(15)^{k_2})$$
$$+ \sum_{j=1}^{8} (k_0 + k_1(\text{age}_j)^{k_2})$$

An additional five year old child thus adds as much to the scale as a young child, and the oldest child as much as an additional adult. The relation between $M - 1$ and age is depicted in figure 7.1.

Estimating (10) subject to M, however, proved difficult in practice with the programme failing to iterate to a solution after 20 minutes of search.[5] However, if k_2 is specified at the outset, the iterative search process rapidly converges to a solution. These estimates, for values of k_2 ranging from 1 to 5, may be found in table 7.4. A glance at the equation standard errors at the bottom of the table suggests why a solution proved elusive: the sum of squared errors varies little in spite of relatively large changes in k_2.

The effect on the scale, M, of an addition to the household aged five, aged 10, and aged 15, is presented below table 7.4 for various values of k_2. As would be expected the coefficient for an additional five year old and an additional 15 year old are not significantly different from the estimates of N_{0-14} and $(N_{15+} - 2)$ in table 7.3.

Finally, let us generalise the Engel curve to allow for regional[6] and seasonal[7] variation in the budget share of food, and introduce further

Table 7.4. *Continuous scales*
Two-adult household = 1.00

$$w_f = a_3 \left(1 - \frac{1}{1 + \delta_3 e^{-\gamma_3[\ln(X) - \ln(M)]}} \right)$$

$$M = 1 + N_{0-4}(k_0 + k_1(5)^{k_2}) + N_{15+}(k_0 + k_1(15)^{k_2}) + \sum_{j=1}^{3} D_j(k_0 + k_1(age_j)^{k_2})$$

	$k_2 = 1$	$k_2 = 2$	$k_2 = 3$	$k_2 = 4$	$k_2 = 5$
a_3	0.7896	0.7895	0.7895	0.7895	0.7895
	(0.008)*	(0.008)*	(0.008)*	(0.008)*	(0.008)*
γ_3	0.8412	0.8421	0.8427	0.8431	0.8434
	(0.035)*	(0.035)*	(0.035)*	(0.035)*	(0.035)*
δ_3	2.3371	2.3342	2.3316	2.3293	2.3275
	(0.126)*	(0.125)*	(0.125)*	(0.125)*	(0.125)*
k_0	0.2542	0.2803	0.2875	0.2904	0.2919
	(0.028)*	(0.022)*	(0.021)*	(0.020)*	(0.020)*
k_1	0.0068	3.6E-4	2.3E-5	1.5E-6	1.0E-7
	(0.002)*	(1.1E-4)*	(6.8E-6)*	(4.4E-7)*	(4.7E-8)*
RMSE	0.09244	0.09242	0.09240	0.09239	0.09238
R^2	0.52984	0.53002	0.53019	0.53033	0.53043
n	2926	2926	2926	2926	2926
$k_0 + k_1 age^{k_2}$					
At age in years:					
5	0.2884	0.2893	0.2903	0.2913	0.2921
	(0.021)	(0.021)	(0.020)	(0.020)	(0.020)
10	0.3226	0.3163	0.3105	0.3058	0.3022
	(0.019)	(0.019)	(0.019)	(0.019)	(0.019)
15	0.3568	0.3614	0.3653	0.3685	0.3710
	(0.023)	(0.023)	(0.024)	(0.024)	(0.024)

Asymptotic standard errors in brackets.

demographic information about the household. Thinking visually, regional and seasonal factors are likely to shift the Engel curve in food share-equivalent expenditure space, or change its slope, or both. A natural way to parametrise changes in the position and shape of the curve is to allow these factors to influence the upper asymptote (a_3) and the point of inflexion ($\ln(\delta_3)/\gamma_3$) of the logistic function. This was done by creating regional dummies (*ZONE1*, *ZONE2*, and *ZONE3*, which equal one when the household falls in the relevant zone) and seasonal dummies (*ROUND1, ROUND2, ROUND3*, which assume the value of one for households sampled in the named round) which were interacted with the parameters of the logistic function. The estimated equation was:

$$w_f = a\left(1 - \frac{1}{1 + \delta\,e^{-\gamma\ln(X/M)}}\right), \quad a, \gamma_3, \delta > 0 \tag{16}$$

where $a = a_3 + \Sigma a_{zi}\,ZONEi + \Sigma a_{rj}\,ROUNDj$,
$\delta = \delta_3 + \Sigma\delta_{zi}\,ZONEi + \Sigma\delta_{rj}\,ROUNDj$.

Deviations from a_3 imply an increase or decrease in the upper asymptote of the Engel curve compared to the reference (located in Zone 4 and sampled in the fourth round) while deviations from δ_3 imply leftward or rightward shifts of the point of inflexion in food share-equivalent expenditure space relative to the reference. (Shifts in the point of inflexion could have been parametrised equally well by holding δ constant at δ_3, and allowing γ to deviate from γ_3 via the dummies.)

The specification of M was widened to include the age of the household head, information on his or her sex,[8] and interaction terms between the age of the head and the normalised number of adults and the number of children in the household:

$$M = 1 + \rho_{23}N_{0-14} + \rho_4(N_{15+} - 2) + \rho_a AGEHEAD + \rho_s SEXHEAD$$
$$+ \rho_{a1} AGEHEAD \times N_{0-14} + \rho_{a2} AGEHEAD \times (N_{15+} - 2)$$

M, as embodied in equation (16), is estimated in column (1) of table 7.5. (The estimates of the coefficients on the seasonal dummies, *ROUND1, ROUND2*, and *ROUND3*, are suppressed in order to confine the results to a single page.) None of the variables in M other than the number of children and the normalised number of adults is observed to be significant. The coefficients on these variables, ρ_{23} and ρ_4 respectively, are not significantly different from the ones in table 7.2B, and are quite close in magnitude to them. It would thus appear that ρ_{23} and ρ_4 are robust to inclusion of other demographic information about the household and the generalisation of the Engel curve.

The effect of error in the measurement of expenditure

Given the emphasis placed in this chapter on regression coefficients, it is important to consider the effect of measurement error on the size of these coefficients. Of the variables used, the age of members of the household is likely to have been recorded with greater accuracy than current expenditure, X. The bulk of total expenditure consists of food expenditure, which

Table 7.5. *Sensitivity of Engel scales to household characteristics*

$$w_f = a\left(1 - \frac{1}{1 + \delta_3 e^{-\gamma_3[\ln(X) - \ln(M)]}}\right)$$

$a = a_3 + \Sigma a_k \times$ zonal, seasonal dummies

$\delta = \delta_3 + \Sigma \delta_k \times$ zonal, seasonal dummies

$M = 1 +$ combinations of demographic variables

	(1)	(2)
a_3	0.7721	0.7716
	(0.015)*	(0.015)*
γ_3	0.8379	0.8366
	(0.034)*	(0.033)*
δ_3	2.4492	2.4652
	(0.293)*	(0.294)*
a_{z1} ($\times$ *ZONE1*)	0.0108	0.0116
	(0.009)	(0.91E-02)
a_{z2} ($\times$ *ZONE2*)	0.0217	0.0222
	(0.010)	(0.010)
a_{z3} ($\times$ *ZONE3*)	0.0544	0.0544
	(0.013)*	(0.013)*
δ_{z1} ($\times$ *ZONE1*)	0.0179	0.0046
	(0.138)	(0.148)
δ_{z2} ($\times$ *ZONE2*)	− 0.1242	− 0.1428
	(0.148)	(0.147)
δ_{z3} ($\times$ *ZONE3*)	0.1710	0.1643
	(0.119)	(0.199)
$(N_{15+} - 2)$	0.4082	0.4095
	(0.029)*	(0.029)*
N_{0-14}	0.3293	0.3059
	(0.026)*	(0.021)*
AGEHEAD	− 0.0015	− 0.14E-03
	(0.001)	(0.91E-03)
SEXHEAD	0.0367	0.0419
	(0.035)	(0.035)
AGEHEAD $\times (N_{15+} - 2)$		0.93E-03
		(0.12E-02)
AGEHEAD $\times N_{0-14}$	0.20E-02	−
	(0.12E-02)	
RMSE	0.0904	0.0904
R^2	0.5501	0.5499
n	2926	2926

Asymptotic standard errors in brackets.

was measured by visiting each sampled household three times during a period of seven consecutive days. This would have partly smoothed any measurement error or error arising on account of daily variation in dietary intake. Nevertheless it is possible that total expenditure was measured with error, particularly those components of X, such as expenditure on clothing, which are based on respondent recall.

Parameter estimates may be purged of measurement error bias through the use of instruments for current expenditure. Measures of medium- and long-term wealth, such as the age and sex of the head of the household, the number of adults or income receivers, dummies for the possession of durables, etc. may be used as instruments for current expenditure, so long as it can be maintained that these variables are uncorrelated with the error term in the regression. A comparison of the least squares coefficients with the confidence intervals of the instrument variables estimates then provides an estimate of the presence and extent of measurement error bias. Finding appropriate instruments is, however, not always straightforward. As an example of a case where the instruments are *correlated* with the error term in the regression, consider the following situation where the presence of guests at meals leads to an overestimation of food expenditure and of food share. Since wealthy households are more likely to have visitors than poor ones, the error term will be systematically correlated with measures of wealth used as instruments for current expenditure. Hopefully, the great care with which the CFS data were collected should make it possible to avoid this kind of error. The number of people present at each meal was recorded, along with whether they belonged to the household or not. Deductions were then made on the basis of points awarded to each meal to account for the presence of visitors.

Table 7.6 estimates equations (6), (12), (13), (14) subject to

$$M = 1 + \rho_{23}(N_{0-14}) + \rho_4(N_{15+} - 2) \tag{17}$$

using instruments for current expenditure.[9] Table 7.6 may be compared with the least squares estimates in table 7.2B. As is usually the case, the instrumental variables estimates have higher standard errors than the least squares estimates. However, the demographic coefficients are well determined and are closed in magnitude to those in table 7.2B. In every case, the least squares estimates of ρ_{23} and ρ_4 lie within the confidence intervals of the instrument variables estimate.

In this chapter, total expenditure is defined to include an average concept of expenditure on durable goods. But this smoothed estimate of expenditure on durables is an imperfect estimate of the value of services

Table 7.6. *Instrumental variable estimates*
Two-adult household = 1.00   Equivalence scale = $1 + \rho_4(N_{15+} - 2) + \rho_{23}N_{0-14}$

	(WL)	(AWL)	(L)	(AL)
	$a_1 = 1.9382$	$a_2 = -1.5651$	$a_3 = 0.7778$	$a_4 = 0.8552$
	(0.041)*	(0.663)*	(0.022)*	(0.214)*
	$\beta_1 = -0.1997$	$\beta_2 = 0.8728$	–	
	(0.006)*	(0.203)*		
	–	$\gamma_2 = -0.0816$	$\gamma_3 = 0.9551$	$\gamma_4 = 0.8379$
		(0.015)*	(0.141)*	(0.282)*
	–	–	$\delta_3 = 2.3304$	$\delta_4 = 1.8579$
			(0.275)*	(1.038)*
	–	–	–	$\theta_4 = 17.0598$
				(44.068)
ρ_4	0.3955	0.4011	0.4027	0.4016
	(0.027)*	(0.029)*	(0.028)*	(0.028)*
ρ_{23}	0.3131	0.3065	0.3066	0.3049
	(0.020)*	(0.022)*	(0.022)*	(0.022)*
RMSE	0.0968	0.0939	0.0923	0.0921
R^2	0.4831	0.5137	0.5307	0.5320
n	2902	2902	2902	2902

Asymptotic standard errors in brackets.

that flow from durable goods. In the framework of this section, the inclusion of expenditure on durables may be responsible for 'error' in the measurement of expenditure and consequent bias in estimation. An alternative to the inclusion of expenditure on durables is to assume that expenditure on nondurable goods is separable from expenditure on durable goods. Equations (6), (12), (13), (14) in table 7.7 do not include durable goods as a part of total expenditure. When compared with table 7.6, the estimates of ρ_{23} and ρ_4 appear to be robust to the change of definition.

Summary and conclusion

Data on food share and household expenditure from rural Sri Lanka were used to compute expenditure-independent or exact equivalence scales based on the Engel model. The restrictions implied by expenditure-independence or exactness were first tested in the context of different parametric forms of the Engel curve. Exactness was not rejected in three

Table 7.7. *Exclusion of expenditure on durable goods*
Two-adult household = 1.00   Equivalence scale = $1 + p_4(N_{15+} - 2) + p_{23}N_{0-14}$

	(WL)	(AWL)	(L)	(AL)
	$a_1 = 1.8084$	$a_2 = -2.0949$	$a_3 = 0.8105$	$a_4 = 0.9365$
	$(0.030)^*$	$(0.221)^*$	$(0.007)^*$	$(0.049)^*$
	$\beta_1 = -0.1767$	$\beta_2 = 1.0338$	–	
	$(0.004)^*$	$(0.068)^*$		
	–	$\gamma_2 = -0.0932$	$\gamma_3 = 0.8903$	$\gamma_4 = 0.7219$
		$(0.005)^*$	$(0.039)^*$	$(0.054)^*$
	–	–	$\delta_3 = 2.4861$	$\delta_4 = 1.7306$
			$(0.135)^*$	$(0.206)^*$
	–	–	–	$\theta_4 = 27.9330$
				(8.521^*)
p_4	0.3880	0.3682	0.3751	0.3711
	$(0.031)^*$	$(0.026)^*$	$(0.026)^*$	$(0.025)^*$
p_{23}	0.3422	0.3049	0.3108	0.3065
	$(0.024)^*$	$(0.020)^*$	$(0.020)^*$	$(0.020)^*$
RMSE	0.0973	0.0923	0.0922	0.0920
R^2	0.4234	0.4812	0.4817	0.4841
n	2926	2926	2926	2926

Asymptotic standard errors in brackets. Standard errors for WL are robust.

of the four parametric forms considered, and was not rejected in the fourth, the AWL form, if one outlying observation was dropped. One imagines expenditure-independence to be quite restrictive but it does not appear to be so in the context of this model of equivalence scales.

The size of the estimated scales appears to be related to the parametric form of the Engel curve, with lower estimates arising in parametric forms which are estimated with a lower equation standard error. While one would hesitate to make a general claim on the basis of this evidence, what it does suggest is that the parametric form of the Engel curve may be significant to the sizes of the estimated equivalence scales and, therefore, warrants careful selection.

In terms of a simple linear function of the (normalised) number of adults and the number of children in the context of the preferred logistic model, the equivalence scale for a child and the equivalence scale for an additional adult appear robust to the inclusion of other demographic information about the household and the generalisation of the Engel curve. A child is seen to be equivalent to approximately 0.3 reference households, while an additional adult is equivalent to approximately 0.4 reference households. The estimate for a child appears to be on the high side relative to the estimate for an adult, though it is significantly smaller. This gives some support to the argument that Engel scales tend to overestimate the cost of children relative to adults. When children are disaggregated into two groups by age (0–4 years and 5–14 years), the equivalence scale for a young child is not observed to be significantly lower than the equivalence scale for an older child. With scales that are continuous in age it should be possible, however, to detect significant effects of the ages of children.

If current expenditure is observed with error, or is not exogenous to the estimation, a standard errors-in-variables argument predicts that the estimated coefficients will be biased. In such cases, measures of long-term wealth such as the number of income receivers in the household, possession of durables, etc. may be used as instruments for current expenditure to purge the estimates of bias. This was not found to alter the size of the equivalence scale for a child or the equivalence scale for an additional adult. When the definition of total expenditure was altered to exclude expenditure on durables this was not seen to affect the estimates.

Appendix A: Description of data

The 1981/1982 survey of consumer finances

The data used in this chapter were collected by the Central Bank of Sri Lanka in 1981–1982 as a part of its *Consumer Finances and Socio-Economic Survey* (CFS).[10] The 1981–1982 survey is fifth in a series that commenced in 1953 and the first since the dismantling of rationing schemes in September 1979. The survey used a stratified two-stage sample design to cover 8,000 households from whom detailed information was obtained on expenditure and other socioeconomics variables.

In the case of household expenditure, information was recorded under three categories: (1) food, (2) nonfood goods and services, and (3) consumer durables. All expenditures were valued in Sri Lankan rupees per month.

In the case of food, expenditure was understood to be the money value of consumption. This was evaluated by multiplying consumption in physical units by prevailing market price per unit. Information on 28 broad categories of food, covering more than 200 individual items, was obtained by visiting each household on three separate occasions during a period of seven days. Each visit by the survey team lasted between 2 and $2\frac{1}{2}$ hours. Actual consumption of food was recorded, as opposed to purchases of food on the part of the household. This was made possible by records kept by respondent households of their daily consumption during the reference period. Expenditure on food thus includes items that were consumed but not purchased (e.g., the produce of the kitchen garden), and excludes purchases made by the household to build stocks. Since the presence of visitors at meals is likely to distort data derived from household consumption, adjustments were made on the basis of the number of persons present at each meal, whether they belonged to the household or not, and the weight given to the meal. The figures for consumption and expenditure were finally scaled upwards to estimate expenditure over a month consisting of 30 days.

In the case of nondurable goods and services, information was collected under 14 heads: housing, clothing, fuel and light, transport and communication, education, recreation, festivals and ceremonies, laundry and cleaning, litigation, gifts and donations, personal services, servants, medication, and infant requirements. Households were asked to recall expenditure during the 30 days prior to interview. A longer reference period (6 or 12 months) was also used for certain items. Values were imputed in the case of owner-occupied houses and subsidised or free accommodation using market rates prevailing in the area for similar dwellings. Where this was done, the difference between market rent and subsidised rent was entered as income in kind. In rented houses where an advance had been paid, only the monthly rent was included as expenditure on rent. Values were also imputed for firewood obtained free of charge or domestically produced. No imputation was made for free medicine or medical attention, nor was any value imputed for domestic labour such as that involved in washing or stitching garments at home or driving vehicles. Expenditure on maintaining vehicles and on animals used to draw carts was treated as expenditure on transport. Where a vehicle was used for both commercial and domestic purposes, total expenditure was apportioned between the two according to the number of hours spent on each type of activity.

For durable goods, information was collected under 41 categories. Households were asked to recollect expenditure incurred on purchasing and maintaining such goods, as well as receipts from sales, for the 30 days prior to sampling, as well as for the previous 6 months.

Definitions used and sample selected

The sample used in this chapter consists of 2,926 households from the rural sector. Having decided to analyse households from rural Sri Lanka, the largest sector in the sample, the first question that arose was the treatment of *multiple spending-unit households*.[11] The category of spending

Table 7A.1. *Nature of multiple spending-unit households, no. of households*

Sector	Urban	Rural	Estate
Type:			
Joint families	97	153	3
Households with servants			
maids, drivers, etc.	51	43	1
Total	148	196	4

Source: Computed from the CFS 1982/1982 survey.

unit, unique to the CFS, is defined as one or more persons taking independent decisions with respect to spending income. A household, on the other hand, is described as a single person or a group of persons living together and sharing common cooking arrangements. A household may thus have more than one spending unit, e.g., a joint family with a common kitchen or a household with live-in servants or boarders. A spending unit conforms more closely to theoretical notions of a household and was thus chosen as the unit of analysis. This raised the question of what should be done with households that had more than one spending unit. While recording expenditure details of such households, consumption and expenditure undertaken jointly was divided among the spending units in proportion to the number of members in each spending unit.[12] Since food consumption from the common kitchen by individual members of a spending unit was not observed, it is not clear that this division reflects actual food consumption or expenditure on the part of the individual spending units. Nor is it clear that this is what food expenditure would have been had these decisions been taken independently. For this reason multiple spending-unit households were dropped from the analysis. One alternative would have been to treat multiple spending-unit households as single entities, i.e., to merge the spending units in a household. But this runs the danger, in households with servants, of conflating spending units with very different expenditure patterns. The number of such households is given in table 7A.1. For these and further accounting discrepancies associated with multiple spending-unit households see Anand and Harris (1990).

Under food, the survey includes the consumption of and expenditure on meals eaten outside the home, and alcohol and tobacco. I exclude expenditure on alcohol and tobacco as a part of food expenditure and instead treat it as a part of expenditure on nondurable goods and services. I define total expenditure as the sum of expenditure on food, expenditure on nonfood goods and service (all 14 survey categories plus alcohol and tobacco), and *smoothed expenditure on durables*. The latter is calculated as follows. As mentioned earlier, the survey contains information on purchases and sales of durables by each household in the 6 months prior to sampling, along with amounts spent on maintenance. A smoothed estimate of expenditure on durables was obtained by subtracting sales receipts from the sum of purchase and maintenance expenditure, and dividing the resulting figure by six. Taking an average of expenditure recalled over a longer reference period partially evens out the inherent lumpiness of durables' expenditure, and provided the data recalled over 30 days and 6 months may be regarded as equally error-prone, is not a bad way of estimating expenditure on durable goods from the data on hand. Note that this average is a poor estimate of the *services* that flow from the possession of durables. To estimate the latter one would require information on the stock and potential economic life of the durables in the possession of the household prior to sampling, as well as the economic life of the net purchases made during the sampling period. In the absence of this information the expenditure on durables, suitably smoothed, is the only way of estimating the consumption of services of durable goods.[13]

The construction of total expenditure is summarised below:

Food +	*Nonfood +*	*Smoothed durables' expenditure*
	Clothing	(purchases over 6 months
	Rent	+ Maintenance over 6 months
	Fuel	− Sales over 6 months)/6
	Alc. & Tob.,	
	etc.	

= *Total expenditure*

It is possible that for some households smoothed expenditure on durables is negative. This would be the case if households made large sales of durables (e.g., of jewellery) in the 6 months prior to sampling. If durables' expenditure is both negative and large, total expenditure may be less than food expenditure, in which case food share will be greater than one. In extreme cases, total expenditure itself may be negative, resulting in values of food share that are less than zero. Since values of food share outside the (0,1) range are not economically meaningful, such households (only a small number in fact) were dropped from the analysis.

The remaining households were classified according to the number of

Table 7A.2. *Sample details*

	No. of households
All island	2,912,941
Rural sector	2,182,914
In survey:	
All island	8,000
Complete responses	7,927
Rural sector:	5,908
of which,	
Single spending-unit households	5,712
0 < Food share	5,708
of which,	
0 < Food share ≤ 1	5,695
Selected family types	2,926

adults and the number of children in them, an adult being defined as any individual who is 15 years of age or older. In Sri Lanka, unlike most western economies where the nuclear family is the norm, the number of household types even in terms of a simple classification like the one above is quite large. I decided to confine the analysis to subgroups with at least 200 observations. The household types selected on this basis were those with either two adults and 0, 1, 2 or 3 children, three adults and 0, 1 or 2 children, or four adults and 0 or 1 child. Household types are represented by ordered pairs, with the first entry for the number of adults and the second the number of children.

The construction of the sample is summarised in table 7A.2. It is followed by averages of the share of various categories in total expenditure, and summary statistics of the two main variables in the analysis (Table 7A.3).

NOTES

I would like to thank John Muellbauer for many helpful comments on various aspects of this chapter. I am also grateful to Richard Blundell and Ian Preston for useful suggestions. None of those mentioned is implicated in any errors in the chapter. I am grateful to Sudhir Anand and Christopher Harris for providing the data in clean and usable form along with access to related material.

Table 7A.3. *Expenditure shares and other statistics*

Family type→ (Adults, children)	(2,0)	(2,1)	(2,2)	(2,3)
Households (no.)	334	414	398	448
Expenditure shares (Unwtd. averages)				
Food	0.64	0.64	0.66	0.68
of which:				
Meals out	0.01	0.03	0.02	0.02
Nonfood	0.35	0.35	0.33	0.31
of which:				
Rent	0.17	0.14	0.13	0.12
Clothing	0.09	0.12	0.13	0.12
Fuel	0.27	0.24	0.24	0.25
Transport	0.07	0.08	0.07	0.08
Alc. & Tob.	0.09	0.11	0.10	0.12
Durables	0.01	0.01	0.01	0.01
Food share:				
Unwtd. mean	0.64	0.64	0.66	0.68
St. dev.	0.13	0.13	0.12	0.12
Lntexp:				
Unwtd. mean	6.51	6.81	6.89	6.96
St. dev.	0.49	0.49	0.46	0.44

1 In this, and the discussion that follows, the error term has been excluded from the equation for food share in order to make the presentation as uncluttered as possible.
2 Many authors (Bhanoji Rao, 1981; Deaton, 1981; Thomas, 1986) report evidence that suggests to them that there is a 'reversal' of Engel's Law at low levels of household expenditure. The evidence is, however, debatable.
3 The rejection of homoskedasticity in (3) makes the use of a conventional F-test inappropriate. White's (1980) consistent estimator of the variance–covariance matrix was used instead to perform a Wald test of the restrictions.
4 AWL is rejected in favour of L at 1% ($\hat{a} = -0.019$, s.e. ($\hat{a}$) = 0.263), while L is not rejected in favour of AWL ($\hat{a} = 1.036$, s.e. ($\hat{a}$) = 0.151).
5 The estimation was programmed on the University mainframe, a VAX cluster, using SAS.

Family type→ (Adults, children)	(3,0)	(3,1)	(3,2)	(4,0)	(4,1)
Households (no.)	302	242	245	233	210
Expenditure shares (Unwtd. averages)					
Food of which:	0.63	0.65	0.67	0.63	0.64
Meals out	0.01	0.01	0.01	0.01	0.01
Nonfood of which:	0.36	0.33	0.31	0.35	0.34
Rent	0.16	0.15	0.14	0.15	0.15
Clothing	0.12	0.12	0.10	0.12	0.13
Fuel	0.25	0.23	0.25	0.21	0.23
Transport	0.09	0.10	0.08	0.10	0.10
Alc. & Tob.	0.08	0.09	0.11	0.09	0.09
Durables	0.01	0.02	0.02	0.02	0.02
Food share:					
Unwtd. mean	0.63	0.65	0.67	0.63	0.64
St. dev.	0.15	0.14	0.12	0.14	0.15
Lntexp:					
Unwtd. mean	6.87	7.05	7.05	7.17	7.23
St. dev.	0.53	0.51	0.46	0.51	0.54

6 Households in the rural sector fall into one of four geographical zones: Zone 1, Zone 2, Zone 3, and Zone 4.

7 Households were sampled in four rounds; the first round of sampling was during the period 1 October 1981–15 December 1981, the second during 4 January 1982–20 March 1982, the third during 20 March 1982–6 April 1982 and 27 April 1982–1 July 1982, and the fourth during 10 July 1982–18 July 1982 and 29 July 1982–30 September 1982.

8 Empirical evidence presented by Haddad and Hoddinott (1990) for the Côte d'Ivoire suggests that the increase in the proportion of cash income accruing to women significantly raises the budget share of food and fuel. The same result applies to households which are dominated, either numerically or economically, by women.

9 The instruments were the age and sex of the head of the household, the square of the age of the household head, the number of income receivers in

the household, the average education in years of the adults in the household, the floor area of the house, a dummy for house ownership, dummies for the possession of radios and televisions, the number of adults and children in various age groups, zonal dummies, and the square of current expenditure 'predicted' from all the variables listed above.

10 Earlier description of the data may be found in Anand and Harris (1985), Appendices 1.A–1.F, and Anand and Harris (1986), Appendix B. The survey is fully described in the *Report of Consumer Finances and Socio-Economic Survey, 1981/1982* (1984) published by the Statistics Department of the Central Bank. Additional details of procedures adopted during enumeration are contained in 'Instructions to Investigators – Consumer Finances and Socio-Economic Survey 1981/1982' (1981).

11 The unsatisfactory application of survey concepts to multiple sending-unit households was first pointed out by Anand and Harris (1986). They suggest that such households be dropped for the purposes of developing methodology.

12 *Report on Consumer Finances and Socio-Economic Survey*, 1981/1982, p. 13.

13 The alternative to including a smoothed estimate of expenditure on durables is to drop this item altogether, making the not unquestionable assumption of separability between expenditure on nondurable and durable goods. Another problem in this context is where to draw the line between durable and nondurable goods; items such as clothing and recreation which are conventionally considered nondurable have a sufficiently lumpy quality to qualify as durable goods. I do not consider the inclusion of durable goods as seriously biasing the results of this enquiry. It certainly does not influence the estimates of demographic effects on food share (see table 7.7).

REFERENCES

Anand, S. and C. Harris (1985) 'Living standards in Sri Lanka, 1973–1981/2: an analysis of Consumer Finance Survey data', World Bank, mimeo

   (1986) 'Food and standard of living in Sri Lanka', paper presented at the conference on 'Food Strategies', WIDER, Helsinki (July)

   (1990) 'Food and standard of living: an analysis based on Sri Lankan data', in J. Drèze and A. Sen (eds.), *The Political Economy of Hunger*, vol. I, Oxford, Clarendon Press

Bhanoji Rao, V.V. (1981) 'Measurement of deprivation and poverty based on proportion spent on food: an exploratory exercise', *World Development*, 9(1), 337–353

Blackorby, C. and D. Donaldson (1988) 'Adult-equivalence scales and the economic implementation of interpersonal comparisons of well-being', University of British Columbia, *Discussion Paper*, 88–27

Browning, M.A. (1988) 'The exact preferences associated with the Engel and Rothbarth methods for measuring the costs of children', Department of Economics, McMaster University, mimeo

(1991) 'Children and household economic behaviour', Department of Economics, McMaster University, *Working Paper*, 91–03 (1993); *Journal of Economic Literature*, 30, 1434–1475

Coulter, F.A.E., F.A. Cowell and S.P. Jenkins (1991) 'Differences in needs and assessment of income distributions', University of Bath, *Discussion Paper in Economics*, 03/91

Deaton, A.S. (1981) 'Three essays on a Sri Lankan household survey', *Living Standards Measurement Study Working Paper*, 11, Washington, DC, World Bank

Deaton, A.S. and Muellbauer, J. (1986) 'On measuring child costs; with applications to poor countries', *Journal of Political Economy*, 94, 720–744

Engel, E. (1857) 'Die Produktions- und Konsumptionsverhältnisse des Königreichs Sachsen', reprinted in 'Die Lebenkosten Belgischer Arbeiter-Familien Fruher und Jetzt', *International Statistical Institute Bulletin*, 9, 1–125

Gorman, W.M. (1981) 'Some Engel curves', in A.S. Deaton (ed.), *Essays in the Theory and Measurement of Consumer Behaviour in Honour of Sir Richard Stone*, Cambridge, Cambridge University Press

Haddad, L. and J. Hoddinott (1990) 'Household expenditures, child anthropometric status, and intra-household divisions in income: evidence from the Côte d'Ivoire', Research Programme in Development Studies, Woodrow Wilson School, Princeton University, *Discussion Paper*, 155

Leser, C.E.V. (1963) 'Forms of Engel functions', *Econometrica*, 31(4), 694–703

Lewbel, A. (1989) 'Household-equivalence scales and welfare comparisons', *Journal of Public Economics*, 39, 377–391

Sri Lanka, Central Bank of (1981) 'Instructions to investigators – Consumer Finances and Socio-Economic Survey 1981/1982', Colombo, Central Bank of Ceylon, mimeo

(1984) *Report of Consumer Finances and Socio-Economic Survey 1981/1982*, Parts I and II, Colombo, Central Bank of Ceylon

Thomas, D. (1986) 'The foodshare as a measure of welfare', Princeton University, unpublished Ph.D. dissertation

White, H. (1980) 'A heteroskedasticity-consistent covariance matrix estimator and a direct test for heteroskedasticity', *Econometrica*, 48(4), 817–838

Working, H. (1943) 'Statistical laws of family expenditure', *Econometrica*, 10(1), 43–56

8 Measuring the life-cycle consumption costs of children

JAMES BANKS, RICHARD BLUNDELL and IAN PRESTON

Introduction

The costs of children can be seen as the additional expenditure needed by a household with children to restore its standard of living to what it would have been without them. To implement this, one might think of comparing the expenditures of two households, one with and one without children, yet sharing a common level of welfare. As documented in a number of studies in this volume, the difficulty in this is in finding a criterion which might allow one to identify when two households of different composition are at a common living standard. While economic analysis of expenditure behaviour can provide important information on the way household spending patterns change in response to demographic change, it cannot identify preferences over composition itself and cannot identify costs of children without making assumptions about these preferences (see Pollak and Wales, 1979; Blackorby and Donaldson, 1991, and chapter 2 in this volume; Blundell and Lewbel, 1991, for example). We argue below that the placing of welfare measurement in an intertemporal context widens the set of parameters that we can identify and clarifies the nature of the welfare information that cannot be recovered from consumer behaviour. Quite simply, consumption *changes* over time following a change in demographic structure probably come closest to reflecting the consumption costs of children.

If intertemporal substitution responses are allowed for then the usual practice of measuring costs by concentrating on effects of children upon the within-period composition of spending seems unappealing. In this chapter we develop a model of life-cycle spending in which households are free to transfer spending between periods by borrowing and saving,[1] and demographic factors affect both within-period and cross-period expenditure allocation decisions. In this case it is not clear why one would want to look simply for compensation that maintained the within-period living

192

standard of, say, a household with children at that of a household without children, holding expenditure in other periods constant. The difference between the within-period expenditure of two such households would seem of limited interest in the study of households other than those suffering extreme liquidity constraint.

One needs to think carefully in this context about what one is trying to capture in the notion of an equivalence scale. A policy maker might, for instance, be interested in compensating a household for the costs of a child and it may be most sensible to think here of the full lifetime costs allowing for intertemporal adjustment to the utility stream. A further contrast might be between the standard within-period measure of child costs and a corresponding life-cycle-consistent measure, thought of as the difference between spending in a particular period for households at points along paths that are consistent with intertemporal reallocation of spending, and yield similar lifetime well-being. Whatever purpose or interpretation we might attach to the scales, it makes little sense to think of scales simply depending on numbers of children of differing ages in any particular period. In the empirical section below we simulate expenditure paths for households with different demographic histories yet common lifetime welfare levels. The timing of children, the anticipation of their arrival, and the anticipation of their future needs, matter.

While costs of children cannot be identified without invoking assumptions or evidence beyond the usual horizon of economic analysis, what can be done is to illuminate the assumptions involved in superficially plausible methods of identifying child costs and in certain cases to test their compatibility with observed behaviour. One example of such an assumption might be that households consuming (or planning to consume) at similar levels in periods before children are present share a common level of lifetime welfare. This would allow one to measure the costs of children simply by observing the increase in spending across the period following the (anticipated) arrival of children. We also consider this possibility at a theoretical level and show that it implies an extreme and implausible unwillingness on the part of households to substitute consumption over the life-cycle. Though implausible, such restrictions would seem necessary if all compensated effects of demographic change could be taken as acting solely on within-budget shares, a view which seems to underlie conventional practices in the estimation of child costs.

The layout of the chapter is as follows. In the next section we consider the theoretical specification of a life-cycle framework and the assumptions necessary to identify equivalence scales. The third section describes the empirical specification we adopt in applying these ideas. The fourth section describes our usage of the pooled cross-sections of the UK Family Expenditure Survey to recover within-period and intertemporal preferences for households of different composition. In the fifth section we outline our simulation methodology and present some simple simulation results. The sixth section draws some conclusions.

Equivalence scales in an intertemporal context

Life-cycle welfare and equivalence scale measurement

To estimate the costs of children in the sense mentioned in the Introduction – which is to say, as the additional expenditure needed by a household with children to restore its welfare to what it would have been without them – requires knowledge not only of preferences over goods but of joint preferences over goods and demographic characteristics. As many authors (Pollak and Wales, 1979; Blundell and Lewbel, 1991) have pointed out, consumer behaviour is at best indicative only of preferences over goods conditional upon household composition and cannot tell us anything about preferences over demographic attributes themselves. Placing household behaviour into an intertemporal context cannot escape this fundamental problem. It does, nonetheless, seem to capture an important aspect of child costs and can be shown to widen the set of parameters which the economist can identify in comparison with conventional procedures. In so doing it also clarifies the precise nature of what remains beyond econometric identification with expenditure data.

To set the scene let the household's preferences over goods and demographics be captured in the following lifetime utility function

$$U = U(\Sigma_t u_t, \mathbf{z}) \qquad u_t = u_t(\mathbf{q}_t, \mathbf{z}_t) \tag{1}$$

where $\mathbf{q}_t$ represents the vector of consumption goods, $\mathbf{z}_t$ a vector of household characteristics in period t, $\mathbf{z}$ the complete lifetime history of these household characteristics and the function $u_t(\ )$ incorporates the household's subjective discount rate. The intertemporally additive specification allows a clear distinction between lifetime and period specific[2] measures of utility, U and u_t. It also allows the results to be placed easily in a world with uncertainty over future incomes, prices and household composition.

We assume that consumers choose their most preferred allocation of expenditures over time subject to a constraint that the discounted value of lifetime expenditures equals the present value of lifetime wealth. The additive separability assumption over time allows us to separate the optimisation problem into two stages. Total consumption is first allocated between time periods, and then, subject to this upper-stage allocation, each period's consumption is distributed between commodity groups (Gorman, 1959). Under such assumptions, within-period preferences may then be represented by an indirect utility function $v_t(x_t, p_t, z_t)$ where x_t is the (discounted) total expenditure allocation to period t and p_t is the vector of discounted commodity prices. Moreover, lifetime utility is given by

$$U = U(\Sigma_t u_t, z) \qquad u_t = F_t(v_t(x_t, p_t, z_t), z_t) \tag{2}$$

where F_t now incorporates the subjective discount rate. As Blundell, Browning and Meghir (1993) show, observation of within-period consumer behaviour, while it may identify the parameters of $v_t(.)$, cannot tell us about the dependence of $F_t(.)$ on z_t. Observation of intertemporal spending behaviour may[3] be able to tell us about both, and therefore enhance understanding even of the determinants of within-period welfare, but cannot inform us about the dependence of $U(.)$ on z. This could be interpreted as the pure benefits or costs of children.

The intertemporal context also has the advantage of directing our attention towards possibly better notions of the cost of children. To outline these we make the following definitions. Let $x^*(U, p, z)$ denote the stream of expenditures minimising the lifetime cost of reaching utility U subject to a particular demographic history z and stream of prices p

$$x^*(U, p, z) = \{x_t^*(U, p, z)\} \equiv \arg \min_x (\Sigma_t x_t \,|\, U(\Sigma_t F_t(v_t(x_t, p_t, z_t), z_t), z) \geq U) \tag{3}$$

and denote the corresponding stream of within-period utilities

$$u^*(U, p, z) = \{u_t^*(U, p, z)\} \equiv F_t(v_t(x_t^*, p_t, z_t), z_t). \tag{4}$$

Lifetime and period specific expenditure functions can then be defined by

$$E(U, p, z) = \min_x (\Sigma_t x_t \,|\, U(\Sigma_t F_t(v_t(x_t, p_t, z_t), z_t), z) \geq U)$$

$$= \Sigma_t x_t^*(U, p, z) \tag{5}$$

$$e_t(u_t, p_t, z_t) = \min_{x_t} (x_t \,|\, F_t(v_t(x_t, p_t, z_t), z_t) \geq u_t).$$

The latter is the cost of keeping the household at a well-defined within-period living standard given period specific prices and demographic composition and is the natural basis for a representation of standard within-period procedures for measuring child costs.

Denote by z_t^1 the demographic composition in period t of a household with children in that period and by z_t^0 that of a household without. Measurements of the cost of children have typically concentrated on the *within-period cost* of keeping a household at a given within-period utility level:

$$e_t(u_t, \mathbf{p}_t, \mathbf{z}_t^1) - e_t(u_t, \mathbf{p}_t, \mathbf{z}_t^0).\tag{6}$$

Note that we cannot identify this without knowledge of the dependence of $F_t(.)$ on $\mathbf{z}_t$ and cannot, therefore, identify it fully from observation solely of within-period behaviour. The best one could do with within-period data alone – and this is possibly the best way of interpreting what conventional methods do – would be to find the cost of keeping a household at a constant level of v_t.

The notion of child costs embodied in (6) is a rather narrow one, however, if households are free and willing to transfer spending between periods of the lifetime by saving or borrowing. Say that one were interested for policy purposes in knowing what compensation would capture all the consumption costs involved in a couple having a child. The relevant notion would be the full lifetime cost and concentrating on the within-period amount could be very misleading. Let $\mathbf{z}^1$ and $\mathbf{z}^0$ be lifetime demographic histories differing only in the presence of a child in period t. Then the full lifetime cost[4] of having a child in that period would be

$$E(U, \mathbf{p}, \mathbf{z}^1) - E(U, \mathbf{p}, \mathbf{z}^0) = \sum_t [e_t(u_t^1, \mathbf{p}_t, \mathbf{z}_t) - e_t(u_t^0, \mathbf{p}_t, \mathbf{z}_t^0)].\tag{7}$$

Again there is an identification problem. Although information on intertemporal allocations might help identify the amount needed to restore $\Sigma_t u_t$, i.e.

$$E(U(\Sigma_t u_t, \mathbf{z}^0), \mathbf{p}, \mathbf{z}^1) - E(U(\Sigma_t u_t, \mathbf{z}^1), \mathbf{p}, \mathbf{z}^0),\tag{8}$$

it cannot identify the full cost (7) without knowing how $U(.)$ depends on $\mathbf{z}$. Given our framework, it is here rather than at (6) that we reach the limit of what observation of consumer behaviour can identify.

Note though that, given that allowance is being made in (8) for the possibility of advantageous cross-period reallocation of utility, standard arguments establish that (6) cannot be less than (8). The costs of children cannot be greater to a household less constrained in the options for adjusting its budget in response.[5] Households clearly can engage in this sort of behaviour, perhaps avoiding restaurant meals and certain forms of leisure activities until children leave home.[6] However, it may well be that the increase in *needs* during periods when children are in the household dominate this effect. The empirical results reported in Banks, Blundell and Preston (1994) and discussed later in this chapter are an attempt to measure the relative importance of these two effects.

Within-period measures of cost also have their uses – say in adjusting within-period measures of living standards such as income or expenditure in studies of poverty or income distribution[7] – and it is worth thinking also whether there are better notions of within-period costs than (6). One obvious idea would be that of a life-cycle-consistent measure. We could define this as the difference between spending in a particular period for households at points along different paths that are consistent with intertemporal reallocation of spending, and yield similar lifetime well-being,

$$e_t(u_t^*(U, \mathbf{p}, \mathbf{z}^1), \mathbf{p}_t, \mathbf{z}_t^1) - e_t(u_t^*(U, \mathbf{p}, \mathbf{z}^0), \mathbf{p}_t, \mathbf{z}_t^0). \tag{9}$$

This will coincide with (6) only under very restrictive assumptions on households' willingness to engage in intertemporal substitution. If we take it that intertemporal reallocation of utility will be away from the periods when children make consuming expensive, i.e., $u_t^0 > u_t^1$ and $u_k^0 \leq u_k^1$ for $k \neq t$, then the life-cycle-consistent cost for the period when the child is present will lie below the partial lifetime cost (8), since part of the cost is being borne in other periods, and therefore also lie below the standard measure (6).

Costs of children are most usually reported in the form of equivalence scales, which is to say as ratios, rather than as differences, between the expenditures of respective households. It will remain true, however, that the scale based on (6) will exceed those based on both (9) and (8) (assuming that costs are positive). Of course, in practice, length of period appropriate to the data used is also unlikely to be the same as the length of a child's stay in the household. In that case, the most interesting concepts of lifetime and period specific life-cycle-consistent costs will relate to the cost across the whole period of parental responsibility and the details of the above formulation will require obvious modification. Nonetheless, it is clear that simply adding up standard measures of within-period cost will still give a very misleading picture of the true financial burden.

Equivalence scales and intertemporal substitution

One way that the existing literature using period specific data has sought to get around the problem of identifying child costs has been to focus on some particular feature of the household's economic behaviour as a supposed proxy for its welfare and thereby to tie down a measure of costs. Examples of such proxies might be the share of the household budget spent on food or on necessities, or the absolute amount spent on some 'adult good' such as alcohol or adult clothing. The variety of such approaches and the implicit restrictions on preferences involved are given a full treatment by Blackorby and Donaldson in chapter 2 in this volume.

The point of what follows is to consider the possibility of extending one such approach to the intertemporal context.

One superficially attractive idea for identifying child costs would be to take households at a common level of spending in periods before child-birth and observe the difference between their subsequent expenditures consequent upon the arrival of a child in one but not the other household. The idea is akin to the idea, introduced by Rothbarth (1943) and mentioned above, of treating expenditure on a group of adult goods as an indicator of the parents' welfare. In the current intertemporal context the proposal amounts to treating expenditure in periods without children as an adult good.

For the method to be legitimate whatever the choice of childless period with common spending on which to base the comparison, two households with like within-period demographic composition and expenditure would need to be guaranteed to be at like lifetime utility. Put another way, within-period Hicksian expenditure would need for any period to be independent of out-of-period demographics, i.e.,

$$x_t^*(U, \mathbf{p}, \mathbf{z}) = h_t(U, \mathbf{p}, \mathbf{z}_t) \qquad t = 1, \ldots, T \tag{10}$$

for some $h_t(U, \mathbf{p}, \mathbf{z}_t)$ where $\mathbf{z}_t$ is the subset of $\mathbf{z}$ relating to the *current* composition of the household.

The exact restriction on preferences implied by (10) is established in the Appendix to this chapter (p. 211). Formally, a necessary and sufficient condition is that the lifetime cost function takes the form

$$E(U, \mathbf{p}, \mathbf{z}) = \Sigma_t \gamma_t(U, \mathbf{p}, \mathbf{z}_t) + \gamma_0(U, \mathbf{p}) \tag{11}$$

where $\gamma_t(U, \mathbf{p}, \mathbf{z}_t)$ is homogeneous of degree zero in each $\mathbf{p}_k$ for $k \neq t$. Note firstly that this imposes no restriction at all on intertemporal preferences conditional on $\mathbf{z}$. What is restricted is the preparedness of the household to substitute child costs over time – compensated cross-period effects of demographic change are ruled out. While nothing in (11) stops households responding to price changes by reallocating consumption towards cheaper periods, they will not respond to anticipated demographic change by shifting consumption expenditure away from periods when children are present. It is as if households choose to bear all child costs (and enjoy all the benefits of parenthood) entirely during the time that children are present. For some costs this may seem reasonable – pushchairs, baby food and so on all need to be bought when the children are in the household; for others it would seem surprising – children, for instance, can make foreign holidays and restaurant meals more expensive and one might expect individuals anticipating children to plan to holiday abroad more

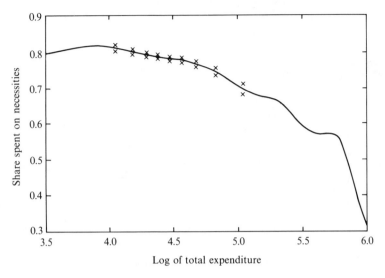

Figure 8.1 Nonparametric Engel curve for 'necessities' (food, fuel and clothing)

often in periods before (and after) the children's presence in the household as a result[8].

Empirical specification

Within-period expenditures

Empirical application of these ideas involves specification of functional forms for the functions $v_t(.)$ and $F_t(.)$ in (2). The specification we adopt below involves a choice of functional form for within-period indirect utility which reflects the need for quadratic Engel curves in line with the growing body of empirical evidence. Figure 8.1 illustrates the presence of such nonlinearity by showing a kernel regression of the share of expenditure spent on 'necessities' (i.e., food, fuel and clothing) on the logarithm of deflated total household expenditure within one demographically homogeneous population.[9] The appropriateness of a quadratic specification is more fully argued in Banks, Blundell and Lewbel (1992) where the underlying indirect utility function is also derived.

In particular the indirect utility function underlying quadratic Engel curves takes the form

$$v_t(x_t, \mathbf{p}_t, \mathbf{z}_t) = [b_t/\ln c_t + \phi_t]^{-1} \quad \text{with} \quad c_t = x_t/a(\mathbf{p}_t, \mathbf{z}_t) \tag{12}$$

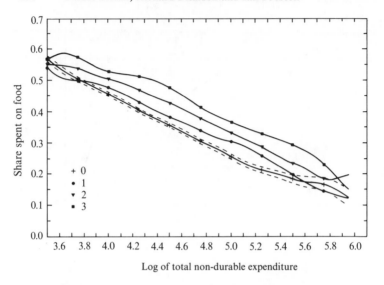

Figure 8.2 Nonparametric Engel curves for food, split by no. of children

where c_t is real expenditure, $a(\mathbf{p}_t, \mathbf{z}_t)$ is a linear homogeneous price index, and $b_t = b(\mathbf{p}_t, \mathbf{z}_t)$ and $\phi_t = \phi(\mathbf{p}_t, \mathbf{z}_t)$ are zero homogeneous in prices.[10] The demographics in the a_t, b_t and ϕ_t functions reflect the possibility that demographic variables may shift within-period preferences. Such a specification reduces to the convenient Almost Ideal type form (see Deaton and Muellbauer, 1980) if ϕ_t is omitted, but otherwise leads to within-period budget shares $\mathbf{w}_t$ quadratic in the log of total expenditure,[11] and given by

$$w_i(x_t, \mathbf{p}_t; \mathbf{z}_t) = \frac{\partial \ln a_t}{\partial \ln p_{it}} + \frac{\partial \ln b_t}{\partial \ln p_{it}} . \ln c_t + \frac{\partial \phi_t}{\partial \ln p_{it}} . \frac{1}{b_t} . \ln c_t^2$$

$$= a_i(\mathbf{p}_t; \mathbf{z}_t) + \beta_i(\mathbf{p}_t; \mathbf{z}_t) . \ln c_t + \psi_i(\mathbf{p}_t; \mathbf{z}_t) . \ln c_t^2. \tag{13}$$

The specification in (13), however, remains flexible enough to sustain linear Engel curves for some goods (if $\psi_i = 0$) and also allow demographic variables $\mathbf{z}_t$ to alter the shape of these Engel curves.

The need for demographic effects is graphically illustrated in figure 8.2 where we present nonparametric Engel curves for food using the same data as figure 8.1. We show four-kernel regressions, split by the number of children in the household, with dotted lines connecting the 95% pointwise confidence intervals around points on the lowermost of the four. There is a clear need to allow the presence of children to shift at least the intercept of any Engel curve. Incidentally, the near-linearity of the food Engel curves indicated here (and the relative size of the food budget share) also implies that the underlying curvature in fuel and clothing expenditures must be strong to generate a kernel regression such as that in figure 8.1.

Intertemporal expenditure allocations

Intertemporal preferences are specified by the following parameterisation of (2)

$$
F_t(v_t(x_t,\mathbf{p}_t,\mathbf{z}_t),\mathbf{z}_t) = \begin{cases} \dfrac{1}{1+\rho_t}\left(\dfrac{v_t(x_t,\mathbf{p}_t,\mathbf{z}_t)}{\delta_t}\right)^{1+\rho_t} & \rho_t \neq -1, \\[2ex] \ln\left(\dfrac{v_t(x_t,\mathbf{p}_t,\mathbf{z}_t)}{\delta_t}\right) & \rho_t = -1. \end{cases} \tag{14}
$$

Here, information in $\delta_t = \delta(\mathbf{z}_t)$ and $\rho_t = \rho(\mathbf{z}_t)$ is important and identifiable *only* within an intertemporal framework.[12] The parameters of both are concerned with intertemporal preferences, as explored by Blundell, Browning and Meghir (1993). The presence of a term like δ_t is attractive because we wish to allow for the possibility that in certain periods children may make spending in those periods more or less appealing independently of the impact of children on the within-period composition of spending.

The term ρ_t is included to allow us to estimate the degree to which parents are prepared to substitute expenditure away from the relatively expensive periods when children are in the household. The within- and cross-period parameters jointly establish the concavity of $F_t(.)$ and hence the intertemporal elasticity of subsitution, σ_t, defined as the reciprocal of the elasticity of marginal utility with respect to period t expenditure (see Browning, 1987, 1989):

$$
\sigma_t = \left[\frac{x_t}{\partial F_t/\partial x_t}\frac{\partial(\partial F_t/\partial x_t)}{\partial x_t}\right]^{-1}
$$

$$
= \left[\frac{[\rho_t b_t - 2\phi_t\ln c_t]}{[b_t + \phi_t\ln c_t]\ln c_t} - 1\right]^{-1}. \tag{15}
$$

The only possible constant value is -1 if ρ_t and ϕ_t are set everywhere to zero, as has been shown by Browning (1989). With values of $\rho_t \leq 0$ and ϕ_t, $b_t \geq 0$, as we find below, willingness to substitute is higher for better off households.[13]

Optimisation, subject to perfect capital markets, leads to a chosen consumption path along which the marginal utility of within-period (discounted) expenditure, $\lambda_t \equiv \partial F_t/\partial x_t$, remains constant (see, for instance, Browning, Deaton and Irish, 1985). The implied equation describing the dynamics of consumption provides a means, given suitable data, of estimating the information necessary to identify $F_t(.)$. With uncertainty,[14] about future real incomes for instance, λ_t evolves according to the familiar stochastic Euler equation (see Hall, 1978 or MaCurdy, 1983, for example):

$$E_{t-1}\lambda_t = \lambda_{t-1} \Rightarrow -\Delta \ln \lambda_t \approx \epsilon_t \qquad (16)$$

where ϵ_t has a positive expectation[15] but is orthogonal to information prior to $t-1$.

For the specification (14) the marginal utility of within-period expenditure is

$$\lambda_t = (\delta_t b_t)^{-(1+\rho_t)} [1 + \phi_t \ln c_t / b_t]^{-(2+\rho_t)} \frac{(\ln c_t)^{\rho_t}}{c_t a_t} \qquad (17)$$

so that the Euler equation (16) takes the form

$$\Delta \ln c_t - \Delta \rho_t \ln \ln c_t + \Delta (2 + \rho_t) \ln[1 + \phi_t \ln c_t / b_t]$$
$$\approx -\Delta (1 + \rho_t) \ln \delta_t - \Delta (1 + \rho_t) \ln b_t + r_{t-1} + \epsilon_t \qquad (18)$$

where r_{t-1} is the real interest rate in the previous period.[16]

Data and estimation

Data

The data are drawn from the repeated cross-sections of the UK Family Expenditure Survey for the period 1969–1988. Selecting all households with two adults gives a total of 83,698 observations. From these we select all households not resident in Northern Ireland that are characterised by the presence of one male and one female adult, both being between the ages of 18 and 65. The size of the remaining sample – 61,216 households – allows us to split the data into four demographic groups on which we estimate separate demand systems: childless households (23,331), households with one child (12,140), households with two children (17,228), and households with three or more children (8,457), where sample sizes are given in brackets.

These individual-level data are pooled within each group to estimate the Quadratic Almost Ideal system. That is to say we estimate a share model which is quadratic in the logarithm of real expenditure on 20 years of observations in five categories – food, fuel, clothing, alcohol and other goods – with monthly price variation. Although this does not represent a very fine level of disaggregation, our grouping does allow us to address all the usual questions associated with the equivalence scale literature. The relative price movement over time allows all parameters of $a(\mathbf{p}_t, \mathbf{z}_t)$,

$b(\mathbf{p}_t, \mathbf{z}_t)$ and $\phi(\mathbf{p}_t, \mathbf{z}_t)$ to be identified. This estimation process is described fully in Banks, Blundell and Lewbel (1992) where the Quadratic Almost Ideal model is also derived and the parameters of our estimated system for childless households (the largest of the five demographic groups) are presented.

Intertemporal parameters are estimated from constructed cohort data, aggregating consistently from the same individual data on the basis of parameters estimated at the earlier stage. Joint estimation across the two stages imposes formidable computational costs and so we follow the methodology of Blundell, Browning and Meghir (1993) and estimate Euler equation (18) conditional on our within-period demand system parameters.

Cohorts are constructed on the basis of birthdate of head of household. We construct 11 cohorts each covering a five year band, resulting in group sizes of between 200 and 500 households with a mean of 354 observations in each cohort. Of these cohorts, five are present for the full sample (i.e., 20 years), while young or old cohorts exist only for shorter periods at either end of the sample. Within-period sampling error in construction of cohort averages leads to a resulting framework econometrically equivalent to errors-in-variables (though with an estimatable variance–covariance structure to the measurement errors) as outlined in Deaton (1985). With sufficiently large cohort sizes, such as those here, it nonetheless becomes admissible to disregard this sampling error and treat the data as genuine panel data (see Verbeek and Nijman, 1992). After allowing for the different periods in which each cohort is observed, and the loss of observations due to lagging the instrument set and taking first differences, the resulting data set comprises 133 data points. For the (individual specific) real interest rate we take the after-tax Building Society lending rate if the household has a mortgage, and the borrowing rate if they do not. This interest rate is then deflated by inflation – which we define as the change in the cohort average of the nondiscounted value of the individual specific linear homogeneous price index $a(\mathbf{p}_t, \mathbf{z}_t)$ described in the previous section.

Cohort average data for number of children and total expenditure are illustrated in figures 8.3A and 8.3B. Each line on the figure illustrates the average value within a single cohort traced over time. The pattern of child bearing over the life-cycle appears from figure 8.3A to be fairly stable across cohorts with little variance over the business cycle. This contrasts somewhat with the expenditure profiles in figure 8.3B in which business-cycle variation, for instance, is clearly visible.[17] It should be noted that conditioning, as we do, on labour market status in the estimation of both the demand system and Euler equation may capture some of these business cycle effects.

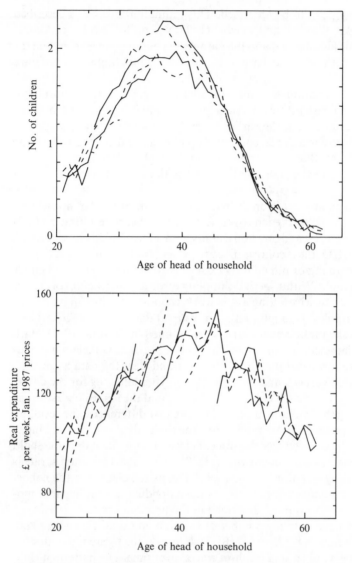

Figure 8.3 Cohort means
A   No. of children in household over the life-cycle
B   Real expenditure over the life-cycle

Estimation

To estimate the intertemporal parameters that govern the evolution of dynamic expenditure paths we assume that p_t is independent of demographics (i.e., $p_t = p$) which allows us to rearrange (18) and write down the estimatable equation

$$\left[\Delta \ln c_t + 2\Delta \ln \left(1 + \frac{\phi_t \ln c_t}{b_t} \right) + \Delta \ln b_t \right] - r_{t-1}$$

$$= p \left[\Delta \ln \ln c_t - \Delta \ln \left(1 + \frac{\phi_t \ln c_t}{b_t} \right) - \Delta \ln b_t \right] - (1 + p)\Delta \ln \delta_t + d_t + e_t \quad (19)$$

where a_t (implicit in c_t), b_t and ϕ_t are calculated from top-stage estimated parameters, and demographics, z_i, are allowed to enter in the following way

$$\Delta \ln \delta_t = \delta_0 + \sum_i \delta_i \Delta z_i \quad (20)$$

Since (19) has a constant which includes both the subjective discount rate and d_t, which represents the conditional expectation of ϵ_t in (2), separate identification of the two cannot be achieved.

We estimate this relationship on the cohort data described above using Generalised Method of Moments (see Hansen and Singleton, 1982). As the terms in square brackets in (19) are nonlinear we construct them at the individual level and then take first differences at the cohort level. Initially, we try a specification that includes demographic and labour market status variables that have been shown to be useful in recent sudies (see, for example, Blundell, Browning and Meghir, 1993, or Attanasio and Weber, 1993). We also include the levels of these demographics at time t, since these might plausibly affect the conditional variance term in d_t in (19) above.

In table 8.1 we report a sequence of alternative models taken from the Banks, Blundell and Preston (1994) study, the first two columns of which contain our most general specifications. In column (3) we present a more parsimonious representation of these results which, as can be seen, would not be rejected by the data and also allows us to focus on the effects of children on the change in δ_t. This retains the influence of head unemployed and in column (4) we show that the p parameter in particular is sensitive to the exclusion of this variable. As a result we choose to use column (3) estimates in the simulations below.

In addition to the estimated parameters, we report the two 'deep' parameters of interest – σ, the elasticity of intertemporal substitution, calculated (from (3.5)) at the sample mean level of c_t, b_t and ϕ_t, and δ_1, the importance of the total number of children in the discount factors (from (20)).

Table 8.1. *Dynamic expenditure model*

	(1)	(2)	(3)	(4)
Constant	0.0435	0.0606	0.0402	0.0219
	$(0.0117)^a$	(0.0300)	(0.0095)	(0.0071)
$\Delta Totkids^b$	0.2629	0.1685	0.1903	0.1802
	(0.1022)	(0.0766)	(0.0826)	(0.0792)
$\Delta Hunemp$	− 1.2745	0.0531	− 1.4135	
	(0.6282)	(0.7170)	(0.4562)	
$\Delta WWife$	0.5734			
	(0.4397)			
$\Delta Mortg$	− 0.3612			
	(0.3758)			
$TotKids$		− 0.0039		
		(0.0177)		
$Hunemp$		− 0.3721		
		(0.1718)		
ρ	− 2.5817	− 1.3357	− 2.2264	− 1.4775
	(0.86339)	(0.9731)	(0.7165)	(0.6475)
σ^c	− 0.6511	− 0.7771	− 0.6827	− 0.7604
	(0.1716)	(0.1914)	(0.1445)	(0.1309)
δ_1	0.1662	0.5019	0.1551	0.3774
	(0.0776)	(1.3387)	(0.0804)	(0.4458)
Sargan^d	18.4270	24.0889	24.7710	37.3044
d.f.	16	16	18	19
St. error of eqn.	0.0070	0.0042	0.0059	0.0054

^{a} Standard errors are given in brackets.
^{b} Variables are levels at time t, or first differences (indicated by Δ). *Hunemp* is a dummy for head of household unemployed; *WWife* is a dummy for working female; *Mortg* is a dummy for presence of a mortgage; *Totkids* is the total number of children of all ages.
^{c} σ is calculated at the mean $\ln c_t$ for the sample of 4.76714 (at January 1987 prices).
^{d} Instruments are no. of children in each of four age groups, *Age of Head, Age of Spouse, Working male* and *Working female* dummies, lending and borrowing interest rates, tenure and region dummies; all instruments are dated $t - 2$.

Simulation methodology

To simulate a lifetime path for consumption we first choose a demo-graphic path for both the reference and the comparison household. This

Table 8.2. *A within-period equivalence scale*

Child's age	Scale[a]
0–2	0.1818
3–5	0.2866
6–10	0.3283
11–18	0.3610

[a] These scales are as reported in Blundell and Lewbel (1991). They coincide with the standard equivalence scales defined in (6) only if δ_t is one in all periods. Higher values of δ_t in periods with children would give higher scales.

includes all the characteristics that enter into the intercept of the esti- mated budget share equations. A child would enter the household when the head reaches some (chosen) age and then stay in the household until the age of 18, with the female adult being constrained to be out of the labour force while the child is less than three years of age. The path is constructed to cover all periods during which the head is between the initial age and 60 years of age. Given such a profile, it is possible to construct a_t, b_t and ϕ_t for each period from the estimated 'top-stage' parameters, and δ_t and ρ_t from the estimated Euler equation parameters.

To simulate we solve forward from the Euler equation as described in Banks, Blundell and Preston (1994) to construct complete expenditure paths. Our model for within-period demands combined with the esti- mated intertemporal parameters allows us to construct life-cycle expendi- ture paths for households with different demographic composition and with different overall levels of real lifetime expenditure. We can then assess the sensitivity of our results to two critical parameters, representing the degree of intertemporal substitution,[18] and the importance of children in the discount factors, δ_1. Intertemporal substitution tends to smooth out the expenditure profile. The δ_t act like prices for within-period utility and, if positively related to children, will tend to lead to substitution away from child rearing periods of the life-cycle. Of course, increases in within- period needs (as reflected in the usual static equivalence scales calculated from our data and reported in table 8.2) tend to counteract this effect. It is also worth noting that the level of initial period consumption for the reference path will influence the resulting scales.[19]

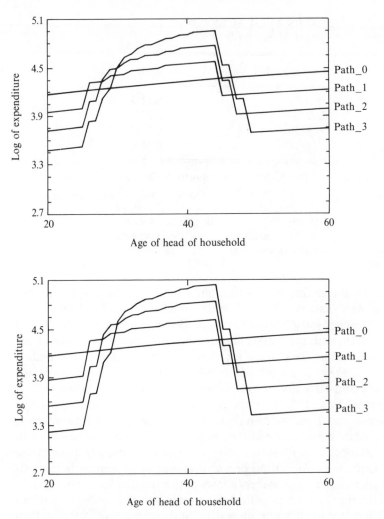

Figure 8.4   Lifetime expenditure equivalent paths
A $\delta_1 = 0.155$, $\sigma = -0.683$
B $\delta_1 = 0.310$, $\sigma = -0.683$

Figures 8.4A and 8.4B present comparisons of 'life-cycle expenditure-constant' paths for households of differing demographic profiles. We take our estimate of the base elasticity of substitution and simulate expenditure paths for two different values of δ_1. The reference household (Path 0) has no children at any point, but its (nominal) expenditure path slopes slightly upward. The demographics of path 1 are identical in every way

Table 8.3. *Simulated life-cycle equivalence scales*

No. of children	Head's age when children born	Lifetime scale	Single-period scale when head is age 40
1	26	0.158	0.334
2	26, 28	0.399	0.848
3	26, 28 and 30	0.753	1.614

except that a child is born when the head of household is 26 years of age. Path 2 has two children – born when the head is 26 and 28 – and Path 3 has three children, born at the ages of 26, 28, and 30. We see that households with more children reallocate expenditure into periods with children, and therefore (since total lifetime expenditure is constant) spend less in the periods before and after the children. Remember that we are considering anticipated changes only, so that households expecting higher costs in the future due to the presence of children will try to save in anticipation of that event. It is clear, however, that a higher value of δ_1 causes household reallocation of expenditures to be more extreme. Period by period needs outweigh intertemporal substitution.

Finally, we turn to the calculation of equivalence scales. If we choose to specify a form for lifetime utility embodying an implicit identifying assumption regarding preferences over children, we can construct paths such that lifetime utility rather than lifetime expenditure is constant. In this case we would not only be able to plot expenditure paths, but would also be able to calculate lifetime equivalence scales and life-cycle equivalence scales defined above.

The obvious choice of identifying assumption would be $U = \Sigma_t u_t$. This turns out, however, to yield scales which are too high, when judged against what seems intuitively reasonable. The scales in table 8.3 are derived by adding an arbitrary linear contribution to lifetime utility from the number of children (chosen such that the scales are of the same order of magnitude as 'traditional' single-period scales) and were simulated from the parameters of the Euler equation presented as column (3) in table 8.1, which is to say using a base-period reference elasticity of intertemporal substitution of -0.68. We assume that all children leave the household at the age of 18. When comparing these scales to those in table 8.2 it must be remembered that they take into account the entire demographic lifetime of the household and therefore are not dependent on the age of the child – unlike most conventional scales. Since the lifetime of the household is assumed to be 40 years in our simulations, whereas a child is in the household for only 18 of those years, the scales in table 8.3 need to be more than doubled to be comparable with those in table 8.2. As a result the lifetime scales are larger, reflecting the incomplete measurement of costs in the standard static approach. Of course, in constructing these scales we have assumed away any part of household utility that cannot be captured by demand analysis. In fact the arbitrariness of any identifying assumption is highlighted in this multi-period setting since it would be possible to get very different scales with reasonably similar functional forms.

Conclusions

Our purpose in this chapter has been to explore the issues raised by measurement of child costs in an intertemporal framework with households able and willing to transfer spending between periods by borrowing and saving. We have stressed that full comparisons of interpersonal welfare are never possible from demand data alone but this is a point equally valid in or out of the intertemporal context. Use of intertemporal information can, nonetheless, extend the range of welfare-relevant parameters open to econometric estimation, clarifying the nature of the identification problem.

The evidence which we have presented for the importance of children in the allocation of expenditures, and therefore consumption costs, over the life-cycle seems empirically compelling. This pattern is also shown to be extremely sensitive to assumptions about intertemporal parameters. By considering the behaviour of household expenditure over time we have exploited the Euler condition to estimate such parameters of interest. Any form of equivalence scale that recognised the intertemporal aspects of household decision making would depend on the shape of these lifetime expenditure profiles. We believe that these intertemporal processes are important, and therefore for policy purposes (given the need for some monetary level of compensation) we need to look outside simple current period models and acknowledge the intertemporal factors that influence the household decision making process.

The main reason why households do not substitute expenditures over time may well not be because they are unwilling, but because they are unable. In particular this may be true at the lower end of the income distribution, where indeed our model suggests willingness to substitute may be lower anyway, and may reduce the importance of these considerations for poorer households. Arguably the most important application of the equivalence scale literature relates to the compensation of such households and may therefore be greater than that which the methodology of this chapter would suggest. In addition, any such 'failure' in the market for credit (e.g., households being unable to borrow against their human capital) could be one justification for the existence of period specific compensation such as child benefit.

Appendix

Theorem: Within-period Hicksian expenditure is independent of out-of-period demographics, i.e.,

$$x_t^*(U, \mathbf{p}, \mathbf{z}) = h_t(U, \mathbf{p}, \mathbf{z}_t) \qquad t = 1, \ldots, T \tag{10}$$

for some $h_t(U, \mathbf{p}, \mathbf{z}_t)$, if and only if the lifetime cost function takes the form

$$E(U, \mathbf{p}, \mathbf{z}) = \Sigma_t \gamma_t(U, \mathbf{p}, \mathbf{z}_t) + \gamma_0(U, \mathbf{p}) \tag{11}$$

where $\gamma_t(U, \mathbf{p}, \mathbf{z}_t)$ is homogeneous of degree zero in each $\mathbf{p}_i$ for $i \neq t$.

Proof: By Theorem 2 of chapter 2 in this volume (p. 59), (10) implies

$$E(U, \mathbf{p}, \mathbf{z}) = \chi_t(U, \mathbf{p}, \mathbf{z}_t) + \psi_t(U, \mathbf{p}, \mathbf{z}) \qquad t = 1, \ldots, T \tag{A1}$$

for some $\chi_t(.)$, $\psi_t(.)$ where $\psi_t(.)$ is homogeneous of degree zero in $\mathbf{p}_t$. Adding across periods of the lifetime gives

$$E(U, \mathbf{p}, \mathbf{z}) = \frac{1}{T} \Sigma_t \chi_t(U, \mathbf{p}, \mathbf{z}_t) + \frac{1}{T} \Sigma_t \psi_t(U, \mathbf{p}, \mathbf{z}). \tag{A2}$$

Noting from (A1) that, for any t, the effect of multiplying $\mathbf{p}_t$ by a positive scalar must be independent of all $\mathbf{z}_i$ for $i \neq t$, it is clear that (A2) can be true only if

$$E(U, \mathbf{p}, \mathbf{z}) = \Sigma_t \gamma_t(U, \mathbf{p}, \mathbf{z}_t) + \gamma_0(U, \mathbf{p}) + \gamma_{00}(U, \mathbf{p}, \mathbf{z}) \tag{A3}$$

where $\gamma_t(U, \mathbf{p}, \mathbf{z}_t)$ is homogeneous of degree zero in each $\mathbf{p}_i$ for $i \neq t$ and $\gamma_{00}(U, \mathbf{p}, \mathbf{z})$ is homogeneous of degree zero in each $\mathbf{p}_i$. But $\gamma_{00}(U, \mathbf{p}, \mathbf{z}) = 0$ by linear homogeneity of $E(U, \mathbf{p}, \mathbf{z})$ in $\mathbf{p}$.

NOTES

This research was supported by funding from the Rowntree Foundation and from the Economic and Social Research Council Research Centre at IFS. We are grateful to the Department of Employment for providing the Family Expenditure Survey. Paul Johnson provided extensive assistance with the creation of our data set, and the chapter has benefited from the useful comments of Guglielmo Weber and one anonymous referee. We alone, however, are responsible for any errors.

1 Perfect capital markets are assumed in much of what follows, but most of the points made here remain relevant provided any cross-period reallocation is possible.

2 It has to be recognised that interpreting u_t as a measure of period specific utility is a little questionable when the mapping from $\Sigma_t u_t$ to lifetime well-being U is mediated in an unspecified fashion by demographic history z. The effect of children on well-being that this captures has to happen sometime. The interpretation is best regarded as of expository value.

3 The concept of a lifetime cost of children was recognised by Pashardes (1991), although some of his analysis is true only when households do not substitute intertemporally.

4 Any additively separated dependence would obviously remain unidentified from intertemporal behaviour.

5 This is not to say that our methodology need imply lower scales than others have found in studies ignoring intertemporal issues since, as we have stressed, there are factors affecting within-period utility which can be picked up only from intertemporal estimation.

6 The significance of intertemporal reallocation upon lifetime utility is, in a sense, second order given the envelope theorem – a point made by Keen (1990, p. 55) as regards the impact of price changes. This is far from implying their unimportance, however, since demographic changes cannot be considered as small.

7 Blundell and Preston (1992) discuss the issues raised by intertemporal considerations in the measurement of welfare from period specific income or expenditure surveys.

8 Note that (11) is compatible with (1) even if it is not a very attractive imposition – one could take, for example, the case in which

$$u_t = F_t(v_t(x_t, \mathbf{p}_t) - \kappa_t(\mathbf{p}_t, \mathbf{z}_t)).$$

9 The data for this figure is a subsample of married couples without children from the Family Expenditure Survey data described on p. 202. In addition we have simply chosen three years of data (1980–1982) to abstract from issues of comparability of prices and incomes across time. All non-parametric calculations were carried out using the kernel regression package NP-REG described by Duncan and Jones (1992).

10 Note that since b_t, ϕ_t and c_t are zero homogeneous it is only when working with a_t that we need to be careful with discounting considerations.

11 This is, in fact, shown by Lewbel (1988) to be the *only* integrable rank three demand system with budget shares linear in a constant, log expenditure and any other function of expenditure.

12 We have omitted any component to $F_t(.,\mathbf{z}_t)$ that cannot be identified from expenditure data alone.

13 The dependence of a_t, b_t, ϕ_t and δ_t on demographics all encourage intertemporal substitution of child costs and rule out (11). Our empirical specification does not allow us to identify child costs by treating expenditure in childless periods as a welfare proxy.

14 What has been said above has ignored uncertainty for simplicity of exposition, but nothing in our estimation methods is undermined if we allow for it.

15 For a simple proof apply Jensen's inequality to (16) and write

$$- E_{t-1} \epsilon_t = E_{t-1}(\ln[\lambda_t/\lambda_{t-1}]) < \ln[E_{t-1}(\lambda_t/\lambda_{t-1})] = 0.$$

If ϵ_t is normally distributed this expectation is equal to half its variance conditional on the given information (see Blundell, Browning and Meghir, 1993).

16 Given that a_t is written in present value terms, $\Delta \ln a_t$ is approximately equal to minus the real interest rate, i.e., the proportional change in the nondiscounted (composition specific) price index less the nominal interest rate.

17 There is some question as to the reliability of the data underlying a sharp upturn in expenditure in the final year. Consequently in these figures we plot 1969–1986 data only. Even so, some cohorts can still be tracked for the full 18 years.

18 For means of comparison we report the elasticity of substitution for the reference household at the initial level of consumption in all the simulations that follow.

19 This arises because the scales are not independent of the level of utility at which they are evaluated. That is they are not 'exact' in the terminology used by Blackorby and Donaldson in chapter 2 in this volume, or 'independent of base' in the terminology used by Lewbel (1989).

REFERENCES

Attanasio, O.P. and G. Weber (1993) 'Consumption growth, the interest rate and aggregation', *Review of Economic Studies*, 60, 631–649

Banks, J.W., R.W. Blundell and A. Lewbel (1992) 'Quadratic Engel curves, welfare measurement and consumer demand', *IFS Working Paper*, W92/14

Banks, J.W., R.W. Blundell and I.P. Preston (1994) 'Life-cycle expenditure allocations and the consumption costs of children', *European Economic Review*, forthcoming

Blackorby, C. and D. Donaldson (1991) 'Adult-equivalence scales, interpersonal comparisons of well-being, and applied welfare economics', in J. Elster and J. Roemer (eds.), *Interpersonal Comparisons and Distributive Justice*, Cambridge, Cambridge University Press, 164–199

Blundell, R.W. and A. Lewbel (1991) 'The information content of equivalence scales', *Journal of Econometrics*, 50, 49–68

Blundell, R.W. and I.P. Preston (1992) 'The distinction between income and consumption in measuring the distribution of household welfare', University College London, *Discussion Paper in Economics*, 92–01

Blundell, R.W., M.A. Browning and C. Meghir (1993) 'Consumer demand and the lifecycle allocation of household expenditures', *Review of Economic Studies*, forthcoming

Browning, M.A. (1987) 'Anticipated changes and household behaviour: a theoretical framework', McMaster University, *Working Paper*
  (1989) 'The intertemporal allocation of expenditure on nondurables, services
and durables', *Canadian Journal of Economics*, 22, 22–36
  (1993) 'Modelling the effects of children on household economic behaviour',
Journal of Economic Literature, 30, 1434–1475
Browning, M.J., A.S. Deaton and M. Irish (1985) 'A profitable approach to life-
cycle labour supply', *Econometrica*, 53, 503–543
Deaton, A.S. (1985) 'Panel data from time series of cross sections', *Journal of
Econometrics*, 30, 109–126
Deaton, A.S. and J. Muellbauer (1982) *Economics and Consumer Behaviour*,
Cambridge, Cambridge University Press
Duncan, A. and A. Jones (1992) 'NP-REG: an interactive package for kernel
density estimation and non-parametric regression', *IFS Working Paper*,
W92/7
Gorman, W. M. (1959) 'Separable utility and aggregation', *Econometrica*, 27,
469–481
Hall, R. (1978) 'The stochastic implications of the life-cycle permanent income
hypothesis', *Journal of Political Economy*, 86, 971–987
Hansen, L.A. and K.J. Singleton (1982) 'Generalised instrumental variables
estimation of nonlinear rational expectations model', *Econometrica*, 50,
1269–1286
Keen, M.J. (1990) 'Welfare analysis and intertemporal substitution', *Journal of
Public Economics*, 42, 47–66
Lewbel, A. (1988) 'Quadratic logarithmic Engel curves and the rank extended
translog', Brandeis University, *Working Paper*, 231
  (1989) 'Household-equivalence scales and welfare comparisons', *Journal of
Public Economics*, 39, 377–391
MaCurdy, T. (1983) 'A simple scheme for estimating an intertemporal model of
labour supply and taxation in the presence of taxes and uncertainty', *International Economic Review*, 24, 265–289
Pashardes, P. (1991) 'Contemporaneous and intertemporal child costs: equivalent
expenditures vs equivalent income scales', *Journal of Public Economics*, 45,
191–213
Pollak, R.A. and T.J. Wales (1979) 'Welfare comparisons and equivalence scales',
American Economic Review, 69, 216–221
Rothbarth, E. (1943) 'Note on a method of determining equivalent income for
families of different composition', Appendix 4 in C. Madge, *War-Time Pattern
of Saving and Spending*, *Occasional Paper*, 4, Cambridge, Cambridge University Press for the National Institute of Economic and Social Research
Verbeek, M. and T. Nijman (1992) 'Can cohort data be treated as genuine panel
data?', *Empirical Economics*, 17, 9–23

9   Family fortunes in the 1970s and 1980s

FIONA A.E. COULTER, FRANK A. COWELL
and STEPHEN P. JENKINS

Introduction

There is continuing debate about how the income distribution has changed over the last decade or so. The arguments in the UK are not so much about whether overall inequality and average real income have increased, since most people agree that they have. The controversy is about whether everyone has benefited from increases in overall living standards, and the size of the changes. How have families with children fared relative to those without children? Are the income changes large or small? In this chapter we provide new answers to such questions, analysing changes in family fortunes in the UK between 1971 and 1986.

Our results also illustrate a more general methodological point: that it is important to have high quality, consistently defined, data for studying income trends. What may at first sight appear to be minor and obvious points about empirical definitions can have a significant impact on the conclusions of interest. Our research shows why official UK income statistics can be unreliable sources about trends in family fortunes. Since most commentators do nevertheless rely on official sources, it is important to document the deficiencies of these series.

Our point about the importance of data quality has been made before of course, but recent empirical work with UK household micro data has focused on the incomes of poor people only.[1] In this chapter we address several new issues.

First we analyse the changing fortunes of middle and high income people as well as low income people. The official statistics reference point for us is thus the series published by the Central Statistical Office (CSO) annually in *Economic Trends* ('The effects of taxes and benefits on household incomes'), rather than the *Households Below Average Income* (*HBAI*) statistics (formerly *Low Income Statistics*) assessed by Johnson and Webb.[2]

A second feature of our research is the information provided about income trends disaggregated by household and family type. Facts about who is better off and who is worse off, and by how much, are of intense policy interest, as illustrated by the publicity and controversy surrounding the research by Roll (1988a), based on published CSO data. Roll found that couples with children had fared worse than childless couples between 1979 and 1985, and that amongst one adult households with children, average real income had fallen in absolute terms as well as relative to other groups. These findings, the second one especially, received extensive publicity in the press and in Parliament.[3] A byproduct of our research is a reassessment of Roll's conclusions. Moreover, we do disaggregations using family income distributions as well as household income distributions; the CSO and Roll use only the latter.

The third distinctive feature of our research compared to that of Johnson and Webb (and of Roll) is that our data span a longer time period – from the beginning of the 1970s to the mid-1980s. To provide this longer perspective, we summarise trends for this period using four years of data; for 1971, 1976, 1981 and 1986. This does raise questions about whether our results are contingent on the specific years compared. For detailed estimates of trends for specific income groups, this is possible, but conclusions about broad trends are likely to be robust according to our previous research (Jenkins, 1991a) which made comparisons with trends from annual data. We are unable to analyse the distributional impact of policy changes after 1986 (notably cuts in direct taxes in 1987 and reform of social security in 1988): the 1986 data were the most recently available when our project began.

The rest of the chapter is organised as follows. The second section explains how we measure 'income' and control for differences in needs and for inflation. It also explains our definitions of the income-receiving unit. The third and fourth sections contain the main empirical results, based on our analysis of micro data from the Family Expenditure Survey (FES). In the third section we focus on changes in the overall income distribution and compare the fortunes of different income groups, giving particular attention to the fortunes of the richest fifth and the poorest fifth of the population. In the fourth, we compare the fortunes of persons from different household and family types: for the most part we compare changes in average living standards across groups, reflecting the emphasis of previous work, but we do also compare the relative chances of being in the poorest and richest fifths for persons of different unit composition groups.[4] The fifth section summarises the results of the chapter concerning who is better off or worse off, and comments on the CSO's *Economic Trends* article methodology in the light of our own analysis. The

Appendix provides details about the derivations of income distributions, sample size and composition, etc.

Important measurement issues

The definition of income

The four main income definitions used in studies like ours have been:

Original income	= income from employment and self-employment, investments and savings, occupational pensions, and other factor income
Gross income	= original income plus cash benefits
Disposable income	= gross income less direct taxes (personal income taxes and employee National Insurance contributions)
Post tax/benefit income	= disposable income less indirect and other taxes (employer National Insurance contributions, domestic rates, taxes on final goods and services, and intermediate taxes).

Series based on each of these definitions are provided by the CSO in its *Economic Trends* articles. However their series for gross and disposable series have not been (and are still not) consistently defined over time. This is a serious problem.

The main changes between 1971 and 1986 arose from the introduction of Housing Benefit in 1982/3, and the Mortgage Interest Relief At Source (MIRAS) scheme in 1983 for most owner-occupiers with a mortgage, both of which led to a change in the way incomes were recorded in the FES from 1983 on.[5] In contrast, our study is based on a specially created, consistently defined, income series.[6] We focus analysis on changes in disposable income, since we believe this gives the best 'feel' for people's comparative living standards.

Another major problem with the CSO *Economic Trends* income data is that household incomes are not adjusted to take account of differences in household composition: a single adult household with an income of £5,000 p.a. is assumed to be as well off as a couple household with children also with an income of £5,000. Furthermore, the income distributions analysed are distributions amongst households, not amongst persons: the income for each household appears once in the data regardless of how many individuals there are in the household. We provide some results based on distributions derived using these same assumptions for comparability's sake and to check robustness.

Our main results, however, are based on distributions of equivalent income amongst persons. The equivalence scale factors used to deflate incomes are those given by the 'McClements scale for income before the deduction of housing costs' (McClements, 1977). This scale is chosen because it is used by CSO in its *Economic Trends* articles (for 1987 onwards), and by the DSS in its *HBAI* tables (DSS, 1990) and in the subsequent updating of these (Social Security Committee, 1991).[7]

To take account of inflation, we deflate incomes using the *monthly* RPI, rather than using an annual average RPI (as Roll did). The choice may have a significant impact on estimates of real income levels: note, for example, that the RPI for January 1976 is 37.63 and for December 1976 42.75 (December 1986 = 100), a difference of almost 14%.

The definitions of the income-receiving unit and population subgroups

CSO *Economic Trends* articles are based on *household* distributions and breakdowns by household type. A distinctive feature of our research is that we also derive results for *family* distributions.[8]

A 'family', according to our definition, comprises either a single adult, or a married couple, plus any dependent children, and our definition is similar to the 'tax unit' definition used by the Inland Revenue for income tax assessments. Clearly a household may consist of several families. Hence, for example, lone parent families (tax units of one adult plus dependent child(ren)) do not comprise the same people as one-adult households with children. We are able to examine the economic circumstances of lone parent families directly.

More generally, having both household and family distributions allows us to draw conclusions about the impact of different assumptions concerning the extent of income sharing within income units. Such comparisons have rarely been done before with the same dataset.[9]

We classify individuals according to their household's composition and their family's composition. 11 groups are distinguished in each case. People are classified according to the age of the head of their income unit (whether under 65 years), and according to the number of adults and children in their income unit.

Our classifications are modelled on tenfold grouping used by the CSO in its *Economic Trends* articles from the late 1970s onwards, but with two main differences. First, we have an extra category including income units for whom a spouse is classifed as absent at the time of the interview. By contrast the CSO series include absent spouse households in the 'one-adult households with children' group for their published breakdowns, even though they have argued elsewhere that this significantly biases estimates of the average income for this group.[10] Given this problem, we always separate out temporarily absent spouse income units in our decompositions by income-unit type (though given their very small numbers, we do not discuss trends for this group explicitly).

The second main difference from the CSO is that our classifications of people by income-unit type are intentionally very straightforward and the same for each of the four years considered. By contrast the CSO uses complicated definitions and has changed them between 1971 and 1986. See the Appendix for a brief discussion of the differences, as well as summary statistics on demographic trends. Coulter (1991a) provides fuller details.

A further feature of our analysis is that, unlike the CSO, we analyse trends in group living standards using median incomes as well as mean incomes. For small groups, and lone parent families in particular, mean income may be less representative of group circumstances than median income is, because the mean is more affected by a few low (or high) incomes.[11]

How the income distribution changed in the 1970s and 1980s

Our first summary of how the income distribution changed in the 1970s and 1980s is provided in table 9.1. This is based on the income definition which gives the best 'feel' for people's comparative living standards – equivalent real disposable income – and shows the distribution amongst persons in households. The picture is a clear one: of rising average living standards for almost all income groups throughout the period but, from 1976 onwards, of rising inequality as well. Let us consider this in more detail.

Changes in average real income

Average real income was some £6,500 in 1971 and £8,600 in 1986, an increase of nearly one-third. It grew by about 6% between 1971 and 1976, but by roughly twice as fast in each of the two subsequent five year periods (1976–1981, 10%; 1981–1986, 13%).

These overall changes disguise significant differences in growth rates across income groups. Between 1971 and 1976, income growth was much greater for poorer groups than richer ones: compare 15% for the poorest tenth with the small negative rate for the richest tenth. However the picture is completely reversed from 1976 onwards. The richer groups then

Table 9.1. *Average real incomes by income group, distributions of equivalent household disposable income amongst persons, £ p.a., December 1986 prices*

	Group mean income as % of overall mean income				Growth in group mean income (%)			Group income share (%)			
	1971	1976	1981	1986	1971–1976	1976–1981	1981–1986	1971	1976	1981	1986
Poorest tenth	41	45	41	39	14.7	−1.2	9.9	4.2	4.5	4.1	3.9
2nd	56	59	55	52	11.9	1.9	8.4	5.6	5.9	5.5	5.2
3rd	67	68	64	62	8.2	4.1	8.3	6.7	6.8	6.4	6.2
4th	76	77	73	71	7.7	4.9	8.9	7.6	7.7	7.3	7.1
5th	85	86	83	81	7.6	5.5	11.0	8.5	8.6	8.3	8.1
6th	95	95	94	93	6.7	8.4	11.5	9.5	9.5	9.4	9.3
7th	105	106	106	106	7.0	9.6	12.9	10.5	10.6	10.6	10.6
8th	119	120	121	122	7.2	10.8	14.2	11.9	12.0	12.1	12.2
9th	140	140	145	145	6.2	14.0	13.3	14.0	14.1	14.5	14.5
Richest tenth	217	202	217	229	−1.5	18.5	19.7	21.7	20.2	21.7	22.9
Overall mean (£ p.a.)	6,518	6,898	7,588	8,601	5.8	10.0	13.4				
Gini coefficient	0.26	0.24	0.27	0.28							
Mean logarithmic dev.	0.11	0.10	0.12	0.14							
Theil coefficient	0.12	0.10	0.13	0.15							
Coefficient of variation	0.55	0.48	0.64	0.71							

Source: authors' calculations from FES micro data tapes.

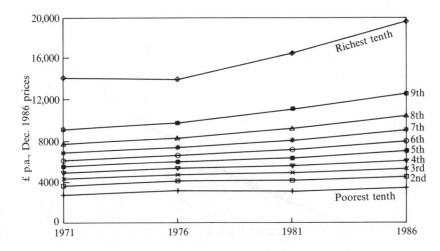

Figure 9.1 Average real income, by income group

experience consistently higher income growth rates. Figure 9.1 illustrates this.

Thus although average income overall grew throughout the 15 years, the incomes of those at the bottom fell relative to the mean from 1976 on, while those at the top rose. To put things another way, in 1971, average income amongst the richest tenth was 5.3 times the average income amongst the poorest tenth. The ratio fell to 4.5 in 1976, but by 1981 it was 5.3, and in 1986 5.7. Between 1976 and 1986, the share of total income received by the bottom fifth of the population fell from 9.6% to 9.1%. Over the same period, the share of the top fifth rose from 36.2% to 37.4%.

Changes in inequality

In fact, the income share figures given in table 9.1 imply that the Lorenz curves for the four years do not intersect, and so all standard indices of inequality will rank the 1976 distribution as the most equal of the four, the 1971 one second most equal, the 1981 one third most equal, and the 1986 distribution the most unequal (see figure 9.2). The four inequality indices shown confirm the inequality ordering. As for the size of the inequality changes, the mean logarithmic deviation increases by some 40% between 1976 and 1986. In contrast, the coefficient of variation, which is more sensitive to income differences amongst richer groups, increased by almost one half over than decade.

These trends are consistent with the year-to-year trends analysed by

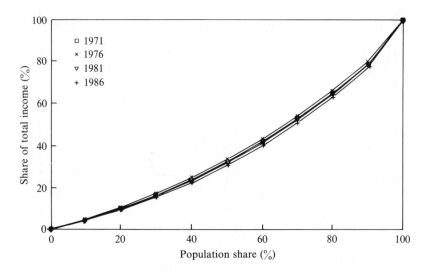

Figure 9.2   Lorenz curves

Jenkins (1991a, 1992a) and Atkinson (1993). As they show, the sub-stantial increase in inequality in the 1980s is unparalleled in recent British history.

How sensitive are the results to changes in definitions?

If we use the 'family' as the income-receiving unit rather than the 'household', but retain the same income definition, then our conclusions about *trends* are robust. For example, using family distributions, overall income growth between 1976 and 1981 is 10.1% (rather than 10.0%) and 32.5% between 1976 and 1986 (rather than 32.0%). The patterns of differential growth between richest and poorest groups are the same too.

The story about *levels* is different. Because we assume that income within each unit is distributed equally, a family distribution for a given year is more unequal than the corresponding household distribution – for example, the Gini coefficient for 1986 is 0.31 rather than 0.28 – but the secular trends in inequality turn out to be the same; falling between 1971 and 1976, rising thereafter. (Again the four Lorenz curves do not intersect.) Using family distributions, the income share of the poorest tenth falls from 4.2% to 3.4% between 1976 and 1986, while the share of the richest tenth rises from 21.1% to 24.1%.

But the CSO's figures (and those published in FES Reports) are based on distributions of household income by households: incomes are not adjusted for differences in composition and each household receives a weight of one irrespective of whether it consists of a single person or a large family. It would be interesting to know whether results are sensitive to switching to an alternative basis (but nonetheless still using consistently defined income series); compare table 9.2 with table 9.1.

If we do not adjust incomes for differences in household composition nor weight by household size then, clearly, we overestimate the degree of inequality in any given year. For example the Gini coefficient for 1986 is 0.35 rather than 0.28, a large difference.

The qualitative conclusions about trends which can be drawn from table 9.2 are broadly similar to those implied by table 9.1, but there are some notable differences in the specific estimates. For example, there is a similar pattern of differential income growth, but raw income growth rates are in many cases smaller in size than the corresponding equivalent income growth rates in table 9.1. Between 1971 and 1986, mean household income amongst households increased by only about one-fifth (22%), compared to an increase of almost a third (32%) for mean equivalent household income amongst persons. Table 9.2 suggests that income growth between 1981 and 1986 was smaller than in the previous five years, in contrast to table 9.1, which shows the reverse.

Recall that table 9.1 shows that the incomes of the poorest tenth of the personal distribution fell between 1976 and 1981. Now we find that the incomes of the poorest fifth of the household distribution grew significantly.[12] As a result, the Lorenz curves for the four distributions corresponding to the table 9.2 income shares intersect (notice that the income share of the poorest tenth does not fall between 1976 and 1981: cf. table 9.1). Table 9.1 estimates imply that inequality was unambiguously higher in 1981 than 1971 according to all standard relative indices, but according to table 9.2 estimates of the Gini coefficient and mean logarithmic deviation it was much the same.

To emphasise the point about sensitivity, we show in table 9.3 how estimates of trends in average disposable income amongst the poorest and richest fifth vary according to the distribution used. We compare the estimates from our consistent series with those from the inconsistent series published in FES Reports and discussed by Townsend (1991).

Our preferred distributions, (1) and (2), provide estimates of average income growth over the five years to 1986 of around 9% for the poorest fifth and 17% for the richest fifth. Both changes are larger than those estimated from our consistent distributions on a household basis (3). By contrast, the FES Report series provides a very different impression of how fortunes have changed.[13] The picture is a little different if we use median incomes to represent group incomes. We now have slightly higher

Table 9.2. *Average real incomes by income group, distributions of equivalent household disposable income amongst households, £ p.a., December 1986 prices*

	Group mean income as % of overall mean income				Growth in group mean income (%)			Group income share (%)			
	1971	1976	1981	1986	1971–1976	1976–1981	1981–1986	1971	1976	1981	1986
Poorest tenth	25	28	28	27	17.1	8.9	6.4	2.5	2.8	2.8	2.7
2nd	39	42	40	39	9.2	5.9	5.9	3.9	4.1	4.0	3.9
3rd	54	55	52	50	3.4	4.9	2.6	5.4	5.5	5.2	5.0
4th	70	70	66	62	1.5	4.5	1.2	7.0	7.0	6.6	6.2
5th	84	84	81	76	1.7	6.2	1.5	8.4	8.4	8.1	7.6
6th	97	98	95	92	3.0	7.7	3.9	9.7	9.8	9.5	9.2
7th	112	112	111	110	2.7	9.4	6.4	11.2	11.2	11.1	11.0
8th	129	130	131	130	2.7	11.2	7.8	13.0	13.0	13.1	13.0
9th	154	154	158	161	2.6	12.9	10.1	15.4	15.4	15.8	16.1
Richest tenth	236	228	239	254	− 0.8	15.7	14.3	23.6	22.8	23.9	25.4
Overall mean (£ p.a.)	7,996	8,186	9,040	9,748	2.4	10.4	7.8				
Gini coefficient	0.33	0.32	0.33	0.35							
Mean logarithmic dev.	0.20	0.18	0.20	0.22							
Theil coefficient	0.18	0.17	0.19	0.22							
Coefficient of variation	0.66	0.61	0.73	0.80							

Source: authors' calculations from FES micro data tapes.

Table 9.3. *Trends in real income for the poorest and richest fifth, 1981–1986*

| | % increase in income | | | | | |
| | Mean | | | Median | | |
Definition of real disposable income distribution	Poorest fifth	Richest fifth		Poorest fifth	Richest fifth
(1) Equivalent household income amongst persons	9.1	17.2		9.7	14.9
(2) Equivalent family income amongst persons	8.7	17.9		10.0	15.4
(3) Household income amongst households	6.1	12.6		9.3	12.1
(4) Household income amongst households (FES Report)	− 12.0	16.2			

Sources: (1)–(3): author's calculations from FES micro data tapes. (4): authors' calculations from Townsend (1991, Table 1).

estimates of income growth for the poorest fifth, and lower growth for the richest fifth. It remains the case, however, that the unadjusted unweighted income distributions (3) provide the lowest estimates of income growth.

In sum, what may seem to be arcane points about definitions can turn out to have a significant effect on the 'big picture' and may thus convey quite different impressions to participants in policy debates about income trends. The definitions of income and income receiver really do matter.

Changing family fortunes

Who are the poorest, who are the richest?

To address the question of who the richest and the poorest groups are, we consider first the breakdowns of the distribution of equivalent household income per person (table 9.4). If we rank groups in terms of their average income, it is clear that those belonging to childless nonelderly households are the richest (average incomes some 30% above the mean for multi-adult households, 15% above for single adults), and that those in elderly households, one adult plus children households, and two-adult households with three or more children are the poorest (average incomes 25% to 30% below the mean). In contrast to those in the last group, those in two-adult households with only one child have an average income some 5% above the overall mean. This reflects another clear pattern in the data: the more children there are in a household, the lower living standards are on average.

It is striking that the relative positions of almost all groups remained stable throughout the 15 years between 1971 and 1986. Moreover, it is not just *rankings* by group mean income that stayed constant, but also many mean income *levels* relative to the mean. Of the exceptions, groups experiencing a decline in income relative to the overall mean were childless households with three or more adults (average income nearly 30% above the overall mean in 1971, but less than 20% above in 1986); one-adult households with children (from about 25% below to almost 30% below); and two-adult households with three or more children (from nearly 20% below to 25% below). In contrast, elderly one-adult households have increased their average income relative to the mean, from two-thirds of the overall mean in 1971 to almost three-quarters of the overall mean in 1986.

What if, like the CSO, we were to look at the distribution of disposable income amongst households, with no adjustments using equivalence scales? The conclusions change in several ways according to table 9.4. Differences in average incomes between richest and poorest groups are exaggerated on this basis, apparently ranging some 60% above and below the average, compared to 30% above and below previously. Different impressions are also given about which groups are richest and which are poorest. This effect is most marked, not surprisingly, for the largest- and the smallest-sized households. According to the nonequivalised unweighted data, two-adult households with two children, two-adult households with three or more children, and three-adult households with children are amongst those with the highest average incomes (ranked third highest, fifth highest, and highest in 1986) whereas on the former basis they had relatively low average incomes (ranked sixth, eighth and fifth highest in 1986). Three-adult households with children have an average income much the same as that for childless three-adult households, 60%–70% larger than the overall average, whereas on our preferred basis, three-adult households with children ranked about fifth richest and had an average income much the same as two-adult households with two children and the overall average. Single nonelderly households are amongst the poorest with an average income some 60% below the overall, whereas the earlier estimate placed them as the third richest with an average income 15%–20% above the overall mean.

One conclusion that does not change is that elderly single adults and one-adult households with children are the poorest groups (though the extent to which they are worse off in relative terms is exaggerated in the unadjusted household data).

Whose incomes have grown the most, and whose the least?

Has everyone shared the benefits of the rise in national prosperity? Consider the growth rates in average equivalent household income per person, as shown in table 9.4.[14]

In the 1970s average real incomes for one-adult households grew faster than the overall average, while those living in households with children tended to do worse than the overall average. Between 1981 and 1986, this position was somewhat reversed, since people in two- and three-adult households with children had above average growth rates then. Only those in elderly households experienced income growth above the average in all three five year periods.

Although there is a diversity in average income growth rates, it is notable that growth rates are positive for all groups and for all three five year periods (with just one exception). In this sense at least it is possible to say that all groups have been benefiting from growing national prosperity.

Of course, focusing on group average incomes ignores potential differences in income growth *within* each group. To investigate the robustness

Table 9.4. *Average real disposable income by household type, distributions of equivalent household income amongst persons and household income amongst households, £ p.a., December 1986 prices*

| | Equivalent household income[a] amongst persons | | | | | | | Household income amongst households | | | | | | |
| | Group mean income as % of overall mean income | | | | Growth in group mean income (%) | | | Group mean income as % of overall mean income | | | | Growth in group mean income (%) | | |
Household type	1971	1976	1981	1986	1971–1976	1976–1981	1981–1986	1971	1976	1981	1986	1971–1976	1976–1981	1981–1986
Elderly: 1 adult	66	70	71	74	12.9	11.8	18.3	33	36	36	40	12.4	11.7	18.4
Elderly: 2 + adults	75	80	80	81	12.9	10.0	14.2	69	74	74	77	9.3	9.8	13.3
1 Adult	111	117	120	115	12.0	12.8	8.4	55	60	62	62	12.0	12.8	8.4
2 Adults	131	129	135	132	3.8	15.2	10.9	108	109	114	118	3.6	15.6	11.1
3 + Adults	125	128	124	117	8.2	6.4	7.0	157	166	164	161	8.0	9.3	6.0
1 Adult & children	74	76	73	69	9.2	5.6	6.6	66	70	66	61	8.0	4.2	− 0.5
2 Adults & 1 child	108	105	105	106	2.8	10.3	13.6	106	107	107	113	3.3	10.4	13.8
2 Adults & 2 children	100	94	93	97	− 0.1	8.4	18.3	115	113	112	122	0.3	9.7	18.2
2 Adults & 3 + children	82	81	79	75	5.4	6.8	8.2	119	123	117	115	5.7	5.6	6.2
3 + Adults & children	97	100	94	99	9.3	3.5	18.6	161	173	158	170	10.2	0.5	16.2
Absent spouse[b]	101	97	165	101	2.0	87.3	− 30.6	100	97	148	96	− 0.6	67.8	− 30.0
All	100	100	100	100	5.8	9.9	13.4	100	100	100	100	2.4	10.4	7.8
Overall mean (£ p.a.)	6,518	6,899	7,588	8,601				7,995	8,186	9,040	9,748			

Source: authors' calculations from FES micro data tapes.

[a] Income definitions are as in tables 9.1 and 9.2.

'Elderly': head of income unit aged 65 years or more.

[b] The 'Absent spouse' group comprises a very small number of income units (see Appendix table 9A.1).

of our conclusions we have also calculated growth rates for people near the bottom of each group income distribution: more precisely, we consider the income of the person one-fifth of the way up the income distribution within each group (group's bottom quintile point). It turns out that the patterns are broadly similar to those provided by the group averages, i.e., two-adult households with one or two children have lower than average growth rates between 1971 and 1981, but relatively high growth rates between 1981 and 1986. There are few incidences of negative growth rates. For example, between 1971 and 1976 there are none. Between 1976 and 1981, the growth rate is negative only for two-adult households with three or more children (− 10%), while between 1981 and 1986, the only group with a negative bottom quintile point growth rate is two-adult households with one child.

These results suggest that Roll's (1988a) conclusion about the fortunes of poorer people in each group is not robust. Roll argues that between 1979 and 1985 the 'income of the worst-off households with children has actually fallen in real terms' (p. 4) and later refers to the figures showing this (table 9.5) as 'probably the most striking results of [her] paper' (p. 5). According to our data, their experience was more diverse than her data suggest.

Income growth if incomes are not equivalised or weighted by household size

Suppose we use the CSO approach (unequivalised and unweighted distributions), but retain our consistently defined disposable income series. This leads to the average income growth rate estimates given in the last three columns of table 9.4, which may be compared with those in columns (5) to (7). It turns out that corresponding estimates differ very little – they are mostly within about two percentage points of each other – with one notable exception, one-adult households with children. Between 1981 and 1986 average unadjusted income growth for this group is negative, the only group for which this is so, a finding which echoes Roll's (1988a) based on post-tax/benefit incomes in 1979 and 1985 (though ours is much smaller in magnitude).

What if medians rather than means are used to summarise group incomes?

If group relative incomes and income growth figures are based on median incomes (rather than means), our conclusions are robust. With a couple of important exceptions, the earlier (qualitative) statements made about group relative incomes (p. 226) and group income growth (p. 227) can be repeated and remain an accurate description of the data.

Table 9.5. *Median real disposable income by household and family type, distributions of equivalent household and equivalent family income amongst persons, £ p.a., December 1986 prices*

| | Equivalent household income amongst persons | | | | | | | Equivalent family income amongst persons | | | | | | |
| | Group median income as % of overall median income | | | | Growth in group median income (%) | | | Group median income as % of overall median income | | | | Growth in group median income (%) | | |
Income-unit type	1971	1976	1981	1986	1971–1976	1976–1981	1981–1986	1971	1976	1981	1986	1971–1976	1976–1981	1981–1986
Elderly:[a] 1 adult	60	70	72	74	24.7	9.7	14.7	59	70	74	76	29.1	11.8	15.2
Elderly: 2 + adults	74	77	78	80	11.9	9.1	12.4	66	73	75	77	18.9	9.1	15.2
1 Adult	106	114	118	105	16.2	10.7	– 1.3	100	102	98	92	10.2	1.7	5.8
2 Adults	131	135	138	133	10.1	10.2	6.2	139	142	147	142	11.0	9.3	8.2
3 + Adults	131	136	132	125	11.6	4.6	4.7	Not relevant				Not relevant		
1 Adult & children	64	69	71	72	16.4	10.8	11.9	68	70	71	75	12.2	7.2	18.3
2 Adults & 1 child	109	107	108	112	5.4	7.6	15.1	116	115	115	120	6.6	6.2	17.1
2 Adults & 2 children	101	97	100	103	2.9	9.9	13.7	107	103	106	108	4.1	9.4	14.0
2 Adults & 3 + children	83	81	78	78	5.4	3.2	9.8	87	85	83	81	6.5	3.6	8.8
3 + Adults & children	100	104	100	103	11.1	2.9	14.6	Not relevant				Not relevant		
Absent spouse[b]	98	93	119	98	1.2	37.7	– 9.1	95	94	117	109	6.7	32.7	3.3
All	100	100	100	100	7.2	7.2	10.6	100	100	100	100	8.3	6.3	11.6
Overall mean (£ p.a.)	5,844	6,265	6,718	7,431				5,491	5,946	6,320	7,052			

Source: authors' calculations from FES micro data tapes.

[a] 'Elderly': head of income unit aged 65 years or more.

[b] The 'Absent spouse' group comprises a very small number of income units (see Appendix table 9A.1).

Compare the first seven columns of table 9.5 with the first seven of table 9.4. Group incomes relative to overall income are slightly lower if means rather than medians are used, but the difference is rarely more than a few percentage points and the pattern of growth rates across groups is very similar.[15]

The main exceptions concern one-adult households. In 1986 childless single adults' incomes are much lower relative to earlier years when medians are used (5% above the overall median, rather than 15% above the overall mean).

More striking is the change in the results for one-adult households with children. According to table 9.5, members of this group *improved* their relative income, from 64% of the overall median in 1971 to 72% in 1986. This is in sharp contrast to table 9.4, which implied the group relative incomes had been *falling* (the group mean fell from 74% of the overall mean in 1971 to 69% in 1986). Although income levels increased according to both means and medians, each of the three median growth rates is nearly twice as high as the corresponding mean growth rate.

What if family income distributions are used rather than household ones?

Compare now the summaries of family income distributions given on the right-hand side of table 9.5 with those for household income distributions on the left-hand side. Note that family and household groups with the same label will not generally comprise the same individuals. In particular the one-adult family groups will include individuals classified as part of two- or three-adult households. For example, multi-adult household groups include lone parent families who share households with their parents or other adults. In our family distributions all lone parent families (and only those families) are included in the one-adult-with-children group, and so we are able to examine their economic circumstances directly.

The other people affected by the change in classification are primarily young adults living in the parental household, and elderly parents living with their adult children. These people are likely to have incomes lower than the average for the other members of their household, but since our household distributions assume equal within-household sharing, they do not reflect this inequality. Our family distributions do incorporate this component of inequality and so we would expect people living in single-adult and elderly families to be worse off than those in the correspondingly labelled household group. This is exactly what the data show.

Compared to those living in childless nonelderly one-adult *households*, those in childless nonelderly one-adult *families* are estimated to have median incomes close to the overall median rather than some 5 to 10 percentage points higher. A similar result describes the position of those in elderly families. In contrast, but also as expected, those living in two-adult families with children are better off relative to the median than those living in two-adult households with children (again by about 5 to 10 percentage points).

People living in nonelderly two-adult families are the richest, and elderly people and those in lone parent families are the poorest, throughout the period 1971–1986. There is a clear association between income and number of children. Take the income for families with two children as a reference point (a little above the overall median in fact). The median income for families with only one dependent child is about 10% higher, and the median for families with three or more dependent children is 10%–15% below the reference point. Relative incomes across family types have remained quite stable between 1971 and 1986, except that elderly and lone parent families have become relatively better off and two-adult families with three or more children relatively worse off.

These findings are similar to the results derived from group medians of the distribution of household income amongst periods. So too are the estimates of group income growth: between 1971 and 1976 the median income of families with children grew more slowly than the overall median, while that for nonelderly families without children grew faster; between 1981 and 1986 this pattern was reversed (except for very large families); and throughout the 15 years, median incomes for elderly families and lone parent families grew faster than the overall median.

Obviously the specific estimates for groups with the same labels differ but in terms of a broad overview, household and family distributions provide similar results. However, this conclusion is based on distributions defined on a fully consistent basis: as we have shown, results based on published household income data may provide very different results.

To emphasise how sensitive income growth estimates are to changes in income definitions, consider table 9.6, which contains 10 different estimates of income growth in the early 1980s for the one-adult-plus-child group. Clearly the range, from − 11% to 18%, is large. But notice that if we take equivalent income on a per person basis, the range of income growth estimates is narrower: 7% to 17%, or 12% to 18% if medians are used. These figures are a sharp contrast to the negative growth figure shown in the readily available published statistics.

The poorest fifth; the richest fifth

We already know which groups did best and which did worst during 1971–1986. Supppose instead we were to focus on the richest and poorest

Table 9.6. *Income growth for the 'one-adult-plus-children'[a] group in the early 1980s*

Definition of real income	Summary measure	Time period	Growth rate (%)
(1) Equivalent disposable household income amongst persons	mean	1981–1986	7
(2) Equivalent disposable family income amongst persons[b]	mean	1981–1986	17
(3) Disposable household income amongst households	mean	1981–1986	– 1
(4) Equivalent disposable household income amongst persons	median	1981–1986	12
(5) Equivalent disposable family income amongst persons[b]	median	1981–1986	18
(6) Disposable household income amongst households	median	1981–1986	3
(7) Post-tax-benefit household income amongst households	mean	1979–1985	– 11
(8) Post-tax-benefit household income amongst households	mean	1979–1985	1
(9) Disposable household income amongst households	mean	1979–1985	9
(10) Equivalent disposable family income amongst persons[b]	mean	1979–1985	12

Notes:

[a] 'one-adult-plus-children' = lone parent family.

(1)–(6): current authors' estimates.

(7): Roll (1988a, Table 4) from CSO *Economic Trends* articles.

(8): CSO revised estimate (see Roll, 1988b, p. 140).

(9)–(10): DHSS estimates (see Roll, 1988b, pp. 145–146).

[b] All estimates are based on FES data and all except (7) exclude absent spouse income units from calculations.

slices of the population – whom would we find inside? Here the picture changes in interesting ways.

To describe this picture we rank everyone according to his/her income and classify people into one of five groups. Those in the richest fifth are labelled α; those in the second richest fifth, β; those in the middle fifth, γ; those in the second poorest fifth, δ; and those in the poorest fifth, ϵ. We study the poorest fifth first, using information about 'ϵ proportions', i.e., for each household type (resp. family type), the number of ϵs divided by the total number of people of that household type (resp. family type). Consider table 9.7.

Both the household and family statistics reveal that the variation in ϵ proportions across types diminished between 1971 and 1986. For groups with high ϵ proportions in 1971, for example elderly households and one-adult households with children, proportions fell dramatically. Non-elderly multi-adult households with children had relatively low ϵ proportions in 1971 and proportions for them increased over time. However, despite the convergence in ϵ proportions, the group with the highest ϵ proportion in 1971 also had the highest ϵ proportion in 1986 (about 30%). There has been little change too in which groups have the lowest ϵ proportions.

There are some interesting differences between the results for household and family distributions. First, although in 1971 the ϵ proportion for elderly two-adult families was much larger than that for elderly two-adult households (51% rather than 35%), in 1986 the proportions were the same (27%). A possible explanation is that elderly people whose adult children live with them benefit from their children's income (hence the lower proportion for households), but over time the incidence of such multi-generation households declined (so the results for households and families converged).

The second difference is for the one-adult-plus-children groups. Notice that the ϵ proportion for lone parent families is distinctly lower than the proportion for one-adult households with children (though proportions for both groups fell by the same amount, about 40%, between 1971 and 1986). The result suggests that those lone parents who share households do so with other adults whose incomes are lower than their own.

The third notable difference concerns nonelderly single adults. Taking the households as the income-receiving unit, the ϵ proportion for this group *fell*, from 25% to 16% between 1971 and 1986. In contrast, with the family as the income-receiving unit, the proportion *rose*, from 24% to 27%. The result probably reflects the worsening fortunes of single adults living with their parents. The group is likely to be younger and have lower skills and work experience, and so be more affected by the relatively large

Table 9.7. *Who had the highest and the lowest incomes?*[a] *Changes in the proportions of each group in the poorest and richest fifth of the income distribution.*[b]

%	The poorest fifth (the εs) Persons in households				Persons in families				The richest fifth (the αs) Persons in households				Persons in families			
	1971	1976	1981	1986	1971	1976	1981	1986	1971	1976	1981	1986	1971	1976	1981	1986
Elderly:[c] 1 adult	68	51	37	29	63	47	31	29	4	4	3	6	4	4	4	6
Elderly: 2 + adults	35	33	30	27	51	42	32	27	6	7	8	8	7	7	9	9
1 Adult	25	20	18	16	24	23	28	27	31	34	35	29	22	22	20	18
2 Adults	9	9	8	11	6	7	7	9	43	45	45	40	44	48	46	42
3 + Adults	5	5	5	7	not relevant				46	49	39	31	not relevant			
1 Adult & children	59	51	46	37	48	47	42	29	6	7	6	5	6	6	6	6
2 Adults & 1 child	9	9	12	17	6	8	10	12	23	21	22	22	24	23	23	25
2 Adults & 2 children	14	15	17	20	8	11	14	14	17	11	13	18	18	14	16	20
2 Adults & 3 + children	28	31	37	36	22	24	31	31	8	7	8	7	8	8	9	7
3 + Adults & children	13	14	17	19	not relevant				14	17	15	19	not relevant			
Absent spouse[d]	22	16	8	21	19	24	12	20	25	19	36	21	20	19	40	34
All	20	20	20	20	20	20	20	20	20	20	20	20	20	20	20	20

Notes:
[a] 'income' = equivalent disposable income.
[b] Income units are weighted by unit size.
[c] 'Elderly': head of income unit aged 65 years or more.
[d] The 'Absent spouse' group comprises a very small number of income units (see Appendix table 9A.1).

rise in youth unemployment rates and hence the fall in the real value of social security benefits relative to earnings (Barr and Coulter, 1991, figure 7.7).

Our results could be used to provide perspectives on the relative chances of being in poverty, but our patterns will differ from those of other studies because the definition of the poverty line is different. (The ϵs are not necessarily poor according to other definitions.) For example, the *HBAI* tables use income cut-offs which are a constant fraction of average income. In contrast, our cut-off point – if it is assumed to be the income of the person a fifth of the way up the distribution (the 'bottom quintile point') – is a fluctuating fraction of the mean. For the distribution of equivalent family income amongst persons, the proportions are: 1971, 59%; 1976, 62%; 1981, 67%; and 1986, 64%.

Such differences in definitions may go part of the way towards reconciling our results that the ϵ proportion for elderly households has been falling over time with the results of others. For example, Barr and Coulter (1991, table 7.8) show that the proportion of pensioner families in constant relative poverty increased from 36% in 1975 to 47% in 1985 (figures derived from Piachaud, 1988).

Changes in the membership of second poorest fifth (the δs) are also relevant for such reconciliations. The reason is that elderly families and lone parent familes, groups for whom ϵ proportions have *fallen*, are the groups for whom δ proportions have *risen* significantly. The δ proportion for elderly single persons in the distribution of family income doubled between 1971 and 1986, from 21% to 40%; the δ proportion for elderly couple families increased from 25% to 34%; and that for lone parent families from 26% to 38%. Increases in the real value of benefits raised incomes, but to a limited extent.

Relative to the results for the poorest fifth (the ϵs), the results for the richest fifth (the αs) show little change over time. It remained the case that people belonging to family types with relatively high average incomes (for example those in nonelderly childless families) were those with the highest α proportions, and those with the lowest α proportions were from family types with relatively low average incomes (elderly families, lone parent families, and couple families with many children).

Summary and concluding comments

We have analysed how incomes changed between 1971 and 1986 and compared the fortunes of people from different income groups and from different household and family types. Average living standards rose for all income groups and all family types but at different rates. Between 1976 and 1986, income growth has been much greater for those at the top of the distribution than for those at the bottom. Overall inequality increased significantly over this period, and for all family type groups.

The picture for family fortunes was a mixture of both stability and change. There was stability because the relative incomes of many family types stayed much the same between 1971 and 1986. Moreover the poorest families in 1971 were also the poorest in 1986, and continued to have the highest ϵ proportions.

However there was also change: some households and families clearly became relatively better off, and some relatively worse off. Who the relative gainers or losers were depends to some extent on which distributions are used, and how they are summarised. The story provided by the distributions of equivalent family income amongst persons and median incomes is as follows.

The gainers. For both elderly people and lone parent families, group average income relative to the overall average improved and the group's ϵ proportion fell. Nevertheless the gains made were somewhat limited, because both groups continued to have the lowest relative incomes and highest ϵ proportions throughout the 15 year period.

The losers. The relative fortunes of childless single people and couples deteriorated, with declining relative average incomes and higher proportions in the bottom fifth. The experience of families with children was more mixed, with some improvement in relative incomes for couples with one or two children. However families with three or more children were relative losers, with lower average incomes relative to the overall average and higher ϵ proportions.

The impressions gained from our results about changes in family fortunes are in several respects different from those that would be gained from official statistics. We have also shown how the choice of income-receiving unit and the use of medians rather than means can influence results. The estimates of income trends for lone parents and for the poorest fifth of the distribution are the two cases we have highlighted. These are of course groups in which there is intense policy interest.

Our results draw attention to several deficiencies in the CSO *Economic Trends* data as a source of information about changes in the distribution of personal economic well-being. First, the published disposable income (and gross income) series are not consistently defined over time. Second, income breakdowns for single-adult households with children continue to include absent spouse households.

Although the *Economic Trends* articles now warn that they are not intended for comparisons over time, this is an inappropriate abnegation of responsibility. Since most people must rely on published tables rather than micro data, it is important for informed policy debate that published data be of good quality.[16] We concur with Roll (1988b, p. 144) that:

> If the *Economic Trends* articles are not designed for making comparisons over time why are they published in such detail each year and with the tables in the same form? The articles *do* sometimes make comparisons over time. The July 1987 one, for example, has a whole section on comparisons since 1975 . . . Clearly, one must accept that definitions occasionally need to be changed but this does not rule out producing a consistent series. The CSO letter [reproduced in Roll's article] does, in fact, set out a consistent series of figures for '1 adult with children' households excluding the absent spouses. So this can be done and should be in future CSO articles.

The CSO *Blue Book* income distribution series provides a good model of how to introduce important changes in definitions: after a change in the treatment of mortgage interest payments in the late 1970s, overlapping series were produced on both the 'old' and 'new' basis for a couple of years. Genuine secular trends could be differentiated from statistical artefacts. Another alternative is to produce a special retrospective analysis applying new definitions to old data, and the CSO has in fact done this, albeit to a limited extent.[17]

A third problem with the *Economic Trends* data for our purposes is that incomes are not deflated by equivalence scales to adjust for differences in composition (as a proxy for 'needs'), nor weighted by income-unit size to derive personal distributions. Not making these adjustments can lead to notable differences in estimates.

CSO articles for 1987 onwards do make greater use of an equivalence scale, but not in the ways we have suggested. In fact the changes make the published data much less useful. As part of a review of methodology, the CSO (1990, 84):

> decided to produce the article on an equivalized basis . . . Equivalization is used in the ranking process, for percentage shares and when calculating Gini coefficients: but the tables show incomes and taxes in ordinary £ a year *not* equivalized £ a year.

Hence in tables on 'the percentage shares of total disposable, gross, and original income by quintile group' the quintile groups are quintile groups of equivalent disposable income in each case. But to discuss inequality from income share data requires income units to be ranked in order of the variable being cumulated and, with different income variables, corresponding income groups comprise different individuals.

We see few merits in the new methodology, and consider the CSO's justification of it unsatisfactory. They said (1990, p. 94):

We have chosen to use equivalization only in the ranking process because we feel that to present all the tables in terms of equivalized income would be confusing and difficult to understand. Equivalized income is a theoretical concept, rather removed from the real money that households actually receive and spend.

One wonders whether they raised the same objection to the income definition used in the *HBAI* tables when they were introduced, for they are all based on distributions of equivalent household disposable income on a personal basis. Experience suggests this aspect of the *HBAI* methodology has not been seen as 'confusing and difficult to understand'.

We are not recommending that the CSO article should always use an equivalent income definition similar to the *HBAI* one: the use of just one equivalence scale also is debatable (Coulter, Cowell and Jenkins, 1992a, 1992b). In any case, we recognise that the statistics presented are used for purposes in addition to analysis of the distribution of economic well-being. The old methodology met the range of demands put on the statistics more satisfactorily, and we prefer it to the way things are done now.

Data appendix

The derivation of our consistent income distributions is described in detail by Coulter (1991a, 1991b). Our demographic and income variables have been constructed using the individual and household micro data provided on the public use FES tapes. The following is a brief summary.

Income definitions

Our definitions of disposable, gross, and original income broadly correspond to those described by the CSO in the Appendixes to their *Economic Trends* articles (which are not consistent over time), but with some notable differences. We draw attention to the following features:

- we use actual earnings rather than 'normal' earnings
- we use current income, rather than CSO 'annualised income'
- we exclude the imputed value of income from owner-occupation
- all housing benefits are treated as cash benefits
- estimates of mortgage interest tax relief are deduced from the income tax payments recorded in the 1986 FES
- all housing-related income and reliefs are allocated to the head of household's tax unit
- we do not deduct housing costs (as in the *HBAI* statistics and related studies)

• we do not include imputations for capital gains and losses, or non-cash income.

Definitions of the income unit, 'adult', 'child', etc.

Our definition of the household is that used in the FES. Our definition of a 'family', is that it is either a single adult or a married couple, plus any dependent children. The definition of a 'dependent child' broadly corresponds to that used for Child Benefit: either (1) aged under 16, or (2) aged under 19, unmarried, and in full-time nonadvanced education, and living with his/her parents. (The CSO has changed to using a similar definition.)

Our definition of an 'elderly' income unit is that its head is aged 65 years or more. We chose this simple definition intentionally. The CSO uses a complicated definition of 'retired' based on age, employment status, and proportion of household income received from retirement pensions, and have changed the details of this definition in the 1980s.[18] We can identify the CSO's retired households in 1971, 1976, and 1981, because the relevant variable is provided on the FES micro data tapes. However it is not in 1986, and despite much experimentation (and correspondence with the CSO), we have been unable to reproduce results published in the CSO's *Economic Trends* article for 1986. Our definition is easy to replicate, and easy to apply to both households and tax units. It is closer to the definition used in the *HBAI* tables (whether the family head is of pension age) though, in contrast to them, we classify single women aged 60–64 years as single adults.

The analysis reported in this chapter is based on those units with positive disposable income. This selection was made because in some of the analysis, we use measures based on log-incomes. The breakdown of our samples by income unit type is shown in table 9A.1. Very few households are removed by the sample selection criterion.

A secular trend towards smaller-sized households is apparent in the FES data.[19] For example, the proportion of elderly one-adult households increased from less than 10% in 1971 to over 12% in 1986. For nonelderly one-adult households without children the corresponding figures are 8% and 12%, and for those with children, 2% and 4%. In contrast, the 'traditional family' grouping, two adults plus children, which formed over 30% of all households in 1971 formed only about 25% in 1986. Similar trends are revealed by the family distributions (see table 9A.1 for a detailed breakdown of sample proportions).

Comparing the CSO *Economic Trends* household sample proportions with our own (shown in the first four columns of table 9A.1), the largest

Table 9A.1. *Sample proportions of income unit types, %*

Income unit type	Households				Families				Persons in households				Persons in families			
	1971	1976	1981	1986	1971	1976	1981	1986	1971	1976	1981	1986	1971	1976	1981	1986
Elderly:[a] 1 adult	9.5	11.3	11.8	12.5	12.6	13.2	13.0	13.0	3.3	4.1	4.3	4.9	5.7	6.2	6.3	6.6
Elderly: 2 + adults	13.5	14.1	13.7	13.3	7.9	8.9	8.6	8.7	10.8	11.3	11.1	11.3	7.3	8.4	8.2	8.8
1 Adult	7.6	8.9	8.8	11.6	27.9	28.3	30.2	32.7	2.6	3.2	3.2	4.6	12.6	13.2	14.4	16.4
2 Adults	20.2	20.1	19.4	20.2	19.4	19.1	18.4	18.6	13.9	14.7	14.2	15.8	17.5	17.9	17.6	18.6
3 + Adults	8.0	7.1	8.2	8.3	not relevant				9.1	8.6	10.2	11.0	not relevant			
1 Adult & children	2.1	2.6	2.9	4.1	2.9	3.5	3.4	4.5	2.2	2.8	3.0	4.4	3.7	4.5	4.4	5.9
2 Adults & 1 child	10.1	8.6	8.6	8.2	10.3	9.0	9.4	8.2	10.4	9.4	9.5	9.6	13.9	12.6	13.5	12.4
2 Adults & 2 children	12.4	13.1	13.3	11.4	11.0	11.5	11.5	9.7	17.1	19.1	19.5	17.8	19.8	21.6	22.0	19.4
2 Adults & 3 + children	8.4	6.4	5.9	5.1	7.5	7.5	5.9	5.1	16.2	12.7	11.5	10.6	18.9	15.0	13.2	11.7
3 + Adults & children	7.4	6.9	7.1	5.1	not relevant				13.5	13.3	13.0	9.8	not relevant			
Absent spouse[b]	0.8	0.8	0.5	0.3	0.6	0.6	0.4	0.3	0.9	0.9	0.4	0.3	0.6	0.7	0.4	0.2
Base (No. with positive disposable incomes)	7,235	7,201	7,517	7,177	9,447	9,229	9,776	9,172	20,980	19,786	20,515	18,328	20,929	19,750	20,440	18,274
Total no. (i.e., prior to selection conditions)	7,239	7,203	7,525	7,178	9,502	9,266	9,859	9,225	20,988	19,793	20,535	18,330	20,988	19,793	20,535	18,330

[a] 'Elderly': head of income unit aged 65 years or more.
[b] The 'Absent spouse' group comprises a very small number of income units.

difference is in the proportion of elderly households with two or more adults. With the CSO definitions they comprise about 8% of the sample in 1971 and 12% in 1986; with our definitions, the corresponding figures are 14% and 13%. The difference in estimated trends probably arises because the CSO group was 'retired-two adult' prior to 1986, but then 'retired-two *or more* adults'. Accordingly we have slightly lower proportions in the nonelderly multi-adult household groups than the CSO does.

Our sample data are not 'grossed up' to better represent the population from which they are drawn because of a lack of suitable grossing up weights.

NOTES

Research supported by the ESRC with grant R000231831 ('The structure of the income distribution'), and a Nuffield Foundation Social Science Research Fellowship (Jenkins). For comments we are grateful to Jo Roll, Jane Millar, a referee, and seminar participants at Jordanstown, Glasgow and Syracuse.

 1 See for example the series of papers by Johnson and Webb (1989, 1990a, 1990b), and their work for the House of Commons Social Security Committee (1990, 1991). Earlier critiques include those by Titmuss (1962) and by the Royal Commission on the Distribution of Income and Wealth in the 1970s. Also see Atkinson's (1983, ch. 3) discussion of 'conceptual problems'. Data issues have been found to be important in other countries besides the UK. See, for example, the leading US study of trends in family fortunes (Congressional Budget Office, 1988).

 2 The CSO articles are the most detailed, up-to-date, and regularly published UK source on the income distribution overall and for different household types, and the statistics are widely quoted. CSO *Blue Book* income distribution articles have been published for only two years during the 1980s (1981/2 and 1984/5), and that for 1987/8 is now well overdue. In any case, these articles have never provided as much detail about incomes in population subgroups as the *Economic Trends* ones have. The DSS's *Households Below Average Income* tables are based on distributions of equivalent disposable household income among persons – like many of ours – but they focus on the bottom of the distribution only. Households from Northern Ireland are excluded from the *HBAI*, whereas we include them. We, like the CSO, but unlike the *HBAI*, do not 'gross up' our sample estimates. Townsend (1991) analyses income changes broken down by household type, but his tables are based on the disposable income series published in FES Reports 1979–1989, which is not consistently defined (an issue he addresses elsewhere in his paper). Jenkins (1991a) examined trends in household income using consistently-defined variables, but focused on gross income rather than disposable income as we do here (see below for definitions). Also he examined trends disaggregated by income group only, and not by household type.

 3 Government ministers criticised the findings, and commissioned further

research by the Central Statistical Office (CSO) and the (then) Department of Health and Social Security (DHSS). Roll (1988b) provides the citations to press reports and parliamentary comments, as well as copies of the letters from the CSO and DHSS containing their critique of her study.

4 We analyse changes in inequality within each group and changes in inequality between groups elsewhere: see Jenkins (1992b).

5 These changes introduce discontinuities in the gross and disposable income series published in the FES Report as well. Appendices to the FES Reports describe the changes in recording made in the survey, but do not discuss the income distribution implications. From 1984 on, gross incomes recorded in the FES for poorer households are lower than they would be on the pre-1984 basis (see Jenkins, 1991a, for an illustration of the implications of the change). The introduction of MIRAS led to higher net direct taxes (and hence lower disposable incomes) being recorded for owner-occupiers with mortgages than would have been on the earlier basis. On this, see Coulter (1991b).

6 The derivation of our income series is explained in detail in Coulter (1991a, 1991b). See also below.

7 We do not examine the implications of choosing this equivalence scale rather than some other one. This is the subject of Coulter, Cowell, and Jenkins (1992a), but there we mainly consider estimation of inequality and poverty indices, rather than average income, the focus of this chapter. Jenkins (1991a) estimates the change in average real gross normal weekly household income between 1976 and 1986 to have been 17% if incomes are not equivalenced, but 25% if a *per capita* equivalence scale is used. (A scale similar to McClements' yields an intermediate estimate.) The 8 percentage point disparity may seem large, but it arises from fairly 'extreme' equivalence scales, and in any case in this chapter, we concentrate on changes over five year periods rather than decades. Nonetheless the sensitivity issue deserves further attention in subsequent work.

8 The derivation of our consistent family distributions is described by Coulter (1991a).

9 We derive our family distributions assuming the total income of a household is shared equally amongst all household members, and our family distributions assuming the total income of a family is shared equally amongst all family members. (The latter assumption introduces some within-household inequality.) Such equal sharing assumptions have been made by virtually all income distribution analysts to date, and while obviously unrealistic, they are at least tractable. See Jenkins (1991b) for a review of previous work on within-unit sharing and a discussion of how alternative within-unit sharing assumptions might be incorporated in further work.

10 When criticising Roll's (1988a) conclusions derived from their own published data, the CSO reworked their figures for the 'one-adult-plus-children' group excluding households with a temporarily absent spouse. They found: 'The number of such [absent spouse] households excluded is small ranging from 23 in 1979 to 5 in 1985, but the effect is dramatic. The post/tax benefit income for the reworked series increased from £2,186 in 1979 to £3,683 in 1985, or *a 1 per*

cent increase in real terms after deflating by the RPI. This is quite a change from the 11 per cent fall shown [by Roll]' (Wilkinson in Roll, 1988b, p. 140, emphasis in original).

11 The argument for using the median is on the grounds of representativeness, rather than statistical precision. For a comparison of the standard errors of the mean and the median estimated using random samples from a normal distribution, see Stuart and Ord (1987, p. 332). Our income distributions are not normally distributed, and the FES is not a pure random sample, which limits application of their results.

12 Remember that the income groups in the equivalised and weighted distribution (table 9.1) contain different people from the corresponding income group in the unadjusted distribution (table 9.2). If we take the distributions of equivalent *family* income amongst persons, the estimates of income growth for the bottom tenth are more like those shown in table 9.1 than in table 9.2. They are, for 1971–1976, 14.5%; for 1976–1981, − 5.2%; for 1981–1986, 6.9%.

13 Further evidence on this point is adduced by the results of Jenkins (1991a), who considers (in part) distributions of equivalent 'gross normal weekly household income' amongst persons. Using the inconsistent FES income definition, he shows that average income for the poorest fifth fell by − 0.8% between 1981 and 1986, while that for the richest fifth grew by 19.3%. If a consistent (pre-1983 basis) series is used the growth rates are 1.3% and 19.6% (calculations from Jenkins, 1991a, table 2).

14 In all our tables, growth rates summarise changes in income levels, not changes in relative income. A positive growth rate can be consistent with group average income relative to the overall mean rising or falling.

15 Comparing corresponding estimates, median growth rates are generally slightly higher than mean growth rates for 1971–1976, but slightly lower in 1976–1981. For 1981–1986, the differences are not consistently in one direction. For each group, the median income lies below the mean income, reflecting the skewed distribution within each group. As the overall median also lies below the mean, the ratio of a group median to the overall median may potentially be higher or lower than the ratio of a group mean to the overall mean.

16 This issue is of ongoing importance, and not simply a one-off problem in the early 1980s. For example CSO *Economic Trends* articles for 1987 onwards deduct domestic rates when defining disposable income (anticipating the abolition of domestic rates and introduction of the poll tax).

17 For example the article for 1988 contains information on 'the effects of taxes and benefits 1977–1988' using the 1987 methodology which ranks households by the same income variable in all key tables. We applaud the provision of such comparisons, though for the case just cited we are sceptical of the usefulness of the statistics *per se* (more on this below).

18 In 1981 the CSO defined 'retired' households to be those where either (1) the combined income of members who are at least 60, and who describe themselves as retired or unoccupied, amounts to at least half the total gross income of the household, or (2) the head is over state pension age and more than three-quarters of the household's income consists of National Insurance retirement and similar state pensions or related Supplementary Benefit.

19 See Ermisch (1990) for a more extensive discussion of demographic trends.

REFERENCES

Atkinson, A.B. (1983) *The Economics of Inequality*, 2nd edn., Oxford, Clarendon
   Press
   (1993) 'What is happening to the distribution of income in the UK?', Welfare
   State Programme, London, LSE, *Discussion Paper*, WSP/87
Barr, N. and F. Coulter (1991) 'Social security: solution or problem?', in J. Hills
   (ed.), *The State of Welfare Since 1974*, Oxford, Oxford University Press
Brown, J.C. (1989) *Why Don't They Go To Work? Mothers on Benefit*, Social
   Security Advisory Committee *Research Paper*, 2, London, HMSO
Central Statistics Office (CSO) (various years) 'The effects of taxes and benefits on
   household incomes', *Economic Trends*, London, HMSO
Congressional Budget Office (1988) *Trends in Family Income: 1970–1986*, Washington, DC, US Government Printing Office
Coulter, F.A.E. (1991a) 'The Family Expenditure Survey and the distribution
   of income: the creation of a consistent income data series for 1971, 1976,
   1981, 1986', University of Bath, *Economics Discussion Paper*, 04/91
   (1991b) 'Mortgage payments in the 1986 Family Expenditure Survey: estimating the incidence of Mortgage Interest Tax Relief', University of Bath,
   Economics Discussion Paper, 05/91
Coulter, F.A.E., F.A. Cowell and S.P. Jenkins (1992a) 'Difference in needs and
   assessment of income distributions', *Bulletin of Economic Research*, 44,
   77–124
   (1992b) 'Equivalence scale relativities and the extent of inequality and poverty',
   Economic Journal, 102, 1067–1082
Department of Employment (various years) *Family Expenditure Survey*, London,
   HMSO
Department of Social Security (DSS) (1990) *Households Below Average Income: A
   Statistical Analysis 1981–1987*, London, Government Statistical Service
   (1991) *Social Security Statistics*, London, HMSO
Ermisch, J.E. (1990) *Fewer Babies, Longer Lives*, York, Joseph Rowntree Foundation
Jenkins, S.P. (1991a) 'Income inequality and living standards: changes in the
   1970s and 1980s', *Fiscal Studies*, 12(1), 1–28
   (1991b) 'Poverty and the within-household distribution: agenda for action',
   Journal of Social Policy, 20, 457–483
   (1992a) 'Recent trends in UK income inequality', in D. Slottje (ed.), *Research
   on Economic Inequality, Vol. 5*, Greenwich, CT, JAI Press
   (1992b) 'Accounting for inequality trends: decomposition analyses for the UK,
   1971–1986', University College of Swansea, *Economics Discussion Paper*,
   92–10
Johnson, P. and S. Webb (1989) 'Counting people on low incomes: the effect of
   recent changes in official statistics', *Fiscal Studies*, 10(4), 53–65

(1990a) *Poverty in Official Statistics: Two Reports*, IFS Commentary, 24, London, Institute for Fiscal Studies

(1990b) 'Low income families, 1979–87', *Fiscal Studies*, 11(2), 44–62

McClements, L.D. (1977) 'Equivalence scales for children', *Journal of Public Economics*, 8, 191–210

Piachaud, D. (1988) 'Poverty in Britain 1899 to 1983', *Journal of Social Policy*, 17, 335–350

Roll, J. (1988a) *Family Fortunes: Parents' Incomes in the 1980s*, Occasional Paper, 7, London, Family Policy Studies Centre

(1988b) 'Measuring family income: a recent controversy in the use of official statistics', *Social Policy and Administration*, 22, 134–149; with correction, 259–260

Royal Commission on the Distribution of Income and Wealth, Chairman Lord Diamond (1979), *Report No. 7: Fourth Report on the Standing Reference*, Cmnd 7595, London, HMSO

Social Security Committee (1990) *Households and Families Below Average Income: A Regional Analysis 1980–1985*, Session 1989–90, House of Commons, 378-I, London, HMSO

(1991) *Low Income Statistics: Households Below Average Income Tables 1988*, First Report, Session 1990–91, House of Commons, 401, London, HMSO

Stuart, A. and J.K. Ord (1987) *Kendall's Advanced Theory of Statistics, 5th edn, Vol. 1: Distribution Theory*, London, Charles Griffin & Co

Titmuss, R.M. (1962) *Income Distribution and Social Change*, London, George Allen & Unwin

Townsend, P. (1991) *The Poor Are Poorer: a statistical report on changes in the living standards of rich and poor in the United Kingdom 1979–1989*, University of Bristol, Statistical Monitoring Unit Report 1

Walker, I. (1989) 'The effects of income support measures on the labour market behaviour of lone mothers', *Fiscal Studies*, 11(2), 55–75

10 Ethically-consistent welfare prescriptions are reference price-independent

CHARLES BLACKORBY, FRANÇOIS LAISNEY
and ROLF SCHMACHTENBERG

Introduction

The best-known measures of welfare changes are the compensating and equivalent variations of Hicks. For a single individual they have the advantage of being monetary measures of welfare change that are also exact. That is, if a positive compensating variation is associated with a project, this indicates that the consumer's utility has gone up because of it. Because these measures are in monetary terms there is a natural temptation to sum them in order to evaluate potential projects. Unfortunately, Boadway (1974) showed that, in a competitive economy, the sum of compensating variations is always nonnegative (positive if prices change) for all possible projects, rendering it an inappropriate tool for project analysis. Roberts (1980), and later Blackorby and Donaldson (1985) extended this result by demonstrating that knowledge of all compensating variations associated with various projects could only be used in Pareto-consistent fashion in rare circumstances even if all consumers face the same prices – a representative consumer would have to exist – and never if consumers face individual prices. The limited usefulness of these surpluses has led more recently to the use of another monetary measure of utility: the equivalent income function. This is the minimum expenditure needed to bring a consumer to a given level of utility at some pre-specified reference prices. Having computed these equivalent income functions, a planner can analyse the worthiness of a project by means of a social welfare function defined on them; see, for example, King (1983a). The weakness of this procedure is that this computation depends upon the reference price vector in such a way that the choice of projects may not be consistent with any Bergson–Samuelson social welfare function, that is, it may not be *ethically consistent*. In fact, as shown below, this procedure is ethically consistent if and only if the project analysis is independent of reference prices.

247

Following the work of King (1983a), a number of studies have evaluated the social welfare impact of price and income changes using equivalent incomes that are computed at some reference price vector, and a *social aggregator function* with these equivalent incomes as arguments in place of a social welfare function (e.g., King, 1983a, 1983b; Colombino and Del Boca, 1989; Patrizi and Rossi, 1989; Baccouche and Laisney, 1990; Nichèle, 1990). However, typically, the impact of the choice of the reference price vector on the results of such exercises has not been clearly delineated.

King (1983a) devoted limited attention to the characterisation of situations (in terms of individual or household preferences and a social welfare function) admitting Reference Price-Independent Welfare Prescriptions (RPIWP), referring loosely to the work of Muellbauer (1974) and Roberts (1980). Roberts studies the robustness of welfare changes using incomes only, and gives partial characterisations of the situations admitting Price-Independent Welfare Prescriptions (PIWP). Slivinski (1983) gives a complete characterisation of PIWP if households face individualised prices.

In our third section, we show that RPIWP implies PIWP on all price domains. In the fourth section we provide a complete characterisation of RPIWP if there are household specific prices. In the fifth section there is a partial characterisation of RPIWP when households face common prices and in the sixth section we discuss some counterexamples.

Notation

We consider H households with preferences over n goods. The preferences are described by an expenditure function whose image is $e^h(u_h, p_h)$ where u_h is the utility level and p_h is the vector of prices faced by household h.[1]

From the expenditure function we can derive the indirect utility function, v^h, of household h

$$y_h = e^h(u_h, p_h) \leftrightarrow u_h = v^h(y_h, p_h) \tag{1}$$

where y_h is the nominal income of household h.

Given a reference price vector[2] q_h for household h, the equivalent income of household h, ξ_h, is given by

$$\xi_h = e^h(u_h, q_h) = e^h(v^h(y_h, p_h), q_h). \tag{2}$$

The equivalent income function is a particular representation of the household's preferences for each reference price vector q_h.[3]

Let $W(u)$, $u = (u_1, \ldots, u_H)$ be a Bergson–Samuelson social welfare function. We define a Bergson–Samuelson indirect social welfare function by

$$V(y,p) = W(\{v^h(y_h,p_h)\})$$ (3)

where $y = (y_1, \ldots, y_H)$, $p = (p_1, \ldots, p_H)$ and $\{v^h(y_h,p_h)\} = (v^1(y_1,p_1), \ldots, v^H(y_H,p_H))$, and W is continuous, increasing, and quasi-concave.

A *tax reform* which moves society from an income-price vector, (y^b,p^b) (b as 'before') to an 'after' income-price vector (y^a,p^a) is a social improvement if and only if

$$W(u^a) \geq W(u^b).$$ (4)

This can also be written in terms of the equivalent income functions $\{\xi_h\}$ by using (1) and (2) to obtain

$$u_h = v^h(y_h,p_h) = v^h(\xi_h,q);$$ (5)

substituting (5) into W yields

$$V(\xi,q) = W(\{v^h(\xi_h,q_h)\}),$$ (6)

where $\xi = (\xi_1, \ldots, \xi_H)$ and $q = (q_1, \ldots, q_H)$.

$V(\xi,q)$ is an attractive form of the social welfare function because it allows the definition of monetary measures of social welfare changes due to a tax reform. Following King (1983a, p. 198) the social gain SG from a tax reform at reference prices q can be defined implicitly by

$$V(\xi^b + SG,q) = V(\xi^a,q).$$ (7)

As a practical problem it can be difficult to find a tractable functional form for V given a social welfare function W and a set of preferences $\{v^h\}$, and one may be tempted to construct a functional form directly on the equivalent incomes themselves, ignoring the primitives from which it must be derived.[4]

Ethical consistency and reference price-independent welfare prescriptions

We noted above that the practical difficulties involved in deriving a tractable V might lead researchers to specify a functional form directly on the equivalent incomes. This is the path followed by King (1983a, p. 196) who posits the existence of an *equivalent income aggregator* whose image is $G(\xi)$ which he then uses to evaluate social changes.[5] Under what conditions is this equivalent income aggregator ethically consistent?

Ethical consistency: G and $\{v^h\}$ are ethically consistent if and only if there exists some Bergson–Samuelson social welfare function W such that

$$G(\xi^a) \geq G(\xi^b) \leftrightarrow W(u^a) \geq W(u^b). \tag{8}$$

Another way to look at the potential problems associated with using the equivalent income aggregator is to note that it depends upon the reference price vector q whereas the indirect Bergson–Samuelson social welfare function does not. Rewriting the equivalent income aggregator as

$$F(y,p,q) := G(\{e^h(v^h(y_h,p_h,q_h)\}), \tag{9}$$

we are interested in the circumstances in which the social changes that it recommends are independent of the reference price vector q.

Reference Price-Independent Welfare Prescriptions (RPIWP): G and $\{v^h\}$ admit RPIWP if and only if for all (y,p), (y',p'), and (q,q') we have

$$F(y,p,q) \geq F(y',p',q) \leftrightarrow F(y,p,q') \geq F(y',p',q'). \tag{10}$$

From Corollary 3.2.1 in Blackorby, Primont and Russell (1978) this is equivalent to the following functional representation.

Proposition 1: G and $\{v^h\}$ admit RPIWP if and only if (y,p) is separable from q in F, that is,

$$F(y,p,q)\hat{F}(E(y,p),q), \tag{11}$$

where $\hat{F}$ is increasing in its first argument.
An immediate consequence of (8) and (9) is Theorem 1.

Theorem 1: G and $\{v^h\}$ are ethically consistent if and only if they satisfy RPIWP.

Proof: If G and $\{v^h\}$ are ethically consistent, then, using (3) and (9), we obtain

$$F(y^a,p^a,q) \geq F(y^b,p^b,q) \leftrightarrow V(y^a,p^a) \geq V(y^b,p^b), \tag{12}$$

which implies (11). On the other hand, if G and $\{v^h\}$ admit RPIWP then

$$F(y^a,p^a,q) \geq F(y^b,p^b,q) \leftrightarrow E(y^a,p^a) \geq E(y^b,p^b). \tag{13}$$

Hence, we can set $q_h = 1_n$ and define, using (9),

$$W(u) := G(\{e^h(u_h,1_n)\}), \tag{14}$$

which satisfies ethical consistency. ∎

On the way we have shown that if G and $\{v^h\}$ satisfy RPIWP, that is if (11) holds, then E is a Bergson–Samuelson indirect social welfare function.
The phrase 'Price-Independent Welfare Prescriptions' was introduced

by Roberts (1980) to describe those situations where policy prescriptions could be made on the basis of incomes alone even though prices had changed. It is defined as follows:

Price-Independent Welfare Prescriptions (PIWP): W and $\{v^h\}$ admit PIWP if and only if the Bergson–Samuelson indirect social welfare function, (3), can be written as

$$V(y,p) = \bar{V}(\tilde{V}(y),p), \tag{15}$$

where $\bar{V}$ is increasing in its first argument. (In this case $\tilde{V}$ can be picked to be positively linearly homogeneous without loss of generality.)[6]

Roberts' notion of PIWP for a Bergson–Samuelson social welfare function leads to two notions of price-independent welfare prescriptions for the equivalent income aggregator:

Local Price-Independent Welfare Prescriptions (LPIWP): G and $\{v^h\}$ admit LPIWP if and only if for all (y,p), (y',p'), and q

$$F(y,p,q) \geq F(y',p,q) \leftrightarrow F(y,p',q) \geq F(y',p',q), \tag{16}$$

and

Global Price-Independent Welfare Prescriptions (GPIWP): G and $\{v^h\}$ admit GPIWP if and only if for all (y,p,q) and (y',p',q')

$$F(y,p,q) \geq F(y',p,q) \leftrightarrow F(y,p',q') \geq F(y',p',q'), \tag{17}$$

Similar to the representation for RPIWP we have two representation results given by Proposition 2 and Proposition 3:

Proposition 2: G and $\{v^h\}$ admit LPIWP if and only if

$$F(y,p,q) = \tilde{F}(D(y,q),p,q), \tag{18}$$

where $\tilde{F}$ is increasing in its first argument

and

Proposition 3: G and $\{v^h\}$ admit GPIWP if and only if

$$F(y,p,q) = \bar{F}(C(y),p,q), \tag{19}$$

where $\bar{F}$ is increasing in its first argument.

LPIWP guarantees price independence for a given reference price while GPIWP requires consistency of these welfare prescriptions across different reference prices.

The relationships between the several definitions of price-independent

welfare prescriptions which hold on both of the price domains considered
are given in Theorems 2 and 3:

Theorem 2: Given RPIWP, LPIWP implies GPIWP.

Proof: From Proposition 3.1, RPIWP implies that y is separable from q
conditional on p whereas from Proposition 3.2, LPIWP implies that y is
separable from p conditional on q. Together these imply GPIWP. ∎

Theorem 3: Assume that prices and reference prices have the same
domain. There exists a G such that G and $\{v^h\}$ admit RPIWP if and only if
there exists a W such that W and $\{v^h\}$ admit PIWP.

Proof:[7] Under RPIWP we have

$$G(\xi^a) \geq G(\xi^b) \leftrightarrow F(E(y^a, p^a), q) \geq F(E(y^b, p^b, q)). \tag{20}$$

Setting $p^a = p^b = q$ and using (2) yields

$$\xi_h = e^h(v^h(y_h, p_h), p_h) = y_h, \tag{21}$$

and hence we obtain

$$G(y^a) \geq G(y^b) \leftrightarrow E(y^a, p) \geq E(y^b, p). \tag{22}$$

Setting $V = E$ yields an indirect social welfare function which satisfies
PIWP.

On the other hand, if W and $\{v^h\}$ admit PIWP, then from (15) we have

$$W(u) = \tilde{V}(\tilde{V}(y), p) = \tilde{V}(\tilde{V}(\{e^h(u_h, p_h)\}), p). \tag{23}$$

Therefore,

$$\tilde{V}(\{e^h(u_h^a, q_h)\}) \geq \tilde{V}(\{e^h(u_h^b, q_h)\})$$
$$\leftrightarrow \tilde{V}(\tilde{V}(\{e^h(u_h^a, q_h)\}), q) \geq \tilde{V}(\tilde{V}(\{e^h(u_h^b, q_h)\}), q) \tag{24}$$
$$\leftrightarrow W(u^a) \geq W(u^b).$$

Setting $G = \tilde{V}$ yields RPIWP. ∎

The equivalence of RPIWP, LPIWP, and GPIWP on household specific price domains

In this section we prove that if all households face different prices, then all
three notions of price-independent welfare prescriptions are equivalent
and require that the Bergson–Samuelson social welfare function and the

equivalent income aggregator must be Cobb–Douglas and that individual preferences must be homothetic (but not necessarily identical).

To do this we first use a result of Slivinski (1983) who proves that PIWP on household specific price domains yields a Cobb–Douglas representation of the Bergson–Samuelson social welfare function and individual homotheticity. Therefore, the equivalent income aggregator must be Cobb–Douglas as well for RPIWP to hold. Second, we show directly that LPIWP implies that the equivalent income aggregator must be Cobb–Douglas and that individual preferences must be homothetic which implies RPIWP. Theorem 2 therefore implies GPIWP. For simplicity we break this argument into a series of Lemmata and assemble the main result at the end. We frequently use the symbol $\overset{\circ}{=}$ to mean 'ordinally equivalent to' in what follows.

Lemma 1: G and $\{v^h\}$ admit RPIWP, on household specific price domains, if and only if the equivalent income aggregator is Cobb–Douglas and individual preferences are homothetic, that is,

$$G(\xi) \overset{\circ}{=} \sum_{h=1}^{H} b_h \ln \xi_h \tag{25}$$

and

$$v^h(y_h, p_h) \overset{\circ}{=} y_h \alpha^h(p_h) \tag{26}$$

where α^h is homogeneous of degree minus one.

Proof: From Theorem 3 RPIWP implies PIWP and on household specific price domains this yields individual homotheticity, (26), and a social welfare function that is ordinally equivalent to a Cobb–Douglas, that is,

$$W(u) \overset{\circ}{=} \sum_{h=1}^{H} b_h \ln u_h \tag{27}$$

by Proposition 4 in Slivinski (1983). From (14) we must have

$$G(\{e^h(u_h, \mathbf{1}_n)\}) \overset{\circ}{=} W(u) \tag{28}$$

for RPIWP to hold, and thus the equivalent income aggregator must be ordinally equivalent to a Cobb–Douglas.

Conversely, given (25) and (26) we can first rewrite (26) as

$$v^h(y_h, p_h) = \phi^h(y_h \alpha^h(p_h)) \tag{29}$$

and hence the expenditure function as

$$e^h(u_h, p_h) = \frac{\psi^h(u_h)}{\alpha^h(p_h)}, \tag{30}$$

where ψ^h is the inverse of ϕ^h. Thus, the equivalent income can be written as

$$\zeta^h = \frac{y_h \alpha^h(p_h)}{\alpha^h(q_h)} .$$ (31)

From the definition (25) of G we then obtain

$$F(y, p, q) \overset{\text{o}}{=} \sum_{h=1}^{H} b_h \ln y_h + \ln \alpha^h(p_h) - \ln \alpha^h(q_h)$$ (32)

which clearly satisfies (11) and thus RPIWP. ∎

Lemma 2: G and $\{v^h\}$ satisfy LPIWP, on household specific price domains, if and only if (25) and (26) hold.

Proof: LPIWP implies that

$$\tilde{F}(D(y, q), p, q) = G(\{e^h(v^h(y_h, p_h), q_h)\}).$$ (33)

Conditional on the vector of reference prices q, (y_h, p_h) is separable from its complement in (y, p) on the right-hand side of (33) and hence must be so on the left-hand side. As the vector y is separable from its complement in (y, p) conditional on q on the left-hand side it must also be so on the right-hand. We have here two overlapping separable sets conditional on q, neither of which is a subset of the other, and can invoke Gorman's overlapping theorem.[8] Let y_{-h} and p_{-h} be the income and price vectors purged of those components indexed by h. Then Gorman's overlapping theorem implies that

$$\tilde{F}(D(y, q), p, q) = A^h(a^h(y_h, q) + b^h(p_h, q) + c^h(y_{-h}, q), p_{-h}, q).$$ (34)

As we can do this for all h this yields, using Lemma 2 in Gorman (1968) or Theorem 4.8 in Blackorby, Primont and Russell (1978),

$$\tilde{F}(D(y, q), p, q) = A\left(\sum_h a^h(y_h, q) + \sum_h b^h(p_h, q), q \right).$$ (35)

From (35) we have that p_h is separable from y_h in $\tilde{F}$ and hence from (33) that p_h is separable from y_h in v^h. From Lemma 3.4 in Blackorby, Primont and Russell (1978) this implies that the preferences of household h are homothetic for all h and the equivalent income of household h can be written as in (31). Substituting this into G yields

$$G(\{e^h(v^h(y_h, p_h), q_h)\}) = G\left(\left\{ \frac{y_h \alpha^h(p_h)}{\alpha^h(q_h)} \right\} \right).$$ (36)

Substituting this into (33) and using (35) demonstrates that each p_h and each q_h are separable from their respective complements in $\tilde{F}$ and hence in A. Setting $\alpha^h(p_h) = t_h$ and $\alpha^h(q_h) = s_h$ allows us to write

$$A\left(\sum_h \bar{a}^h(y_h, s) + \sum_h \bar{b}^h(t_h, s), s\right) = G\left(\left\{\frac{y_h t_h}{s_h}\right\}\right) \tag{37}$$

where $s = (s_1, \ldots, s_H)$. Setting $s_h = t_h = 1$ for all h demonstrates that W is additively separable in its arguments and hence we can rewrite (37) as

$$A\left(\sum_h \bar{a}^h(y_h, s) + \sum_h \bar{b}^h(t_h, s), s\right) = \bar{G}\left(\sum_h G^h\left(\frac{y_h t_h}{s_h}\right)\right). \tag{38}$$

Next, setting $y_h = 1$ and $t_h = 1$ we see that the left-hand side of (38) must be additive in s as well and hence can be rewritten, in an abuse of notation, as

$$A\left(\sum_h a^h(y_h) + \sum_h b^h(t_h) + \sum_h c^h(s_h)\right) = \bar{G}\left(\sum_h G^h\left(\frac{y_h t_h}{s_h}\right)\right). \tag{39}$$

This however is a Pexider equation whose solution is (25); to see this, use sequentially Theorem 3.5.5 in Eichhorn (1978). This establishes the Lemma. ■

Thus RPIWP and LPIWP are equivalent in this situation, and using Proposition 2 we obtain Theorem 4.

Theorem 4: On household specific price domains, RPIWP, LPIWP, and GPIWP are equivalent and yield (25) and (26).

This completes our characterisation on household specific price domains. As a practical matter, we note that the empirical results of King (1983a, 1983b), Colombino and Del Boca (1989), and Nichèle (1990) are based on individualised prices. In addition they assume a family of equivalent income aggregator functions parameterised by an index of inequality ϵ. Theorem 4 asserts that the only acceptable value for this parameter is one if the prescriptions are to be free of the reference price vector, and this only if preferences are homothetic. The latter is satisfied in the studies of King and Nichèle but not in the study of Colombino and Del Boca. There, the methodology used does not warrant any safe welfare prescription.

RPIWP on common price domains

The case of price domains is more difficult. To date no one has provided a complete characterisation of PIWP on common price domains; and we certainly have not succeeded in providing a complete characterisation of RPIWP. We do, however, have several partial characterisations which are of some interest.

Roberts (1980) gives a wide range of results concerning PIWP on a common price domain which are closely related to the characterisations available for RPIWP. We stress in the sequel only those that have direct empirical relevance.

Proposition 4: If G and $\{v^h\}$ satisfy RPIWP, then G is homothetic.

Proof: Given RPIWP, we obtain from (9) and (11), after setting $p = q$,

$$G(\xi) = \hat{F}(E(\xi,p),p) \tag{40}$$

where E is a Bergson–Samuelson indirect social welfare function. From Theorem 3 we know that RPIWP implies PIWP and hence we can write

$$E(E(\xi,p)) = \bar{E}(\tilde{E}(\xi),p) \tag{41}$$

where $\tilde{E}$ is linearly homogeneous. Combining (40) and (41) yields the result. ■

Proposition 4 is the analogue of Proposition 3 in Roberts (1980). The analogue of his Proposition 4 follows from Theorem 3.

Proposition 5: Suppose that all households have identical homothetic preferences. Then, G and $\{v^h\}$ satisfy RPIWP if and only if G is homothetic.

In our sixth section we give three counterexamples which show that, generically, none of the three assumptions of Proposition 5 can be omitted.

Finally, an analogue to Roberts' Proposition 6 in our context follows.

Proposition 6: If G is linear, then G and $\{v^h\}$ satisfy RPIWP if and only if preferences are quasi-homothetic with identical slopes. Conversely, in the latter case, the only member of the Kolm–Atkinson family of equivalent income aggregators G leading to RPIWP is linear.

Proof: If G is linear, then

$$G(\xi^a) \geq G(\xi^b) \leftrightarrow G(\xi^a - \xi^b) \geq 0. \tag{42}$$

By setting q equal to the status quo price vector the first part of the proposition follows from the characterisation of ethical consistency for functions of individual equivalent variations by Blackorby and Donaldson (1985).

Conversely, consider quasi-homothetic preferences with identical slopes:

$$\xi^h = \alpha^h(q) + \frac{\beta(q)}{\beta(p)}(y^h - \alpha^h(p)) \tag{43}$$

and the symmetric Kolm–Atkinson family

$$G(\xi) = \frac{1}{1-\epsilon} \sum_h (\xi^h)^{1-\epsilon} \quad \text{for } \epsilon \neq 1 \tag{44}$$

$$G(\xi) = \sum_h \ln \xi^h \qquad (\epsilon = 1).$$

If (y, p) is separable from q in F (see equation (9)), in particular p is separable from q. Given differentiability as above, this means that the ratio $\partial G / \partial p_i$ over $\partial G / \partial p_j$ must be independent of q for all pairs of goods $\{i, j\}$. But this ratio is equal to

$$\frac{\partial G / \partial p_i}{\partial G / \partial p_j} = \frac{\sum_h (\xi^h)^{-\epsilon}[\alpha_i^h + (y^h - \alpha^h(p))\beta_i(p)/\beta(p)]}{\sum_h (\xi^h)^{-\epsilon}[\alpha_j^h + (y^h - \alpha^h(p))\beta_j(p)/\beta(p)]} \tag{45}$$

and it will be independent of q only if $\epsilon = 0$. ∎

In addition, Proposition 6 shows that RPIWP is *not* characterised by Proposition 5. Proposition 6 is, however, of direct relevance for the study of Baccouche and Laisney (1990). They present results for quasi-homothetic individual preferences with identical slopes in terms of the Kolm–Atkinson family of equivalent income aggregators: only their results for $\epsilon = 0$ are robust to changes in the reference price. How much the other results would be affected by a drastic change of the reference price remains to be studied.

Patrizi and Rossi (1989) specify piglog individual preferences and consider values of 0.5, 1, 2 and 5 of the parameter ϵ of the Kolm–Atkinson family of equivalent income aggregators. Proposition 6 of Roberts suggests that the only value of ϵ warranting RPIWP is $\epsilon = 1$, and indeed this is easily checked directly.

Counterexamples

We turn to some counterexamples showing that relaxing any of the assumptions of Proposition 5 generically results in loss of RPIWP. In Counterexample 1 we relax the assumption of identical consumers and show that this can result in very large departures from RPIWP indeed. In Counterexamples 2 and 3, we relax homotheticity of G and v, respectively, while retaining the assumption of identical preferences. All counterexamples concern the special case where $H = 2$ and $n = 2$, and the merely technical details of the proofs are gathered in the Appendix (p. 260).

Counterexample 1: We assume linear direct utility for each household:

$$u(x) = ax_1 + bx_2 \quad a,b > 0. \tag{46}$$

This corresponds to homothetic preferences $v(y,\mathbf{p}) = \phi(yg(\mathbf{p}))$ with

$$g(\mathbf{p}) = \begin{cases} a/p_1 & \text{if } p_1/p_2 \leq a/b \\ b/p_2 & \text{if } p_1/p_2 > a/b \end{cases} . \tag{47}$$

Taking the second good as numeraire, and denoting by p resp. q the prevailing price and the reference price of the first good, we have:

$$\xi/y = g(p)/g(q) = \begin{cases} q/p & \text{if } p,q < a/b \\ \dfrac{a}{pb} & \text{if } p < a/b < q \\ qb/a & \text{if } q < a/b < p \\ 1 & \text{if } a/b < p,q \end{cases} . \tag{48}$$

Specifying a linear equivalent income aggregator[9]

$$G(\xi) = A\xi_1 + B\xi_2, \quad A,B > 0 \tag{49}$$

and choosing

$$q,p < a_1/b_1 < p' < a_2/b_2 < q' \tag{50}$$

we show that if the post-reform income of consumer 1 exceeds a minimum level (function of all other incomes and prices, except the reference prices), which would ensure that society appears to be indifferent between the status quo and the reform when the reference price q' is used, then RPIWP will be violated if the real income (in terms of the price of good 2) of consumer 2 is increased by the reform, as long as constellation (50) holds.

Counterexample 2: We now assume identical homothetic preferences and a quasi-homothetic equivalent income aggregator. We choose:

$$G(\xi) = \left[\frac{g(p)}{g(q)} y_1 - \gamma_1\right]\left[\frac{g(p)}{g(q)} y_2 - \gamma_2\right]. \tag{51}$$

RPIWP will be violated if, for given γ_1, γ_2, we find y, p, y', p', q, q' such that

$$\begin{aligned} &[g(p)y_1 - g(q)\gamma_1][g(p)y_2 - g(q)\gamma_2] \\ &\geq [g(p')y_1' - g(q)\gamma_1][g(p')y_2' - g(q)\gamma_2] \end{aligned} \tag{52}$$

and

$$[g(p)y_1 - g(q')\gamma_1][g(p)y_2 - g(q')\gamma_2]$$
$$\geq [g(p')y_1' - g(q')\gamma_1][g(p')y_2' - g(q')\gamma_2]. \tag{53}$$

Choosing $q' = p$ and $q = p'$ (which is an interesting case in its own right, corresponding to the familiar EV and CV measures of individual welfare change) and calling η the ratio $g(p)/g(p')$, this means:

$$(\eta y_1 - \gamma_1)(\eta y_2 - \gamma_2) \geq (y_1' - \gamma_1)(y_2' - \gamma_2) \tag{54}$$

and

$$(y_1 - \gamma_1)(y_2 - \gamma_2) \geq (\eta^{-1}y_1' - \gamma_1)(\eta^{-1}y_2' - \gamma_2). \tag{55}$$

These inequalities can be expressed in terms of the signs of second degree polynomials in η with coefficients for η^2 equal to $y_1 y_2$ (> 0) for (54) and $y_1 y_2 - y_1 \gamma_2 - \gamma_1 y_2$ for (55). Choosing γ_1 and γ_2 so as to make the latter quantity negative ensures that for any choice of y_1' and y_2' there will exist a threshold value of $g(p)/g(p')$ beyond which RPIWP will be violated. Here we see that RPIWP will be satisfied (in a weakened sense) for some intervals of variation of prices and reference prices, the width of these intervals depending on the income distributions in the situations compared.

Counterexample 3: Consider G linear and symmetric (i.e., $G = \xi_1 + \xi_2$) and identical preferences defined by:

$$\ln v(y,p) = a(p) + \beta(p)\ln y \tag{56}$$

We know from Proposition 6 that RPIWP will be violated since (56) does not correspond to quasi-homothetic preferences. However, it is of interest to see how critical the violations are in this particular instance. Indeed, assuming as in Counterexample 2 that $q' = p$ and $q = p'$, that the functions a and β are identical that that prices move in such a way that $\beta(p)/\beta(p') = 2$, and supposing further that incomes change proportionally:

$$\frac{y_1}{y_2} = \frac{y_1'}{y_2'} = a, \tag{57}$$

we show that RPIWP will be violated everywhere except if $a = 0$ (a value which (56) excludes *a priori*) or $a = 1$, which is a trivial case of absolutely identical consumers.

The interpretation is that the distance between p and p' corresponding to the assumption that $\beta(p)/\beta(p') = 2$ is sufficient to enable us to find equiproportional income distributions y and y' that lead to reverted

260   Charles Blackorby, François Laisney and Rolf Schmachtenberg

evaluations of the move from (y,p) to (y',p') if these evaluations take place at p and p', except if consumers have identical incomes.

Conclusions

Having accumulated negative evidence against the possibility of RPIWP as we have, we must stress the fact that, in the case of differentiable v^h and G and with (y',p') in a neighbourhood of (y,p), one can expect from definition (10) to find no violation of reference price-independence over a reasonably large neighbourhood of a given q. This comment applies to the study of Patrizi and Rossi, for instance, where the VAT reforms considered do not alter prices dramatically and the distribution of income is left unchanged in most cases.

A potential extension of this work would be to focus on independence of welfare prescriptions with respect to the choice of reference characteristics, which becomes necessary if households differ but one still insists on anonymity of the equivalent income aggregator. Given the negative results obtained here for a global definition of RPIWP one should probably focus attention on local results, at least as regards prices and incomes. This problem, as well as that of the choice of a reference price is also discussed by Willig (1981), in the related context of social welfare dominance. Some interesting results are given by Donaldson (1992): in particular, for a given reference household, the requirement of RPIWP is less stringent than here, as it places restrictions only on the preferences of the reference household and on the SWF.

Appendix: proofs for the counterexamples

Counterexample 1: Given constellation (50) we have:

(i) $F(y,p,q) = A \dfrac{q}{p} y_1 + B \dfrac{q}{p} y_2$

(ii) $F(y',p',q) = Aq \dfrac{b_1}{a_1} y_1' + B \dfrac{q}{p'} y_2'$

(iii) $F(y,p,q') = A \dfrac{a_1}{pb_1} y_1 + B \dfrac{a_2}{pb_2} y_2$ (A1)

(iv) $F(y',p',q') = Ay_1' + B \dfrac{a_2}{p'b_2} y_2'.$

According to the definition, RPIWP will be violated if we have simultaneously (i) > (ii) and (iii) < (iv). The second inequality is equivalent with:

$$y_1' > \frac{a_1}{pb_1} y_1 + \frac{Ba_2}{Ab_2} \left(\frac{y_2}{p} - \frac{y_2'}{p'} \right) = : y_{-1}' \tag{A2}$$

where y_1' is the post-reform income of consumer 1 as a function of all other incomes and prices, except the reference prices, which given the constellation (50) ensures that society appears to be indifferent between the status quo and the reform when the reference price q' is used. Note that y_1' exceeds y_1 if $y_2/p = y_2'/\mathbf{p}'$. A sufficient condition for the inequality (i) > (ii) to hold is then:

$$A \frac{y_1}{p} + B \frac{y_2}{p} > A \frac{b_1}{a_1} y_1' + B \frac{y_2'}{p}, \tag{A3}$$

or, since, A, B, and $b_1 > 0$:

$$\frac{y_2}{p} > \frac{b_1 a_2}{a_1 b_2} \left(\frac{y_2}{p} - \frac{y_2'}{p'} \right) + \frac{y_2'}{p'}. \tag{A4}$$

Taking account of the negative sign of $a_1 b_2 - b_1 a_2$ (see (50)), this yields

$$\frac{y_2}{p} < \frac{y_2'}{p'} \tag{55}$$

as sufficient condition for the violation of RIWP given our choices.

Counterexample 3: Here

$$\xi = \exp[(a(\mathbf{p}) - a(\mathbf{q}))/\beta(\mathbf{q})] \, y^{\beta(\mathbf{p})/\beta(\mathbf{q})}. \tag{A5}$$

A violation of RPIWP will obtain if, for instance:

$$e^2 y_2^2 (1 + a^2) > e y_2' (1 + a) \quad \text{and} \quad e y_2 (1 + a) < \sqrt{e y_2'} (1 + \sqrt{a}). \tag{A6}$$

In that case we have:

$$y_2^2 > \frac{1}{e} \frac{1+a}{1+a^2} y_2' \quad \text{and} \quad y_2^2 < \frac{1}{e} \left(\frac{1+\sqrt{a}}{1+a} \right)^2 y_2'. \tag{A7}$$

We will be able to find values of y_2 and y_2' satisfying these inequalities iff

$$\left(\frac{1 + \sqrt{a}}{1 + a} \right)^2 > \frac{1 + a}{1 + a^2} \tag{A8a}$$

or equivalently

$$(1 + b^2)^3 - (1 - b^4)(1 + b)^2 < 0, \tag{A8b}$$

where b denotes the square root of a. Easy algebra shows that the polynomial on the left-hand side of this inequality admits only 0 and 1 as real roots and takes negative values everywhere else.

NOTES

This chapter is an extended version of Blackorby, Laisney and Schmachtenberg (1993) which in turn is a revision of Laisney and Schmachtenberg (1989). Blackorby was partially supported by a grant from SSHRCC. Laisney wishes to thank the Deutsche Forschungsgemeinschaft for support. The benefits of discussions with Rafiq Baccouche, Salvador Barbera, Walter Bossert, François Bourguignon, Russell Davidson, David Donaldson, Mervyn King and Ian Preston are gratefully acknowledged.

1 We assume that e^h is a continuous and increasing function of its arguments and that it is linearly homogeneous and concave in prices. In the third section we permit prices to be household specific whereas in the fourth we require all households to face the same price vector.

2 When households face different prices we allow the reference prices to be household specific as well. In the fourth section where we require households to face a common price vector we require the reference price vector to be common as well. The equivalent income is also known as the indirect money metric. See Weymark (1983) or Blackorby and Donaldson (1988).

3 Is it possible to pick all ordinal representations of a preference ordering by changing the reference price vector? The following example shows that this is not possible. Let a household consume only good 1 so that $V(y,p) = \phi(y/p)$. Then $\xi = q\psi(u)$ where ψ is the inverse of ϕ. Hence changing reference prices can only pick up all linear transforms of $x = \psi(u)$ and no others.

4 Even this exaggerates somewhat the value of $V(\xi, q)$. In general, the equivalent income functions are not concave representations of preferences; see Blackorby and Donaldson (1988). Hence the function defined above may not be able to pick up all favourable reallocations of resources.

5 For example, suppose that households 1 and 2 consume only goods 1 and 2 respectively. If $u^h(x) = x$ for $h = 1, 2$, the sum of the equivalent income functions is $q_1 u^1 + q_2 u^2$. That is, the utilities are weighted in an arbitrary and capricious manner. Of course, this can easily be undone in this simple example by dividing the first argument by q_1 and the second by q_2. In general this is difficult to do and to the best of our knowledge no one has ever bothered to do it.

6 See Roberts (1980) or Blackorby and Donaldson (1985).

7 This was discovered independently and given as Proposition 1 in Laisney and Schmachtenberg (1989) and Theorem 1b in Donaldson (1992). We present the proof given by Donaldson because of its simplicity.

8 See Theorem 1 in Gorman (1968) or Theorem 4.7 in Blackorby, Primont and Russell (1978).

9 Since the assumptions of Proposition 6 are met, but the slopes differ across households, we know that RPIWP will not hold. The justification of the example is to show how easy it is for RPIWP to fail if consumers have different tastes.

REFERENCES

Atkinson, A.B. (1970) 'On the measurement of inequality', *Journal of Economic Theory*, 2, 244–263

Baccouche, R. and F. Laisney (1990) 'Simulation of VAT reforms for France using cross-section data', in J.P. Florens, M. Ivaldi, J.J. Laffont and F. Laisney (eds.), *Microeconometrics: Surveys and Applications*, Oxford, Basil Blackwell

Blackorby, C. and D. Donaldson (1985) 'Consumers' surpluses and consistent cost-benefit tests', *Social Choice and Welfare*, 1, 251–262

(1988) 'Money metric utility: a harmless normalisation?', *Journal of Economic Theory*, 46, 120–129

Blackorby, C., F. Laisney and R. Schmachtenberg (1993) 'Reference price independent welfare prescriptions', *Journal of Public Economics*, 50, 63–76

Blackorby, C., D. Primont and R.R. Russell (1978) *Duality, Separability and Functional Structure: Theory and Economic Applications*, New York, North-Holland

Boadway, R. (1974) 'The welfare foundations of cost-benefit analysis', *Economic Journal*, 84, 926–939

Colombino, U. and D. Del Boca (1989) 'The effect of taxes and labor supply in Italy', Turin University, mimeo

Donaldson, D. (1990) 'On the aggregation of money measures of well-being in applied welfare economics', *Journal of Agricultural and Resource Economics*, 17, 88–102

Eichhorn, W. (1978) *Functional Equations in Economics*, London, Addison-Wesley

Gorman, W.M. (1968) 'The structure of utility functions', *Review of Economic Studies*, 35, 369–390

King, M.A. (1983a) 'Welfare analysis of tax reforms using household data', *Journal of Public Economics*, 21, 183–214

(1983b) 'An index of inequality: with applications to horizontal equity and social mobility', *Econometrica*, 51, 99–115

Kolm, S.-C. (1969) 'The optimum production of social justice', in J. Margolis and H. Glutton (eds.), *Public Economics*, London, Macmillan

Laisney, F. and R. Schmachtenberg (1989) 'For welfare prescriptions *reference price* independence implies *price* independence', *Beiträge zur Angewandten Wirtschaftsforschung*, 404–489, Universität Mannheim

Muellbauer, J. (1974) 'Inequality measures, prices and household composition', *Review of Economic Studies*, 41, 493–504

Nichèle, V. (1990) 'Effets redistributifs et gain d'efficacité d'une réforme de l'allocation de logement en France', *Economie et Prévision*, 91, 19–34

Patrizi, V. and N. Rossi (1989) 'The European internal market and welfare of Italian consumers', Universita degli Studi di Venezia, *Discussion Paper*, 8906

Roberts, K.W.S. (1980) 'Price-independent welfare prescriptions', *Journal of Public Economics*, 13, 277–297

Slivinski, A.D. (1983) 'Income distribution evaluation and the law of one price', *Journal of Public Economics*, 20, 103–112
Weymark, J.A. (1983) 'Money-metric utility functions', *International Economic Review*, 26, 219–232
Willig, R.D. (1981) 'Social welfare dominance', *American Economic Review*, 71, 200–204

11 The effect of systematic misperception of income on the subjective poverty line

MARTIJN P. TUMMERS

Introduction

Empirical evidence indicates that respondents misperceive their own household after-tax income (see Kapteyn *et al.*, 1988); respondents appear to underestimate their household after-tax income. As will be explained below, this underestimation turns out to have a downward-biasing effect on the subjective poverty line in empirical implementation. Walker (1987) also pointed out that the concept of income the respondent has in mind may not always be the same as the researcher's. In Kapteyn *et al.* (1988) a method is presented to remedy this bias. One can adjust the responses to subjective questions if these questions are preceded by a question which measures the respondent's perception of his household after-tax income. The misperception of income can be calculated from a comparison of the respondent's perception of the income with the measurement of income as the sum of a lengthy list of components. Next the responses to the subjective questions can be corrected. An alternative is of course to avoid the misperception, by prefacing the subjective questions with the detailed questions about household income components. Here, the focus is on the former case.

Kapteyn *et al.* (1988) assume that the answers to the subjective questions are biased in the same proportion as income is underestimated by the respondent. In this chapter, this assumption is tested within the context of the so-called Subjective Poverty Line (SPL) (see Goedhart *et al.*, 1977). The second section concisely introduces the SPL concept. The third section presents the adjustment procedure as proposed in Kapteyn *et al.* (1988) and indicates how their assumption can be empirically relaxed.[1] An alternative assumption is also given through more direct use of the measurement of the respondent's perception of income in explaining subjective answers. The fourth section contains the estimation results. For comparisons the same specification as in Kapteyn *et al.* (1988) is adopted. The fifth section draws some conclusions.

The Subjective Poverty Line

The SPL was introduced in Goedhart *et al.* (1977). It is called 'Subjective' because it springs from the respondents' answers to a survey question, the Minimum Income Question (MIQ). Callan and Nolan (1991) classified the SPL under the 'Consensual Income Poverty Lines', as the SPL is based on views in the population about minimum needs. The MIQ tries to measure these views. It runs as follows:

Which after-tax income for your household do you, in your circumstances, consider to be absolutely minimal? That is to say that with less you could not make ends meet.

The MIQ answer, given by the head of household n, is referred to as the respondent's minimum income $y_{min,n}$.

The SPL is operationalised by specifying a relation between $y_{min,n}$, on the one hand and household income and a vector of household characteristics, on the other. To facilitate comparison, the SPL equation will initially be specified as in Kapteyn *et al.* (1988):

$$\ln y_{min,n} = a_0 + a_1(1 - a_2)fc_n + \psi(1 - a_2)fc_n \ln y_n + a_2 \ln y_n$$
$$+ (1 - a_2)m_n + a_1(1 - a_2)hc_n - \psi(1 - a_2)hc_n m_n + \epsilon_n \qquad (1)$$

where

fc_n composition of household n
y_n household after-tax income
m_n mean ln income in the reference group of household n
hc_n mean household composition in the reference group of household n
ϵ_n error term.

The specification in equation (1) originates from a 'theory of preference formation' as developed in Kapteyn (1977); for details see Kapteyn *et al.* (1985). Equation (1) explains the financial wants of a household by household composition, its income, and by a mean of incomes in the reference group adjusted with a mean of household compositions in the reference group. The product terms of income and household composition account for an income-related change in costs if household composition changes. Household composition is specified such that account is taken of both the number of persons in the household and their ages:

$$fc_n = 1 + \ln fs_n + f(a_1) + \sum_{j=2}^{fs_n} f(a_j)\ln(j/(j-1)) \qquad (2)$$

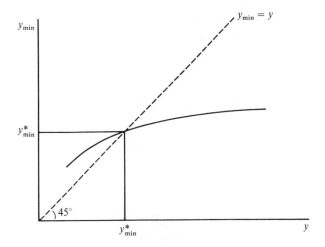

Figure 11.1   The subjective poverty line y^*_{min}

where

fs_n number of persons in household n

$$f(a_j) = 0 \qquad\qquad a_j > 18$$

$$f(a_j) = \gamma_2(18 - a_j)^2 + \gamma_3(18 - a_j)^2(36 + a_j) \qquad 0 \le a_j \le 18$$

where a_j refers to the age of person j and γ_2 and γ_3 are parameters to be estimated. The third order polynomial in ages lower than 18 has the effect that children under 18 are not only logarithmically weighted like all household members but also on the basis of their age.

From equation (1), $y_{min,n}$ can be written as a function of y_n, for given values of the other variables on the right-hand side, as set out in figure 11.1. The MIQ answers are aggregated into the SPL by the following reasoning. Suppose one obtains an income to the right of $y^*_{min,n}$ in figure 11.1. Take the corresponding minimum income level and return it as income. Through an iterated habituation process that person will end up in the fixed point of the function set out in figure 11.1. The SPL is defined by this fixed point of that function, $y^*_{min,n}$, which equals

$$\exp\frac{a_0 + a_1(1 - a_2)fc_n + (1 - a_2)m_n - a_1(1 - a_2)hc_n - \psi(1 - a_2)hc_n m_n}{(1 - a_2)(1 - \psi fc_n)}.$$

(3)

The income level $y^*_{min,n}$ is the point where a household can just make ends meet. Eventually, a household with less income is not able to manage and a household with more income is able to manage. Having estimated the

Table 11.1. *Comparison of two income measures, Dfl. per year*

Income bracket (1)	Average income (2)	N_b (3)
< 17,500	17,201	564
17,500–20,000	25,085	355
20,000–24,000	28,690	521
24,000–28,000	32,128	632
28,000–34,000	38,305	635
34,000–43,000	45,412	686
> 43,000	65,006	698

Column (2) gives the average income of all households in the corresponding income bracket according to the detailed measurement of income.
N_b shows the number of respondents in the income bracket.
Socio-economic Panel (October 1986).

parameters in equation (1), the SPL can be evaluated for various household compositions.

Adjusted for downward bias

In the definition of the SPL, the respondent's income appears to be a crucial variable, so it is important to know which estimate of his own household income the respondent has in mind when answering the MIQ. If the respondent underestimates this income, it is likely that he will also underestimate $y_{min,n}$. As mentioned before, the factor of downward bias can be calculated from comparison between the respondent's estimate of income and a more accurate measurement of income. Just before the MIQ in the survey, the respondent's perception of his household after-tax income is measured by the following question where the respondent can choose out of seven income brackets:

Can you indicate roughly what the total after-tax income of your household has been during the past 12 months? Less than Dfl. 17,500; 17,500–20,000; 20,000–24,000; 24,000–28,000; 28,000–34,000; 34,000–43,000; 43,000 or more.

In order to analyse the systematic difference in table 11.1 between the results from the two income measures, Kapteyn *et al.* (1988) postulate the following relation between income y_n^*, the answer to the income question in brackets, and the income components y_{ni} ($i = 1, \ldots, I$) recorded at the end of the questionnaire

$$y_n^* = \left(\sum_{i=1}^{I} \beta_i \, y_{ni} \right) e^{\eta_n} \tag{4}$$

where β_is are parameters to be estimated and η_n is a normally distributed error term with mean zero and variance σ_η^2. The values of β_i are expected to lie in the unit interval $[0, 1]$. The smaller a parameter β_i, the more the respondents 'forget' the ith income component in response to the income question in brackets. The parameters β_i and σ_η^2 can be estimated by means of maximum likelihood.

Denote the factor of underestimation by g_n. The parameters β_i being estimated, this factor can be evaluated as $\hat{g}_n = \Sigma_{i=1}^I y_{ni} / \Sigma_{i=1}^I \hat{\beta}_i y_{ni}$. Kapteyn et al. now assume that the respondent underestimates his minimum income $y_{min,n}$ by the same proportion as his current income y_n. It is, however, not entirely obvious why the adjustment of y_{min} should be proportionate to the underestimation of y, for in equation (1) y_{min} and y are not linearly related. Moreover it appears that it is possible to let the data determine the extent of correction of y_{min}. After substituting the adjusted value $y_{min,n} g_n^\delta$ for $y_{min,n}$, equation (1) becomes

$$\ln y_{min,n} = -\delta \ln g_n + a_0 + a_1(1 - a_2)fc_n + \psi(1 - a_2)fc_n \ln y_n + a_2 \ln y_n$$
$$+ (1 - a_2)m_n - a_1(1 - a_2)hc_n - \psi(1 - a_2)hc_n m_n + \epsilon_n \tag{5}$$

where δ indicates the extent of adjustment. Note that it is now possible to test whether proportional adjustment fits the data, i.e., $\delta = 1$ vs. $\delta \neq 1$.[2]

From equation (1) an alternative specification readily suggests itself. In the response to the MIQ, income serves as a frame of reference. This is represented by $\ln y_n$ in equation (1). However, $\ln y_n^*$ seems a more natural candidate to capture this frame of reference, or perhaps a combination of $\ln y_n$ and $\ln y_n^*$ is best. So the alternative specification reads

$$\ln y_{min,n} = a_0 + a_1(1 - a_2)fc_n + (\psi(1 - a_2)fc_n + a_2)((1 - \lambda)\ln y_n + \lambda \ln y_n^*)$$
$$+ (1 - a_2)m_n - a_1(1 - a_2)hc_n - \psi(1 - a_2)hc_n m_n + \epsilon_n. \tag{6}$$

Equations (5) and (6) are identical if $\ln g_n = \ln y_n - \ln y_n^*$ and $\delta = \lambda(\psi(1 - a_2)fc_n + a_2)$. For equation (5), $\ln y_{min,n} + \delta \ln g_n$ is substituted for $\ln y_{min,n}$ in equation (1) and for equation (6), $\ln y_n$ in equation (1) is replaced by $(1 - \lambda)\ln y_n + \lambda \ln y_n^*$. The specification in equation (5) has the disadvantage that it still suffers from a specification for adjustment in the MIQ answers: $y_{min,n} g_n^\delta$. The specification in equation (6) suffers less from this kind of disadvantage, since it needs a specification for income as a frame of reference: $(1 - \lambda)\ln y_n + \lambda \ln y_n^*$, and that seems more in line with the 'theory of preference formation' mentioned before.

In estimation, equation (6) results in particular, but nonnested cases of equation (5). The concurrences in specification are tabulated in terms of δ and λ in table 11.2.

Table 11.2. *Concurring specifications*

δ	λ
0	0
$\lambda(\psi(1 - a_2)fc_n + a_2)$	λ
$\psi(1 - a_2)fc_n + a_2$	1
$\hat{\delta}$	$\hat{\delta}/(\psi(1 - a_2)fc_n + a_2)$
1	$1/(\psi(1 - a_2)fc_n + a_2)$

In the next section, the estimation results for equations (5) and (6) are given. Assuming that ϵ_n and η_n are independent and follow a normal distribution the parameters are estimated by maximising the log-likelihood

$$L = \sum_{n=1}^{N} \left(\ln P_n - \tfrac{1}{2} \ln(\sigma_\epsilon^2 + \delta^2 \sigma_\eta^2) - \tfrac{1}{2} \frac{\zeta_n^2}{\sigma_\epsilon^2 + \delta^2 \sigma_\eta^2} \right) \tag{7}$$

where

$$P_n = \Phi \left(\frac{\ln ub_n - \ln \sum_{i=1}^{I} \beta_i y_{ni} - \dfrac{\delta \sigma_\eta^2}{\sigma_\epsilon^2 + \delta^2 \sigma_\eta^2} * \zeta_n}{\sigma_\epsilon \sigma_\eta / \sqrt{\sigma_\epsilon^2 + \delta^2 \sigma_\eta^2}} \right)$$

$$- \Phi \left(\frac{\ln lb_n - \ln \sum_{i=1}^{I} \beta_i y_{ni} - \dfrac{\delta \sigma_\eta^2}{\sigma_\epsilon^2 + \delta^2 \sigma_\eta^2} * \zeta_n}{\sigma_\epsilon \sigma_\eta / \sqrt{\sigma_\epsilon^2 + \delta^2 \sigma_\eta^2}} \right)$$

where $\zeta_n = \epsilon_n + \delta \eta_n$, Φ is the cumulative standard normal distribution function and ub_n and lb_n are respectively the upper and lower bound of the income bracket y_n^* is part of.

Estimation results

The data are from the October 1986 wave of the Social Economic Panel survey conducted by the Netherlands Central Bureau of Statistics. Table 11.3 lists the income components distinguished, y_{ni}.

Table 11.4 presents the estimation results for equations (4) and (5). The estimated parameters $\hat{\beta}_i$ indicate that the head of household's wages, etc. appear to be recalled almost completely. Components like incomes of children and other household members, rent subsidies and head of household's other income are often forgotten.

Table 11.3. *Income components*

Head of household's wages, salaries, benefits	β_1
Head of household's fringe benefits	β_2
Rent subsidies	β_3
Household allowances	β_4
Profits, employer's contribution to health insurance premiums, scholarships	β_5
Head of household's other income	β_6
Spouse's income	β_7
Eldest child's income	β_8
Other household members' income	β_9

Table 11.4. *Estimation results, equations (4) and (5)*

δ	0	$\lambda(\psi(1-a_2)fc_n + a_2)$		0.40(0.02)	1
λ	0	1.11(0.05)	1	$\delta/(\psi(1-a_2)fc_n + a_2)$	
$\hat{a}_0$	$-0.43(0.03)$	$-0.38(0.01)$	$-0.39(0.01)$	$-0.38(0.01)$	$-0.30(0.01)$
$\hat{a}_1$	$3.88(0.78)$	$-0.12(0.25)$	$-0.13(0.25)$	$0.48(0.32)$	$-2.00(0.21)$
$\hat{a}_2$	$0.54(0.04)$	$0.34(0.03)$	$0.35(0.03)$	$0.39(0.03)$	$0.29(0.04)$
$\hat{\gamma}_2$	$0.05(0.01)$	$0.03(0.01)$	$0.03(0.01)$	$0.03(0.01)$	$0.03(0.01)$
$\hat{\gamma}_3$	$-1*10^{-3}$	$-1*10^{-3}$	$-1*10^{-3}$	$-1*10^{-3}$	$-1*10^{-3}$
	$(3*10^{-4})$	$(2*10^{-4})$	$(3*10^{-4})$	$(3*10^{-4})$	$(2*10^{-4})$
$\hat{\psi}$	$-0.35(0.07)$	$0.03(0.02)$	$0.03(0.02)$	$-0.03(0.03)$	$0.21(0.02)$
$\hat{\beta}_1$	$0.91(0.01)$	$0.91(0.01)$	$0.90(0.01)$	$0.90(0.01)$	$0.90(0.01)$
$\hat{\beta}_2$	$0.95(0.07)$	$0.77(0.06)$	$0.78(0.06)$	$0.79(0.06)$	$0.84(0.04)$
$\hat{\beta}_3$	$0.39(0.08)$	$0.42(0.08)$	$0.41(0.08)$	$0.42(0.08)$	$0.63(0.08)$
$\hat{\beta}_4$	$0.44(0.07)$	$0.79(0.07)$	$0.79(0.07)$	$0.78(0.07)$	$0.75(0.06)$
$\hat{\beta}_5$	$0.73(0.02)$	$0.68(0.02)$	$0.68(0.02)$	$0.68(0.02)$	$0.69(0.02)$
$\hat{\beta}_6$	$0.45(0.03)$	$0.45(0.03)$	$0.45(0.03)$	$0.45(0.03)$	$0.48(0.03)$
$\hat{\beta}_7$	$0.87(0.02)$	$0.90(0.02)$	$0.90(0.02)$	$0.90(0.02)$	$0.86(0.02)$
$\hat{\beta}_8$	$0.43(0.03)$	$0.42(0.03)$	$0.42(0.03)$	$0.42(0.03)$	$0.41(0.03)$
$\hat{\beta}_9$	$0.48(0.04)$	$0.48(0.05)$	$0.48(0.05)$	$0.48(0.05)$	$0.48(0.04)$
$\hat{\sigma}_\epsilon$	$0.31(0.003)$	$0.29(0.003)$	$0.29(0.003)$	$0.29(0.003)$	$0.31(0.004)$
$\hat{\sigma}_n$	$0.29(0.004)$	$0.30(0.004)$	$0.30(0.004)$	$0.29(0.003)$	$0.29(0.004)$
L	-3543.6	-3312.2	-3315.3	-3312.5	-3803.0

$N = 4,091$. Standard errors in parentheses.

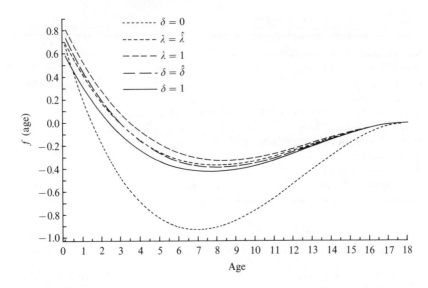

Figure 11.2   Age functions

Clearly, the hypothesis $\delta = 1$ has to be rejected. A striking result is that $\delta = 0$ in the first column performs even better than $\delta = 1$ in the fifth column in terms of the likelihoods. In the fourth column, an estimated value of 0.40 is found for δ significantly different from zero and one. The estimation result $\lambda > 1$ in the second column is difficult to interpret. At a high significance level ($\chi^2_{1;0.01} = 6.63$), however, the restriction $\lambda = 1$ in the third column holds, which signifies that only income as perceived by the head of the household, y_n^*, is the frame of reference when completing the survey.

To compare the results between the columns in table 11.4, figure 11.2 presents the five corresponding age functions $f(age)$ and table 11.5 shows the implied poverty lines for various household compositions. The poverty lines have been computed according to formula (3) with m_n and hc_n set equal to their sample means.

Except for $\delta = 0$, the age functions look rather similar. Although the age functions show a dip, the poverty lines in table 11.5 rise whenever the number of persons in a household increases. Household size compensates for the age dips below zero. For $\delta = 1$, i.e., overadjustment of $\ln y_{min,n}$ according to table 11.4, the poverty line for a one-person household appears to be overestimated with respect to δ unrestricted. Similarly, the economies of scale are overestimated in this case.

Just for comparison the last column of table 11.5 contains the levels of

Table 11.5. *Poverty lines, Dfl. per year*

Household composition	$\delta = 0$	$\lambda = \hat{\lambda}$	$\lambda = 1$	$\delta = \hat{\delta}$	$\delta = 1$	Statutory poverty line
1 Adult	14,239	15,310	15,181	15,091	15,489	13,218
2 Adults	18,095	17,415	17,091	17,537	16,387	18,882
2 Adults + 6[a]	18,298	18,359	18,017	18,564	16,832	19,963
2 Adults + 12	19,100	18,481	18,070	18,702	16,942	20,233
2 Adults + 12,6	19,240	19,199	18,772	19,462	17,337	22,071
2 Adults + 12,6,1	20,575	20,430	19,969	20,788	18,158	23,360
2 Adults + 12,6,2,1	21,222	21,290	20,811	21,681	18,834	24,933
2 Adults + 18,12,6,1	21,996	21,335	20,742	21,723	19,000	28,281

[a] + a child aged 6, etc.

the statutory poverty line for the selected household compositions. The levels are based on the Social Assistance Act and include holiday and family allowances. The steeper household composition compensation does offset the lower starting level of a one-person household. Whatever the specification, the statutory poverty-line levels end up higher than the subjective poverty-line levels for all selected household compositions, except for the first one.

Conclusions

If in a questionnaire, the MIQ is not preceded by detailed questions on household income to avoid misperception of this income by the head of the household when answering the MIQ, the answer should be corrected. Prefacing the MIQ with a measure of the perception of household income enables adjustment in explaining the answer to the MIQ. If one prefers to adjust the answers, it is possible to estimate the size of adjustment. Also the measurement of perceived income may be used more directly in explaining the MIQ answers. Both approaches show that adjustment proportionate to income misperception leads to both an overestimation of the SPL, for a one-person household, and an overestimation of the economies of scale if there is an increasing number of household members.

NOTES

The research reported was conducted while the author was at the department of econometrics of Tilburg University. The author thanks Peter Kooreman, Arie Kapteyn and Bertrand Melenberg, and a referee for their invaluable comments. Ruud Muffels took care of the statutory poverty line levels that appear in table 11.5. The Netherlands Central Bureau of Statistics kindly released the data for publication.

1 This was suggested by a referee of Kapteyn *et al.* (1988).

2 Since we do not observe correctly perceived minimum income, the most that we can identify is the degree to which perception of minimum income varies with misperception of income. The implication of the current specification that minimum income is accurately assessed if and only if actual income is, i.e., $g_n = 1$, is an assumption, and one that is important since it determines the level of the derived poverty lines in table 11.5.

REFERENCES

Callan, T. and B. Nolan (1991) 'Concepts of poverty and the poverty line', *Journal of Economic Surveys*, 5, 243–261

Goedhart, T., V. Halberstadt, A. Kapteyn and B.M.S. van Praag (1977) 'The poverty line: concept and measurement', *Journal of Human Resources*, 12, 503–520

Kapteyn, A. (1977) *A Theory of Preference Formation*, Leyden University, unpublished Ph.D. thesis

Kapteyn, A., P. Kooreman and R. Willemse (1988) 'Some methodological issues in the implementation of subjective poverty definitions', *Journal of Human Resources*, 23, 222–242

Kapteyn, A., S. van de Geer and H. van de Stadt (1985) 'The impact of change in income and family composition on subjective measures of well-being', in M. David and T. Smeeding (eds.), *Horizontal Equity, Uncertainty, and Economic Well-Being*, Chicago, University of Chicago Press, 35–64

Walker, R. (1987) 'Consensual approaches to the definition of poverty: towards an alternative methodology', *Journal of Social Policy*, 16(2), 213–226

Index of names

275

Index of subjects